Balancing Water for Humans and Nature

Dedication

To the memory of the late Professor Mark I L'vovich, Moscow, whose groundbreaking work on soil moisture as a more important element than river water, from the standpoint of human interest, influenced our thinking profoundly.

Balancing Water for Humans and Nature

The New Approach in Ecohydrology

Malin Falkenmark and Johan Rockström

With contributions by Hubert Savenije

London • Sterling, VA

First published by Earthscan in the UK and USA in 2004

ISBN: 1-85383-927-2 paperback
        1-85383-926-4 hardback

Typesetting by MapSet Ltd, Gateshead, UK
Printed and bound in the UK by Cromwell Press, Trowbridge, Wiltshire
Cover design by Danny Gillespie

For a full list of publications please contact:
Earthscan
8–12 Camden High Street, London, NW1 0JH, UK
Tel: +44 (0)20 7387 8558
Fax: +44 (0)20 7387 8998
Email: earthinfo@earthscan.co.uk
Web: **www.earthscan.co.uk**

22883 Quicksilver Drive, Sterling, VA 20166-2012, USA

A catalogue record for this book is available from the British Library

Library of Congress Cataloging-in-Publication Data

Falkenmark, Malin, 1925-
    Balancing water for humans and nature : the new approach in ecohydrology / Malin
Falkenmark and Johan Rockström.
     p. cm.
    Includes bibliographical references (p.).
    ISBN 1-85383-927-2 (pbk.) – ISBN 1-85383-926-4 (hardback)
     1. Ecohydrology. 2. Human ecology. 3. Water use. I. Rockström, Johan. II. Title.
QH541.15.E19F35 2004
333.91–dc22
                                                                                    2003023956

Earthscan publishes in association with WWF-UK and the International Institute for
Environment and Development

This book is printed on elemental chlorine-free paper

Contents

List of Plates, Figures and Tables

Plates

Figures

Tables

Foreword

Water is life. It nourishes our ecosystems, powers our industry, grows our food, and makes life itself possible.

Freshwater systems are created by water that enters the terrestrial environment as precipitation and flows both above and below ground towards the sea. This constant cycle of water between the oceans, atmosphere and land sustains life on Earth. All organisms on the planet need water to survive. There is scarcely any human activity that is not, in one way or another, linked to water. Without water, microorganisms that decompose organic matter could not exist, there would be no recycling of matter and energy, and no complex ecosystems.

Fresh water, once so abundant on our planet, is now rapidly becoming a scarce resource. Water-related conflict is already beginning to erupt from the desperation of deprivation, not only among states and territories but also within communities. And, as usual, the poor are paying the heaviest price for water; both to obtain it and because of the lack of it.

The evolution of an economy in a country or a region is significant for future patterns of water use. Two major implications arise. First, direct impacts occur as a result of water demands from different uses. Second, indirect impacts occur as a result of growing regional income and higher standards of living, which usually result in higher levels of water use. Thus, it is important to be able to estimate both the size and shape of future regional economies.

However, estimating the nature of a future economy is fraught with difficulties. Calculations are required regarding the number and mix of industries, (manufacturing, service, etc), the future demand for goods and services, the comparative advantage of a region relative to competing regions, and effects of changes in public policies on the economy. Water is usually a minor cost relative to total production costs, but when real water scarcity occurs, it can be a significant constraint on economic development.

Water security is a principal concern for sustainable development in the 21st century. The global statistics speak for themselves. Approximately one in three people live in regions of moderate to high water stress and it is estimated that two-thirds of people will live in water-stressed conditions by 2025. This issue is complicated further by the evolving trend of global warming.

The conventional approach to meeting water-use needs has been to expand existing sources, or to create new sources. This approach has been labelled as the 'supply management approach', since the emphasis has been upon enhancing or increasing the supply of water. As the most suitable dam and reservoir sites became developed, and as awareness grew about some of the negative environmental and social impacts of major structural works, attention has turned increasingly to what has been labelled as a 'demand management approach'. In this approach, the focus shifts away from providing additional water supplies to meet anticipated use and towards modifying human behaviour, and especially to reduce wasteful use of water resources.

It has never been suggested that the demand management approach should replace the supply management approach. Instead, the argument has usually been that water managers have over-relied on the supply management approach. The emerging view is that supply and demand management approaches should and can be used together, to develop a package custom-designed for any given situation.

To correctly address this major issue of water-use needs, a better understanding of the links between water security, food security and environmental security is required. This is what this book is all about. It is not another book addressing one or other single approach to studying fresh water. It is addressing, among so many others, the issues of incorporating water for ecosystem services and finding the balance between water for humans and water for nature, and introducing soil water into the water-balance equation. It also addresses a number of very controversial subjects, including the issues of virtual water or invisible water; increasing the productivity of fresh water (more crop per drop) and water as an economic good, or the burning issue of water pricing. These issues, together with the issue of shared water resources, come at the top of the global water agenda in the 21st century.

This book is a truly authoritative basis for a better understanding of the complex issues surrounding fresh water. I strongly believe that fresh water experts as well as policy-makers will benefit tremendously from the excellent approach followed in this book to the maze of issues involved in freshwater management.

Mostafa K Tolba
Former Executive Director
United Nations Environment Programme

Preface

Human welfare is built on beneficial use of natural resources, but has generated environmental problems that continue to escalate in spite of 40 years of efforts to contain them. The UN Millennium Declaration (UN, 2000) exposes a deeply felt willingness on the part of state leaders to get out of this disastrous dilemma and eradicate problems of poverty, hunger and ill health – all of them linked to human interactions with the global ecosystem that constitutes the planet's life-support system. But the ability to reach those goals will depend on a less fragmented perception of the life-support system, how it functions and how humanity must manipulate its components. In particular, we need to find out how to balance two partly incompatible imperatives: human welfare and protection of the environmental resource base on which that welfare is built.

This book has its focus on four key areas in which society interacts with water, which involve quite different functions: water supply to humans and industry; water as a component of the plant production process; water as a silent, but active, actor involved in generating the many environmental impacts of human activities; and water in relation to droughts.

Achieving the goals of the Millennium Declaration will therefore be an issue of socio-ecohydrological balancing between beneficial use of water, and the fundamental goods and services that it provides (such as food, fibre, timber, energy, etc), and protection of essential ecosystem functions. Whereas earlier studies of the link between water and ecosystems have been limited to aquatic ecosystems, this book also focuses on terrestrial ecosystems. The presentation builds on the groundbreaking ecohydrological analyses of biomass production in different world biomes by the late Professor M I L'vovich, of Moscow University, to whose memory we are dedicating the book. His conceptualization has been captured within the green water flow concept, introduced at a Food and Agriculture Organization (FAO) seminar in 1993, which refers to the vapour flow involved in the photosynthesis process in which two-thirds of the precipitation over the continents is being literally consumed.

The book enters ecohydrology from the perspective of water, paying due attention to its many parallel functions. In doing so, it builds on thoroughgoing discussions with Professor Carl Folke and his group at the Department of Systems Ecology, at Stockholm University, and members of the international Resilience Alliance. These discussions resulted in 1999 in the first calculation of the green water flow from the main biomes.

In order to make the book readily accessible for readers with a variety of specializations – whether biophysically or socio-economically oriented – each chapter ends with a summary of its main messages.

In developing the book we have been strongly influenced by three savanna-region scientists: Professor M M Sivanappan (Coimbatore, Tamil Nadu) and the late Dr Anil

Agarwal (New Delhi), both in India, and Professor Nuhu Hatibu (Sokoine University, Tanzania). These contacts clearly revealed to us the importance of learning to live with droughts and dry spells. In view of the untapped water resources in savanna regions, the book pays particular attention to the challenges and possibilities there. This is further motivated by the deep poverty of these regions, the scale of ill health and hunger that they suffer, and the extremely rapid population growth.

This book would not have been possible without the resources provided by the Volvo Environment Prize 1998 and the institutional support of the Department of Systems Ecology, at Stockholm University, in close cooperation with UNESCO-IHE Institute for Water Education, in Delft. Particularly valuable has been the contribution of the Stockholm International Water Institute (SIWI), and in particular Stephanie Blenckner, who prepared most of the illustrations. Special thanks are due to Professor Carl Widstrand and his wife, Rede, from Ottawa in Canada, for their efforts in improving the English and readability of the text.

Malin Falkenmark   Johan Rockström
Professor   Associate Professor

Stockholm
July 2003

List of Acronyms and Abbreviations

CFWA	UN Comprehensive Freshwater Assessment
CIMMYT	Centro Internacional de Majoramiento de Maiz y Trigo, Mexico
CWR	crop water requirement
CV	coefficient of variation
D	deep percolation, or drainage
E	evaporation
EIA	environmental impact assessment
ET	evapotranspiration
Etot	total evaporation
FAO	Food and Agriculture Organization
FAOSTAT	Food and Agriculture Organization statistics
GNP	gross national product
GWP	Global Water Partnership
IAHS	International Association for Hydrological Science
ICRAF	International Center for Research in Agroforestry (World Agroforestry Center)
IIASA	International Institute for Applied Systems Analysis
IRRI	International Rice Research Institute, Phillipines
IWMI	International Water Management Institute, Sri Lanka
IWRM	Integrated Water Resources Management.
kcal	kilocalorie
p	rainfall
PAI	Population Action International
PET	potential evapotranspiration
Roff	surface runoff
SD	standard deviation
SIWI	Stockholm International Water Institute
t	tonne (metric)
T	transpiration
UN	United Nations
UNCED	United Nations Conference on Environment and Development
UNCFA	United Nations Comprehensive Freshwater Assessment
UNDP	United Nations Development Programme
UNEP	United Nations Environment Programme
UNESCO	United Nations Educational, Scientific and Cultural Organization
UNESCO-IHE	UNESCO-IHE Institute for Water Education
UNFPA	United Nations Population Fund
WCD	World Commission on Dams

WP	water productivity
WUE	water use efficiency
WWC	World Water Council
WWF	World Water Forum
y	yield

Introduction

Water is the elixir of life on Planet Earth; it is equally fundamental for humans and ecosystems. Our planet is the only one in the solar system where liquid water can exist (National Research Council, 1991). The most fundamental role of water is as the bloodstream of the biosphere. However, the tendency among policy-makers and the general public is to see water mainly as a technical issue. This tendency is a barrier to sustainable development, but it is a natural consequence of past experiences in human history. Such experiences go back a long way.

Early civilizations developed in regions where water was a dominant component of the environment and a challenge to human ingenuity (Leopold and Davis, 1968). The Euphrates and Tigris river system supported Mesopotamia, Egyptian culture developed around the Nile, and other agricultural cultures that were created along the Indus River and the Yellow River. Brilliant engineering supported all these early civilizations by securing easy access to river water for irrigation and transport.

In the Euphrates–Tigris system, the Mesopotamians built both urban water supply systems and a network of water highways for navigation. The Babylonians developed regulations for water use. The Assyrian capital of Nineveh was located on the Tigris, but a 60 km canal, bringing water from the mountains to water the famous gardens, regulated the irregular behaviour of the river. Equally technologically advanced was the great Harappan civilization in the 1600 km Indus valley, where the river was used for irrigation, communication and trade. A fourth river-fed civilization developed along the Yellow River in China, where people settled around 5000 BC. Cold winters with a frozen river and ice clogging on certain stretches were additional challenges to that of river flooding. The Chinese also excavated a 1500 km canal that is still partly in use 2500 years later.

However, none of these cultures was able to master water completely. Floods caused immense problems. Those of the Nile were most predictable with their clockwork regularity. In other rivers, the floods were more irregular. The floods of the Yellow River, for instance, gave it the name 'China's sorrow', as a single flood could take the life of millions. Beside the flooding, silting, waterlogging and salinization also caused severe problems in the river valleys.

Thus, while water is a vital ingredient of human life, it can also be destructive. Societies tried to adapt to disastrous floods, which became part of human life. But in addition, what we may call water's 'pick up and carry away' function was manifest in the development of erosion, silting, and salinization. In the end, these functions and their ecological and social consequences led to cultural breakdowns.

Over the centuries people have benefited from water in other ways than merely the support of navigation and irrigation of crop production. Water was part of the breakthrough invention in the 18th century of the steam-driven engine, which transforms the heat energy of water vapour into mechanical energy by acting on a piston in a closed cylinder. This water-driven engine became the key to the UK's Industrial Revolution. This was later followed by the development of hydropower for the generation of electricity. Engineering skills kept on improving and water projects grew larger and larger, culminating in huge dams for storage of wet-season water, and large-scale water transfers. Such projects made arid California inhabitable, for example, while in Central Asia, huge irrigation schemes were made possible along the rivers Amy Darya and Syr Darya, facilitating socioeconomic development upstream of the Aral Sea. However, since water is a finite resource, downstream of the Colorado River and in the Aral Sea there was severe degradation of the aquatic ecosystems due to lack of water.

The propensity of water to be a clandestine destroyer also pertained in these cases. Additionally, beside erosion and salinization, water pollution has become an increasingly serious problem. Socioeconomic development since World War II has been accompanied in most of the developing world by expanding environmental degradation. Although such degradation is now a worldwide phenomenon, there is what can be described as paralysis in terms of the efforts needed to mitigate the situation. The quality of natural water continues to deteriorate due to pollution from human activities. This problem is expanding in the developing world where small-scale industry constitutes the backbone of employment and economic development (Agarwal, 2001). Even in Western countries there is a similar paralysis when it comes to dealing with so-called diffuse pollutants: both Europe and the US have failed to overcome the continuous bleeding of nutrients and pesticides from agricultural land to groundwater, rivers, lakes and coastal waters.

Water is therefore a truly 'double-edged' resource. It saves lives but it can also take lives. It supports ecosystems, but can also degrade them by acting as a vector for pollutants and excess nutrients. As a result, water management is a challenge that is becoming more and more complex as humanity expands and its expectations keep increasing. There is scarcely any human activity that is not, in one way or another, linked to water.

Today, the world is experiencing what we may refer to as a set of arid zone surprises – for example, where immigrants from the temperate zone have settled in dry climate regions. European immigrants from the temperate zone transferred their bush- and forest-clearing habits to Australia and this eventually produced serious waterlogging and salinization problems. In regions where water is scarce for climatic reasons there are difficulties in securing both safe water for the population and enough water for adequate food production. Today, the regions with the greatest difficulties in terms of socioeconomic development, are the dry climate regions in sub-Saharan Africa and South Asia. In these regions, large-scale poverty and malnourishment remain, and rapid population growth continues. Beside problems of water supply, there are also problems caused by careless land use. Upstream land degradation tends to produce severe silting problems in water reservoirs further downstream.

These are some of the threats involved in what has been called an impending water crisis. Although the crisis has been discussed since the 1970s, when it was first highlighted by the book *Water for a Starving World*, presented in preparation for the United Nations Water Conference in 1977 (Falkenmark and Lindh, 1976), it was still neglected in the report *Our Common Future* of the World Commission on Environment and Development in 1987. The issues of environment and development and their links were discussed at the UN Conference on Environment and Development (the 'Earth Summit') in Rio in June 1992. Its outcome, Agenda 21, contains a long chapter on conventional water issues, but disregards the fundamental role of water in sustaining all ecological lifeforms on Earth.

In March 2000, in The Hague, the Second World Water Forum was organized by the World Water Council and attended by some 5000 participants. At this meeting, finally, a 'World Water Vision' was presented (Cosgrove and Rijsberman, 2000). The above introductory exposé of water-related challenges around the world shows that water is an extremely complex substance that, besides producing expected benefits, creates a whole set of unexpected phenomena. To be successful, water management will not only have to incorporate straightforward technological efforts but must also respond to the problems and benefits caused by the evident links between land use and water, between upstream and downstream regions, and between water and ecosystems. As understanding is increasing, a shift in thinking is now developing that links water security, food security and environmental security. This shift in thinking is what has prompted this book.

There is a Limited Understanding of the Constraints

Currently, some 800 million people suffer from malnutrition, and among them there are 200 million children below five years of age. Other fundamental weaknesses in the developing world are that 1.1 billion people still lack an organized water supply to their household for everyday use. Safe sanitation is lacking for 2.5 billion people, a fact that strongly contributes to the widespread occurrence of infectious diseases spread by bacterial and other pollutants from human faeces. All over the world there are examples of unsustainable water withdrawals, which cannot continue. The Colorado River, the Aral Sea tributaries and the Yellow River are the most flagrant examples of large-scale river depletion that seriously impact on downstream regions.

Besides all the above water-related problems, the driving forces exacerbating them are extremely strong. Population growth, urbanization, industrialization and globalization all contribute to increasing the pressure and are continuously 'squeezing' the planet's life support system and its life elixir, fresh water. Population growth, although having diminished during recent years, is still strong, and current projections indicate that it will continue for the next two decades (UN medium projections). The problem is that there seems to be a limited overall understanding of these constraints.

Although the world has been calling for sustainable development for some decades, it has failed to come close to that goal. The processes by which the global life support system is becoming more and more undermined are not yet broadly enough understood. Many of the water-related natural processes in the landscape are neither part of the agenda of policy-makers and politicians, nor that of the general public, which tends to see this issue as the realm of experts.

Several life-supporting processes in the landscape are linked to water, its functions and its movement in the hydrological cycle. Water is a unique solvent, continuously on the move through the landscape above and below the ground, and it is a key substance in the process of photosynthesis. Water contributes to a large part of the natural greenhouse effect and thus also affects the climate. With its atmosphere the Earth is 33°C warmer than it would be without it, and of those 33°C, 30°C are due to the water vapour in the atmosphere.

It took almost two decades for professionals to become alarmed over the water crisis and to take decisive action through the formation of the World Water Council and its project World Water Vision. What are the consequences of the fatal omission of water from the conceptualization of our planetary life support system?

- The pollution of groundwater – the drinking-water source of possibly the majority of the world's inhabitants – has been allowed to continue without few countermeasures.
- The leaking of nutrients from agricultural land all over the world has been allowed to continue decade after decade, now culminating in mats of toxic algae in lakes and coastal waters.
- There has not been enough conscious valuation of water as a resource, while what has dominated is a narrow perspective concentrating only on liquid water and only on sectoral approaches.

Only limited value has been given to water flows sustaining terrestrial ecosystems such as grasslands and forests.

Only recently, in a few countries, has the securing of water to sustain aquatic ecosystems in lakes and rivers become part of water management.

A New or Alternative Form of Knowledge is Needed

The present dilemma is that the experts tend to see only a minor part of the overall water-related issue. First, the dominant perception of what constitutes the renewable freshwater resource is truncated. Surface water is linked to locations in a river where stream flow can be measured, rather than to runoff formation. Groundwater is linked to storage rather than to groundwater renewal. While water professionals have only been able to master part of the pollution problem, there is also only a poor understanding of the implications for environmental problems of an expanding human population. The food production dilemma is poorly understood and so is the obvious conflict of interest in the area of protection of ecosystems.

In addressing the above difficulties two key perspectives will have to be properly highlighted: the involvement of water in the development of environmental problems and in the threats to viable ecosystems; and, the food production dilemma, especially in water-short semi-arid regions. Both these perspectives are closely linked to the function of water as the bloodstream of the biosphere. It is evident that managing the life elixir of our planet cannot remain the business of experts only! Because, ultimately, there has to be social acceptance of the way conflicting issues are balanced against each other.

In view of the central functions of water in our life support system, something must be fundamentally wrong when enormous interest and financial resources are devoted to finding water on Mars rather than the water on which our personal survival and quality of life depend. Part of the explanation is that in water-rich environments, ideas and actions are focused either on how to technically cope with various water problems, or on issues linked to water as a highly valued landscape amenity. People may be aware of details and peculiarities: of a certain well or spring in the neighbourhood; the water tap that provides the household with its water supply; the amount of water wasted in the toilet; the industrial wastewater flows; the fish in lakes and rivers; and of algal blooms in lakes and coastal waters. In contrast, there is poor awareness of the fundamental role played by fresh water in sustaining biological life in nature, and in determining the biological structure of ecosystems.

Evidently the approaches taken in the past have not been effective in protecting the world against the multidimensional water crisis now in view. Essential to our thesis, then, is that there is a need for a different type of knowledge and a better-integrated understanding of how water enters into the planet's life support system and how humanity can better cope with the constraints of that system. The role of water in all living systems can no longer remain in a conceptual void. The term 'ecohydrology' can no longer refer only to aquatic ecosystems, since terrestrial ecosystems are equally water-dependent. The role of water in ecosystem production can no longer remain neglected if we are going to be able to cope in a controlled way with the life support system of our human-dominated planet (Lubchenko, 1998).

Consequently, what is now needed is a wider knowledge base that makes it possible to take an ecological approach to land and water resources. A basis was laid by the UNESCO book *Comparative Hydrology: An Ecological Approach to Land and Water Resources* (Falkenmark and Chapman, 1989), which highlighted hydrological differences between different hydroclimates and between different landscape elements, in particular sloping lands and flatlands.

The Fundamental Dilemma

If we are worried today about a water scarcity crisis (Falkenmark, 1989; World Water Commission, 2000), how will it be possible to feed another 2–3 billion people in the next two to three decades (which would be the active professional years of today's graduate students)? We know that producing food is equivalent to getting water taken up by the roots to rise through a plant for the plant production process. As will be shown later, 1300 m^3/person/year would be needed as a generic water requirement to produce food at an acceptable nutrition level. This is more than 70 times the per capita amount of 50 litres per person per day used to indicate basic household needs of water. To produce food for another 3 billion in the next 50 years – whether in rainfed or irrigated agriculture – we will need an additional amount of water that is almost three times the amount presently used in irrigated agriculture.

Allowing such large additional amounts to evaporate might produce negative side effects on ecosystems, which could be seen as unacceptable. This means that we may envisage a conflict of interest between eliminating hunger and nutrition deficiencies on one hand and protecting ecosystems on the other. It is against this background that this book has been developed. It aims to bring together the mass of knowledge needed for addressing the food versus ecosystem dilemma. We must take an integrated approach to land, water and ecosystems as well as broaden the perception of water. We must take into account the involvement of water in terrestrial as well as aquatic ecosystems. We must also increase our understanding of the multiple water functions in the planetary life support system; of the value of ecosystem water; and of the value of water for socioeconomic development.

Blue and Green Water Flows

While two-thirds of total continental precipitation is involved in biomass production in terrestrial ecosystems (Rockström et al, 1999), only one-third (or 40,000 km^3/year) takes the liquid route to the sea. We refer to this as 'blue water flow'. Since in conventional water assessments only these 40,000 km^3 are seen as humanity's freshwater resource, the water needed for food production tends to be incorrectly understood as only the volume used for irrigation. In reality, however, 60–70 per cent of food production is rainfed and based on vapour flow from infiltrated rainfall, hereafter referred to as 'green water flow'.

To feed almost 2 billion more people in the next 25 years some say that most of the increase will have to come from irrigation. Others, however, see irrigation expansion as a more limited option, since a certain amount of water must remain in rivers in order to protect aquatic ecosystems. This leaves us with the fundamental question as to what degree rainfed production in the tropics could be made much more productive. Plants do not mind what sort of water reaches the root zone, whether rain or irrigation water.

Since water use as green water involved in food production is so large, the most vulnerable areas, and indeed the world's hot spots, are obviously the semi-arid tropics, the savanna zone. This is the region where a high degree of malnourishment and rapid population growth are increasing dramatically, and where large water-related difficulties tend to create very low crop yields in rainfed agriculture. We know that there is plenty of rainwater, but we also know that as much as two-thirds of the rainfall in Southern Africa, for example, goes back to the atmosphere unused as pure evaporation from moist surfaces. This represents a huge amount – in fact a hidden resource – that might be put to better use to bring up farmers' yields. Experiments suggest that doubling or even trebling crop yields even in water-scarce regions is feasible if nutrients are also added. If the elimination of hunger could be achieved in such regions, other regions with a less extreme hydroclimate would be expected to have fewer problems. For that reason, part of this book is dedicated to a more thorough analysis of the crop production challenge in the savanna zone.

The Book

Two conclusions can be drawn: First, it is essential to broaden the international discussion of food production from seeking solutions only in the increase of irrigated agriculture. Second, it will be necessary to address the conflict between tomorrow's food production needs and the need to save more water for ecosystems, which was the message of the environmentalists at the Hague Forum. In response to the latter problem, a large consortium of ten international organizations initiated (in 2001) formed for the Global Dialogue on Water for Food and Environment. This book is a contribution to the knowledge base supporting such dialogue. It aims at facilitating a better understanding for both agronomists and environmentalists of the joint problem: how to best benefit from and protect the fresh water passing through inhabited landscapes.

Both authors of the present book work in a university department of systems ecology, and thus have striven to properly link the presentation to ongoing discussions in systems ecology as well as in hydrology and water management. The discourse develops around crucial concepts: the water cycle, which can be seen as the bloodstream of both the biosphere and the anthroposphere; plant production, which is a process of consumptive water use; and rainwater partitioning into green and blue water flows that determines the productive use of water. A proper distinction between terrestrial and aquatic ecosystems, and the balancing of water between humans and nature, are other concerns of the authors.

The book begins with global-scale analyses of freshwater resources; it clarifies the many parallel roles of water and its functions in relation to both humans and ecosystems; it explains rainwater partitioning in different regions, the different modes of water use, both direct and indirect, and both blue (liquid) and green (vapour) water flows. Moreover, the book discusses in some depth the problem of where to find the additional green water that needs to be appropriated in order to produce enough food for the next two generations. How much can be gained by different ways of maximizing 'crop per drop' in irrigation, and what remains to be looked for elsewhere? And where is that elsewhere?

As already indicated, special focus will be on the semi-arid tropics, since they represent the largest challenges. While pollution problems dominate the humid region, and a very dry climate and pastoralism dominate the arid region, the semi-arid tropics, or the savanna zone, is the region where the conflict between more food production and protection of ecosystems stands out particularly clearly.

The extremely broad scope of water-related issues makes it important to make clear what the book does *not* cover – ie the limits the authors imposed on their analyses. The focus is on water resources management, not on water quality management or big-business involvement in water; on crop and meat production, not on fishery and coastal products; on water consumed in food production, not on irrigation; on the particular problems of the most vulnerable regions as seen from a water scarcity perspective, not on the problems of the temperate zone and the humid tropics.

The book is divided into three main parts:

1   Part 1, Chapters 1–5, takes a generic ecohydrological overview focusing on water functions and the water flows involved in those different functions.
2   Part 2, Chapters 6–8, deals with the predicament of the savanna zone with its rapid population growth and malnourishment, which is analysed in some detail from an ecohydrological aspect.
3   Part 3, Chapters 9–10, focuses on balancing water for humans and ecosystems, with a final chapter addressing issues related to the search for hydrosolidarity between upstream and downstream activities in a catchment, and between humans and ecosystems.

This book aims to be an eye-opener for a large community of experts involved in some aspect of these problems and challenges, whether old or young, whether from the North or South, whether agronomist, hydrologist, ecologist or economist. It will:

- Explain the development of human-generated environmental problems (Chapter 1).
- Clarify the links between humans, water and ecosystems (Chapters 1 and 9).
- Link the conventional approach to water resources with the broader view encouraged in studying water use and water functions in society as well as in ecosystems (Chapters 2, 3 and 4).
- Clarify fundamental regional differences in hydroclimate and in water-related degrees of freedom in view of both a remaining water reserve that can be mobilized and put to additional use, and the level of 'water-crowding' and dispute proneness due to high population pressure on a finite resource (Chapter 5).
- Put particular focus on the highly vulnerable semi-arid tropics and how the huge remaining water reserve there can be put to better use to prevent non-productive evaporation (Chapters 6, 7 and 8).
- Integrate the crucial water functions into a catchment perspective by an analysis of various hydrosolidarity aspects involved (Chapter 10).

Part 1

Water Functions in the Life-support System

1

Water – The Bloodstream of the Biosphere

Water is always on the move in the hydrological cycle. It is the very foundation for all biological life on Earth, and the basic link between the biosphere and the anthroposphere.

Water as the Liquid of Life

Water is the most essential component for the life of all beings. Hardly any economic activity can be sustained without water (Haddadin, 2001).

The water cycle links human society with ecosystems

In view of past failures, a better idea is now needed of the roles and functions of water in the global life support system. For example, the conventional conceptions of water related to plant production are increasingly unsatisfactory from a hydrological perspective. Through its physical, chemical and biological involvement, water has fundamental balancing functions in the water cycle (Ripl, 1995). It dissipates solar energy variations in space and time. This is performed through three main interactive processes with mutually balancing components:

1   Physical processes. The interaction between evaporation and condensation is of major importance for the distribution of energy around the planet.
2   Chemical processes. The interaction between crystallization and dissolution is of fundamental importance for the distribution of soluble substances around the planet.
3   Biological processes. The interaction between splitting water molecules in the first step of the photosynthesis process and their later re-assemblage through respiration creates sugar and oxygen in the process.

Figure 1.1 illustrates in a schematic way the linkages between the freshwater cycle, human livelihoods and ecosystems. The terrestrial system, fed by precipitation, returns green water to the atmosphere through the biomass production process. Aquatic ecosystems thrive in the habitats formed by the liquid blue water. Human society benefits from freshwater services for settlements and industries, and from crop

---

Box 1.1 Water – A Most Remarkable Substance

Water is a most remarkable substance. Water molecules have pervasive effects on macromolecules of proteins and nucleic acids (Chaplin, 2001). The water molecule is among the smallest of all molecules, but in spite of this it has highly complex properties, such as a large heat capacity and a high latent heat of evaporation. Water is an excellent solvent due to its polarity, high dielectric constant and small size. The complexity of its properties seems to fit ideally into the requirements of the carbon-based life on this planet as no other molecule can. Chaplin (2001) therefore stresses that we should always be alert to the central role that water plays in the rich diversity of biological processes.

The water cycle is an essential part of the life support mechanism of the planet. The interaction with the biota adds water vapour – an active greenhouse gas – to the atmosphere. The result is that the planet's temperature is kept 30°C higher than it would be without water in the atmosphere. Carbon dioxide (CO_2)contributes another 3°C. The resulting temperature rise allows liquid water to exist on Earth, something that makes this planet exceptional among all the planets in the solar system.

The human body is 65–70 per cent composed of water. None of this water is stagnant. Water is the body's busiest substance (Leopold and Davis, 1968). All the water molecules in one part of the body at any moment are somewhere else seconds later, and have been replaced by new molecules. Although the molecular formula is H_2O, the hydrogen atoms are constantly exchanged between neighbouring oxygen atoms. At pH7 the average time that a water molecule exists between gaining and losing a proton is only a millisecond.

The unique hydration properties of water to a large extent determine the three-dimensional structure of biological macromolecules, and hence also their functions in solution. Water networks around proteins link secondary structures and so determine fine details of a protein's structure. Hydrophobic interactions with surfaces to which water cannot form hydrogen bonds encourages a surface minimization that drives protein folding.

By introducing the concept of 'ecosystem goods and services' the ecological research community has increased the attention given to ecosystems among groups concerned with natural resource management. Gretchen Daily (1997) defined ecosystem services as 'the conditions and processes through which natural ecosystems, and the species that make them up, sustain and fulfil human life'. We also include in this definition the various forms of agricultural land, which can be seen as ecosystems manipulated by humans. Ecosystems provide a wide spectrum of essential 'goods' for supporting life, such as timber, food and biodiversity, as well as 'services', such as maintenance of genetic resources, partitioning of rainfall, and pollination for our food consumption needs. Some ecological services are evident, but others are not immediately obvious. Based on a systematic approach, we may structure the 'services' as follows (FAO, 2000):

- Physical services, such as phosphorus absorption in the soil, erosion and sedimentation of silt, interception of rainfall, and facilitating rainwater infiltration into the soil.
- Chemical services, such as oxygen production and CO_2 uptake in the photosynthesis process, denitrification, and nutrient release through biodegradation.
- Biological services, such as photosynthesis, pollination, seed dispersal, pest control, production of biomass, and macropore creation in the soil.

---

irrigation. When linking this figure to Ripl's balancing processes (1995), one finds that the different branches of the water cycle are basically dominated by different key functions. The physical functions in the atmospheric green water branch of the hydrological cycle involve a balancing of evaporation from land and water surfaces

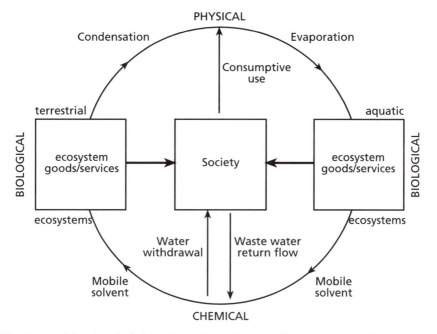

Note: The terrestrial system is fed by the water cycle, aquatic ecosystems thrive in the habitats formed by the water, and society withdraws water for its needs and returns the water either as a (polluted) return flow of wastewater or as a green water flow/evaporation.

Figure 1.1 *Schematic illustration of links between the cyclic movement of fresh water, the terrestrial and the aquatic ecosystems, and human society*

and condensation of vapour into water droplets that combine and form rainfall. The lower left section of Figure 1.1 shows the blue water branch of the hydrological cycle with its biological and chemical functions. Blue water flows are important determinants of aquatic habitats. Biological functions in terrestrial ecosystems are closely linked to green water flow. Blue water derives its quality from interactions within terrestrial ecosystems, and carries out chemical functions. It is important to realize that the planetary life support system is composed of both a non-negotiable biological sphere, which includes the interactions between the biosphere and the water cycle, and a negotiable socioeconomic sphere, which includes human activities (FAO, 2000).

Distinguishing between green and blue water flows

We have already used the terms blue and green water, so this would be a convenient place to explain more fully what is represented by these concepts. The picture of the principal partitioning of rainfall into green and blue water flows at the soil surface is shown in Figure 1.2.

Blue water flow is the visible liquid water flow moving above and below the ground as surface or sub-surface runoff, respectively (FAO, 1995b, 1997). Blue water flow can thus be in the form of surface runoff in rills, gullies and rivers, or water flowing

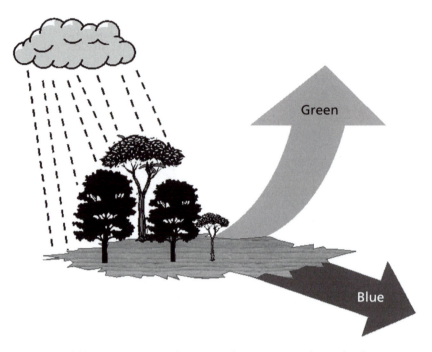

Figure 1.2 *Rainfall partitioning – the vertical green water branch of water vapour and the semi-horizontal blue water branch of liquid water*

underground, recharging water tables and aquifers. Green water flow is defined as the invisible flow of vapour to the atmosphere (FAO, 1995, 1997). Productive green water flow is defined as the transpiration from plants or trees, which directly contributes to biomass growth. Non-productive green water flow consists of the evaporation flows from soil (direct evaporation from water puddles on the soil surface and evaporation of water from the soil), and evaporating interception (rainfall trapped in the canopies of trees and plants). Green water flow thus equates to the commonly used term evapotranspiration, which combines productive and non-productive vapour flows in one term. We will return to this discussion in Chapter 2.

Both blue and green water flows support ecological functions and delivery of ecosystem goods and services. Both are also a precondition for human survival and societal development.

Another important difference between green and blue water flows is that green water flow (evaporation + transpiration) always involves a consumptive use of water, which is not the case with blue water use. Green water cannot be used again further downstream. Blue water, on the other hand, can be recycled and reused again. For example, because irrigation is so inefficient, only a fraction of the blue water withdrawn from the system is consumed as green water flow. A large portion percolates and recharges groundwater, and can therefore be reused further downstream.

As will be seen later, the distinction between green and blue water flows is useful in hydrologically based projections of water needs for food production for a growing world population. The idea of dividing water flows into green and blue water is a new concept and the terms will therefore be used consistently throughout this book. This will allow a discussion in later chapters of the consumptive use of water for crop production compared to the water involved in biomass production in the main biomes of the world.

The green/blue concept will also be useful in a closer analysis of water balance alterations linked to land-use changes and referred to as 'blue/green redirections'. We will show through examples that a land-use decision is also a decision about water. Consumptive use phenomena have in the past often been subsumed under the term 'environmental impacts'. Such phenomena need to be a topic for discussion so that incompatible water uses can be properly analysed. Serious conflicts of interest can be foreseen between human activities and biomass production upstream in a river basin and the activities downstream. The conflicts will be particularly difficult in basins with a rapid population growth and escalating food needs.

Society and ecosystems share the same water

If we look at the planetary life support system on the landscape scale, there is only one water source and that is precipitation. Since we will not be discussing the peculiarities of cold climates and snow in this book, we will speak of precipitation solely as rainfall. On sloping land, all water-dependent human activities and all the ecosystems are enclosed in nature's own water delivery system, the catchment or drainage basin. This is the area inside a water divide, such as a mountain or other ridge. All rain falling inside that water divide constitutes the shared water resource of all the water-dependent activities there. After reaching the land surface the water is partitioned into the green water flow and the blue water flow. The former consists of evaporated water (see above) while the latter moves downhill from land to water systems (see Figure 1.3).

The green water flow system incorporates the water consumption by forests, grasslands and rain-fed croplands. It sustains terrestrial ecosystems as well as rainfed crop production. The blue water system sustains aquatic ecosystems and constitutes the water resource directly available to, and 'harvested' by humans. After use, this blue flow goes back to the water system as a return flow of wastewater, often loaded with pollutants. Blue water is also withdrawn to support irrigation, and during use part of that water, the consumptive portion, will turn into green water flow, while the surplus, the non-consumptive portion, forms a return flow of blue water. When agrochemicals are used, and when runoff carries sediments from erosion, the return flow is often loaded with leached agrochemicals and soil nutrients, causing eutrophication in the water system and coastal waters.

These are some of the characteristics of the basic hydrological landscape unit, the catchment, in which rainfall is shared between terrestrial and aquatic systems, and between nature and human society. This is the unit in which a balance between man and nature must be struck. Before we proceed to a few policy directions that follow from the considerable complexity of water issues, we will address human manipulation of the landscape and its environmental consequences.

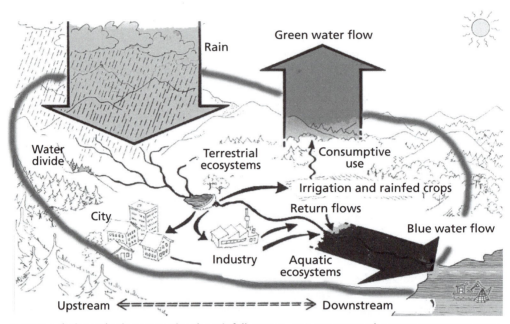

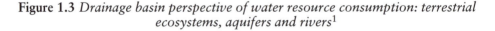

Note: In a drainage basin perspective the rainfall over an area represents the proper water resource, part of which is consumed in terrestrial ecosystems by vegetation and evaporation from moist surfaces (green water flow), while the surplus goes to recharge aquifers and rivers (blue water flow), becoming available for societal use and aquatic ecosystems.

Figure 1.3 *Drainage basin perspective of water resource consumption: terrestrial ecosystems, aquifers and rivers*[1]

Focusing on Invisible Water

The past focus on visible water

Human history is more or less the product of successful water control, through which fundamental human needs could be met, such as everyday household water supply and the requirements of crop irrigation to supply food to the population.

The utilitarian function of water has caught the human imagination and throughout history a wealth of ingenious devices has been developed to transfer water from wetter to drier areas. It was also realized early on that falling water could be used as an energy source. Since World War II water pollution has attracted increasing attention. There are many severe diseases caused by toxic or polluted water, such as the mass poisoning episodes dues to cadmium and mercury (*minamata* and *itai-itai* in Japan from the 1940s to the 1960s (Nash, 1993). There have also been problems with agrochemicals, such as fertilizers and pesticides, since the development of mechanized and chemically dependent agriculture. Nitrate leaching has contaminated groundwater, and many potential water sources have become degraded.

Until the last decade two major professional groups dominated thinking about water: engineers and aquatic ecologists. Both focused on visible blue water, with the engineers interested in the direct function of water and the methods of controlling the flows, while the freshwater and marine ecologists focused on the indirect ecological functions of visible water.

Until the last two decades, all the attention of managers was concentrated on visible water in rivers and aquifers. In spite of the fact that water is one of the two raw materials in plants – the other being carbon dioxide from the air – ecologists focused on energy and nutrient flows. Among engineers, on the other hand, crop production was thought of as an irrigation issue and remains so among most water professionals today. For the crops themselves, however, it is not pertinent where the water available to their roots comes from – whether it is infiltrated rainwater or water added through irrigation. In fact, some 60–70 per cent of world food production originates from rainfed agriculture (Wood et al, 2000). Similarly, huge amounts of water are consumed in plant production in the main biomes of the world: the forests and the grasslands. As will be shown in more detail in Chapter 4, almost 90 per cent of the vapour flow from the continents is involved in the plant production of terrestrial ecosystems.

This water blindness is quite fascinating. In view of the rapidly growing world population, and the warnings from environmentalists that large-scale expansion of irrigation will be unacceptable, it is absolutely essential to focus on the invisible water in the soil that is necessary for plant production. In large parts of the semi-arid tropical region no large-scale expansion of irrigation can be foreseen in the next few decades. This further stresses the need to focus on the function of invisible water in rainfed agriculture.

The scale of water consumption in plant production

The water primarily involved in plant production – ie the soil moisture – has in ecological texts tended to be lumped together with soil. Water itself has been seen as an abiotic factor in soil, one without biological functions and simply considered as an attribute of the soil. This is also evident from the concepts involved in production ecology. The presence of water is taken for granted and production refers to the interaction of energy and matter and is seen as energy accumulation rather than the formation of new organic matter from water and CO_2 (Falkenmark and Lundqvist, 1997). In agricultural production the growth potential is understood as the potential realized when crops grow with ample supply of water and nutrients. The growth potential concept is rather deceptive as it invites the false conclusion that by simply multiplying it by the arable land area available one can arrive at a figure for the potential agricultural production of the world. Such an approach to water in relation to land productivity disregards the fact that the scarcity of soil moisture is a fundamental characteristic of dry climate regions, for example in sub-Saharan Africa.

Brismar (1996) conducted a conceptual study on land production constraints and desertification that was based on a set of basic and widely acknowledged sources. The aim was to see how much proper attention was paid to important water related conditions, and what processes and linkages were limiting land productivity. The study

Table 1.1 *The multiple uses and benefits of water*

	Visible	*Invisible*
Direct	Water supply	Food production
Indirect	Aquatic ecological services	Terrestrial ecological services

made it clear that widespread 'water blindness' characterized the approaches, with the result that water was indeed subsumed within the term soil. Phenomena were discussed in terms of short-cut linkages between soil and land productivity, and between rainfall and land productivity. Authors tended to focus on the visible rather than the key invisible phenomena that affect productivity in dry climate regions.

The invisibility of water is twofold: there are the direct functions of water as manifested in plant production; and the indirect functions related to the involvement of water as a fundamental determinant in terrestrial ecosystems. Table 1.1 shows this twofold invisibility. First, it shows the multiple usefulness of water both directly for water supply and for food production; second, it shows the indirect usefulness of water for the production of ecological services produced in both aquatic and terrestrial ecosystems.

Scientific literature, however, reveals that the prevailing focus remains on visible ecosystem goods such as food, fish and biomass, without attention to how the ecosystems function and the ways in which they produce those goods (FAO, 2000; Baird and Wilby, 1999).

To summarize, the water in the plant root zone, consumed in the photosynthesis process, constitutes part of the local water balance. If more water is used to produce plant mass, less water will remain to recharge aquifers and rivers. Since rivers around the world are rapidly becoming depleted, it is crucial that we relate the green and blue water branches to each other. The flow that is inherently linked to plant production has to be made 'visible' and integrated into the analysis.

Only part of the vertical branch of the water cycle passes through plants. The particular ecohydrological conditions of the semi-arid tropics have resulted in natural ecosystems and agro-ecosystems that are characterized by sparse vegetation with trees and plants standing at a distance from each other. The implications of this are that a large part of the green water flow is unproductive, as it goes back to the atmosphere by evaporation from wet soil between the plants and trees. We find an example of this in Southern Africa, where it is common for two-thirds of the incoming rainfall to immediately go back to the atmosphere via evaporation from wet soils, while only 20 per cent takes the productive route through the root zone. Only about 15 per cent of the rainfall remains as surplus available to recharge aquifers and rivers (Heyns, 1993).

The role of green water flow in sustaining rainfall

An important but often ignored aspect of the water cycle is that green water vapour flows support the formation of rainfall over the landscape, forming an important moisture feedback loop. On a global scale we know that about 40 per cent of terrestrial rainfall stems from oceanic moisture that is transported inland by wind. It is, however, not widely known that about 60 per cent of rainfall stems from vapour produced from the land surface. This means that the hydrological 'bloodstream' that supports the biosphere and the anthroposphere is, to a large extent, generated by the biosphere itself. This leads to the important conclusion that natural or manmade changes in the landscape can have significant impacts on the sustainability and reliability of rainfall.

The origin of rainfall, terrestrial or marine, depends primarily on the size of the landmass. On small islands the contribution of local evaporation is negligible, whereas on large continents the effect of moisture feedback through terrestrial evaporation is dominant (Savenije, 1995, 1996a and 1996b). As a rule of thumb, if the path of the moisture over the land is longer than 500–1000 km, then the effect of local evaporation becomes dominant over oceanic moisture. In the Sahel belt, for instance, 90 per cent of the rainfall stems from continental evaporation. In the central US recycling of moisture can amount to up to 60 per cent of the rainfall (Bosilovich and Schubert, 2001).

Evaporation from the land surface thus recycles moisture to the atmosphere and sustains rainfall. The amount of rainfall (on a monthly timescale) is a linear function of this moisture content in the atmosphere. If the amount of atmospheric moisture is reduced, then the rainfall is reduced until it reaches a lower threshold, below which there is no longer any significant rainfall (De Groen and Savenije, 1996). If evaporation were completely eliminated – that is, if all rainwater flowed directly to the river – then the rainfall in West Africa, for instance, would be limited to a belt stretching about 500 km inland from the coast. Currently, the rainfall reaches some 2000 km from the coast; but this distance is getting shorter. The reason for this is that land-use change causes an increasing percentage of rainfall to be converted to runoff. If the percentage of rainfall that becomes runoff is increased, then the amount of moisture feedback to the atmosphere is reduced at the same rate. This percentage is directly proportional to the distance that rainfall penetrates inland.

In the savanna and steppe belts of West Africa, there has been significant land-use change. Where there was originally shifting cultivation with a high degree of natural vegetation, permanent settlements have become dominant and natural vegetation is reduced. Cropland always evaporates less than natural vegetation, simply because of the limited root depth of a monoculture. In a natural habitat biomass production is optimal, which includes maximum use of the water for transpiration by vegetation. Ploughing and cultivation generally promote surface runoff, thus reducing evaporation. In summary, land-use change reduces evaporation during the rainy season, reduces moisture recycling, and moisture feedback to the atmosphere and, thereby, reduces rainfall further inland. During dry years, people expand their forest-clearing activities even more, which exacerbates the limited moisture recycling.

The consequences for both ecosystems and agricultural production can be dramatic. In the Sahel, they have suffered enormously, and the equilibrium that existed before the 1970s has gradually been disturbed, with the sequence of dry years during the 1980s accelerating the process.

Most scientists in the 1980s blamed climate change for the disastrous Sahelian drought. Now the idea is becoming more accepted that the drought period was only the trigger. Human activities that were driven by drought, rather than the drought itself, intensified the land degradation and led to the persistence of drought effects. A series of wet years was required to partially restore the system.

Different Scales of Water–Plant Interactions

Basic water–plant interaction

Our first focus here is on how plants use water and how water moves in plants. As already stressed, photosynthesis starts with the splitting of the water molecule. This is followed by a second biochemical reaction in which the hydrogen molecule, which has now become free, reacts with CO_2 from the air to form the sugar molecules that constitute the basic building blocks of plant biomass (Waterlow et al, 1998). The plant absorbs CO_2 by opening the stomata in the leaves. At the same time, plants lose water by diffusion of water vapour into the air through the stomata. Water ascends cellulose pipes inside the plants to replace the lost water. The driving force is generated by surface tension at the leaf surface and the tension is transmitted through the continuous water columns to the root tips (Tyree, 1999). Plants can thus be seen as highly sophisticated and strong suction pumps, where the roots do all they can to even out the large pressure difference between the wet root (low pressure or tension) and the dry leaf (high pressure or tension) following the thermodynamic law on conservation of energy. The result is a water flow driven by differences in water potential or pressure between the soil and evaporating surfaces in the leaves.

The 'pump' is only active during sunlight hours when photosynthesis occurs, and it stops during the night when the stomata close. During periods of plant water stress, the soil around the roots becomes dry, which evens out the pressure between the leaf and the soil (high tension or pressure in both ends) and the pump stops. The dryness at the leaf–air interface, which determines the pressure gradient between root and leaf, is regulated by the dryness of the air close to the leaf surface. This dryness is, in turn, determined by the potential evaporation of the air – the 'thirstiness' of the air or the capacity of the air to transform liquid water into vapour. If the same plant is grown in a cold and a warm climate, productive green water flow will be much higher in the warm climate (where the dryness at the leaf–air interface will be much higher) compared to the cold climate.

This water movement can be seen as purely passive from the biological perspective, in the sense that it is a spontaneous process in a system striving towards equilibrium. There is no input of biological energy, and the plants act like standing wicks: the roots extract water from the soil to replace the water that evaporates from the leaves during the process of photosynthesis. It may seem paradoxical to say that one of most water-consuming biological processes on Earth – productive green water flow through plants – is not an active process but a passive effect of active CO_2 uptake during photosynthesis. The 200–1000m³ transpiration flow required to generate 1 tonne of biomass flows off to the atmosphere and can thus be seen as a non-negotiable side effect of photosynthesis. However, as we mentioned earlier, this is not completely true, as the water flowing from soil to plant carries plant nutrients from the soil, keeps the plants cool, and secures the turgor of the plants.

Furthermore, there are other strong plant–water interactions. Roots are able to send chemical signals to the leaves, thereby mediating stomata closure to avoid further losses to the atmosphere. With soil water deficiency, plants wilt by drooping when turgor pressure in the cells falls, which leads to loss of conductance due to gas bubbles in the plant vessels (xylem).

Plant species have evolved in adaptation to their environment. In arid regions, various forms of succulent such as cacti have developed mechanisms to store water in inner compartments of the leaves. In wetter tropical environments plants have developed the capacity to store CO_2 in compartments of the leaf, thereby reducing the exposure of the stomata to the atmosphere. These so-called C4 plants include such important food crops as maize, millet and sorghum, while rice, wheat, barley, oats and rye are examples of so-called C3 crops with no similar mechanism for regulating CO_2 uptake.

Plants and water in terrestrial ecosystems

Landscape ecosystems are our next focus. These can be distinguished by hydroclimate, which is generally the relation between rainfall and potential evaporation. *Savanna and steppes* – namely arid, semi-arid and dry-sub-humid ecosystems – are at the drier end of the hydroclimatic gradient. They are generally defined as steppes in cold temperate climates and savannas in hot tropical climates. Savannas and steppes are characterized by low biological productivity, with an annual biomass growth in the order of 300–700 g/m^2 (Wainwright et al, 1999). Rainfall is subject to strong seasonal, inter-annual and long-term variability. The evaporative demand of the atmosphere is high so that canopies are open, with often less than 30 per cent plant cover. Vegetation patterns are quite complex with large bare patches. The supply of water forms the dominant control on the growth and maintenance of plants. Due to the extreme variability, plants must adapt. The low vegetation cover makes the soil–vegetation–atmosphere transfers complex, and land surface degradation has atmospheric feedbacks. The timing, intensity, and seasonality of rainfall determine the hydrological fate of the rainwater.

Forests and woodlands are another dominant type of terrestrial ecosystem. They may be discussed both from the perspective of the importance of water for the trees and from the perspective of the importance of trees for the water in the landscape. Trees often have extensive and deep root systems that exploit water beyond the reach of shallow rooted vegetation, and they can survive long rain-free periods (Roberts, 1999). They represent the principal green water route from the continents, with a total evaporation of almost 20,000 km^3/year (Rockström et al, 1999).

One component of this green water flow is the interception loss from the foliage (direct evaporation of rainfall trapped on the surface of leaves and stems of plants and trees). The losses are often less from seasonal canopies (Roberts, 1999). Forest transpiration tends to be of the order of 3–4 mm/day, which is well below the potential evaporation. There are only small differences between temperate and tropical forests.

Trees in tropical forests may have 15 m deep roots. The function of such deep roots remains unclear, however, but might produce insurance for the driest years. Infiltration may be aided in dry conditions by root shrinkage during dry periods, but there may also be other conduits and macropores in the soil. Soil moisture is subject to considerable local variations caused by differences in infiltration and root uptake. Most woody vegetation may have 50 per cent of its roots in the upper 30 cm. In humid forests, the lateral spread of roots corresponds to the size of the canopy, but in semi-arid woodlands it is much larger and defines the distance between trees on the savanna, as shown by Eagleson's classical analysis (Eagleson and Segarra, 1985). Runoff production is of particular interest from the erosion aspect. The emphasis conventionally put on tree planting to mitigate soil degradation by erosion originates from simplistic analyses based on temperate zone experiences in the UK and US. Due to the open canopy patterns and large exposed soil surfaces, sediment yield is of special importance in drylands, as will be further elaborated in Chapter 6.

Trees are important for the routing of incoming rainfall. They determine whether rain infiltrates or forms rapid runoff. Much attention is therefore being paid to forests in upper catchment locations where groundwater is being recharged. Protection of upstream forests is important for a stable stream flow further downstream. Forests are also feeding the atmosphere with water vapour, thereby influencing precipitation patterns in neighbouring areas. This function is reflected in popular debate, where forests tend to be credited with a number of vague effects in terms of impacts on water balance, and the generation of runoff (Sandström, 1995). Forests are thought of as behaving like sponges, providing buffer-stock supplies of dry-season flow. Opinions differ, however. Thus, for experts with temperate zone experience, deforestation is known to cause an increase in streamflow, while developing country farmers in the tropical zone have observed that deforestation reduces the dry season flow in the river. Sandström analysed these opposite opinions, concluding that the differences relate to the fact that the infiltrating rainfall (as will be clarified in Chapter 2) passes two partitioning points, the visual one at the land surface, and the invisible one in the root zone.

Plants and water in wetlands

The next type of ecosystem to analyse is *wetlands*. The links to water have been much more thoroughly analysed for this type than for drylands and forests. The term wetland already represents an extremely broad concept in ecology and mainly stands for a land that is rather wet, irrespective of what type of water keeps the land wet. A basic distinction can be made between aquatic wetlands, which are part of an aquatic ecosystem, and wet terrestrial systems. The reason for having one term for such different conditions is the shared characteristics of water saturation and low oxygen content and low potential for reduction and oxidization (Wheeler, 1999). The basic characteristic used in ecology to define wetlands is that the land is wet enough to support typical wetland vegetation, which differs clearly from the vegetation of well-drained land (Pielou, 1998). In other words, its vegetation defines a wetland, not its hydrology.

Wetlands are particularly abundant in regions where drainage systems are incompletely developed. For example, North American wetlands are more productive in terms of plant growth, compared to either agricultural land or natural grassland

(Pielou, 1998). They are storehouses for biodiversity. They are irreplaceable habitat for vast numbers of birds, which breed there or stop there to feed while migrating. Basically, wetlands form wherever poorly drained land collects enough water to be submerged or saturated most of the time.

Wetlands have been classified since the early 1900s according to different aspects, including flooding depth, dominant vegetation and salinity regimes (Mitsch and Gosselink, 2000). For the purpose of this book, a simple classification based on hydrological flow is most useful. From this perspective there are several main types of wetland (Pielou, 1998): bogs, fens, marshes and swamps. The first two are known as peatlands. The water in the bog is mainly rainwater, stagnant and poor in nutrients, while the water in the fen can be either seeping groundwater or surface runoff water, which are both nutrient rich and slowly moving. The result is spectacular differences in vegetation.

The second group of wetlands dries out from time to time and peat cannot form since the land is only seasonally flooded. Such non-peaty wetlands tend to develop in warmer, drier climates than do peat-lands. The two main forms, swamps and marshes, differ by their vegetation: the former has trees, the latter grass-like plants. In swamps the water table sinks below the root zone during the dry season, whereas marshes have vegetation that can grow in constantly wet soil. Wet meadows with waterlogged soil and with a more varied vegetation are intermediate between marshes and dry land.

It follows from the above distinctions that the main water determinants of terrestrial wetlands are rainfall (bogs), lateral water flow (fens), flood water (swamps and marshes), and groundwater seepage (fens and wet meadows). The conclusion has been drawn that soil moisture may be more important than the level of the water table (Wheeler, 1999). When the water table is high the aquifer may be supplying water to the wetland, whereas when it drops the water starts moving downward, recharging the groundwater (Acreman, 2000).

Flood pulses are of fundamental importance in many wetlands where the ecosystems have developed in close relation to the flood regime of the adjoining river. The importance of this phenomenon for sustaining the biological life of wetlands led ecologists to develop systems of flood wave mimicking in dammed rivers. This was done through improved control of discharge from a dam in order to allow, for instance, flooding of downstream riparian pastures (World Commission on Dams, 2000).

Many wetlands are fed mainly by groundwater seepage, such as those in valley floors where the groundwater recharged in the surrounding hills reappears as seepage in the bottom flat lands of the catchment areas (Acreman, 2000).

How do wetlands function hydrologically in a catchment? We indicated that wetlands might recharge groundwater during periods when the water table of the land area surrounding the wetland is reduced. Other fundamental functions are flow regulation and water quality modifications due to biochemical reactions in the wetland ecosystem. Due to the biochemical reactions between the water in the wetland and its chemical components, wetlands are sometimes spoken of as 'kidneys in the landscape' (Acreman, 2000), referring to water quality improvements in terms of sedimentation and absorption/biodegradation of nutrients and certain pollutants.

All wetlands require water, associated sediments and nutrients to survive (Acreman, 2000). Today, wetlands are seen as respected water users in catchment management. Securing a threshold ecological flow is therefore sometimes recommended to sustain a minimum habitat and keep target species alive. Overall, wetlands are water-consuming components of the landscape and do not produce water. They may facilitate groundwater recharge during flood season, a fact that may have contributed to the false idea that they are water producing.

Water/plant/biota in aquatic ecosystems

The links between water and freshwater biota in waterbodies tend to be addressed under the concept of hydroecology or limnology. In many studies the focus has mainly been on the role of water quality in determining habitat for flora and fauna in aquatic ecosystems. Since much attention has been paid to hydroecology, reflected not least in the rich literature in the field, this section will be kept short and raise only issues of particular relevance for this book. Three complementary perspectives may be discussed here: the water system as a habitat determining the diversity of freshwater biota; the influence of freshwater plants on hydraulic properties in a river; and evaporation from vegetation in shallow lakes (Dunbar and Acreman, 2001).

In streams, water movement is considered to be the most important factor affecting plant distribution (Large and Prach, 1999). Stream habitats tend to have a patchy distribution of large plants due to a mix of localized low and high flow velocities and differences in sediment distribution. At the same time, conditions are interactive in the sense that the large plants tend to reduce flow velocity and enhance sedimentation, thereby offering habitats for invertebrates and fish. Flow variability is one of the primary determinants of species distribution in riverine systems. The relative contribution of groundwater outflow is also important (Wood et al, 2001).

A lake ecosystem is closely linked to the water and chemical inflows from the catchment (Wetzel, 1999). Lakes are topographic depressions that have become filled with water from a drainage basin. The lake water is modified by vertical water exchange through the combination of precipitation and evaporation over the lake surface. The chemical components in the blue water inflow from the drainage basin provide an ionic input to the lake. Once in the lake, biochemical processes and the vertical water exchange will modify the water quality. In lakes where there is a net vertical input, the inflow is diluted by the precipitation, reducing the ionic content. In lakes with a net vertical loss of water, there is a hydrological enrichment of the ionic content.

As a consequence, habitat characteristics of lakes differ according to the relative roles of horizontal and vertical water exchange (Falkenmark, 1975). Some lakes, like those in the rivers draining the mountain chain along the inner parts of Northern Sweden, are dominated by horizontal water exchange, with negligible vertical influences. The volume of water in the lakes is primarily renewed by blue water inflow and outflow, and not through vertical precipitation and evaporation fluxes to and from the lake surface. Therefore, they are characterized by the throughflow system, with a fairly rapid overall renewal of the lake water mass.

Other lakes with small drainage basins may have water renewal that is dominated by vertical exchange, which makes them climate controlled and vulnerable to climate fluctuations. For example, the Aral Sea is climate controlled – ie the level of the sea depends on the difference between precipitation and evaporation. The dramatic lowering of the water level has arisen in response to the depletion of the two main tributaries as a result of large-scale irrigation development in the drainage basins.

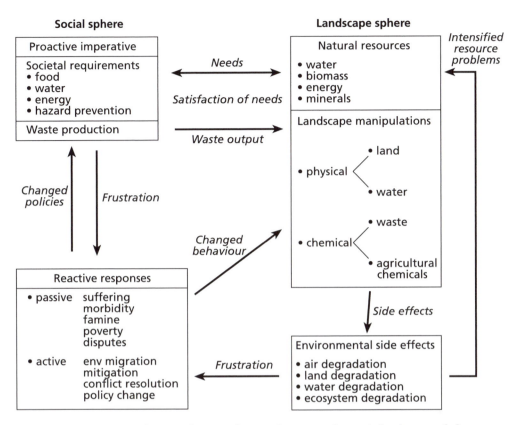

Figure 1.4 *Fundamental interrelations between the social sphere and the landscape sphere (adapted from Falkenmark, 1999)*

Human Landscape Interventions

Landscape manipulations and their environmental consequences

Humans manipulate various landscape components: the vegetation, the soil and the water. Two main types of human influence are the addition of contaminants and the direct modification of landscape components (Falkenmark and Mikulski, 1994).

Vegetation may be cut down (deforestation) or altered (agricultural development, reforestation) in efforts to meet societies' needs for food, fibre, fuel and timber. Soils are manipulated by remodelling the land surface, by tilling, draining, and by shifting permeable soil to impermeable surfaces such as those in urban areas. In addition, water flows are manipulated in a number of ways. Drilling wells and pumping groundwater contribute to rural and urban water supply. Construction of pipelines and canals make it possible to carry surface water to cities and industries and irrigation schemes. Reservoirs and dams may provide water storage from a season with water surplus to a season with deficiency, or from a wet year to a dry year. Reservoirs may be used for flow control both to reduce downstream flood risks and to secure water supply during dry periods of the year.

The links between society and the landscape are important for understanding the main phenomena behind the development of environmental problems and ecosystem degradation. These links are illustrated in Figure 1.4 (Falkenmark, 1999). Human activities are driven by societal demands for life support – water, food, timber, energy and shelter. There is a political imperative for leaders to secure, or at least facilitate, access to the goods and services that are fundamental to eradicate poverty and to develop human welfare.

The long-term human challenge is to balance the provision of freshwater services to human populations and to water-dependent ecosystems. At the same time, the capacity of the natural resource base has to be preserved not only to provide such goods and services for future generations, but also to maintain a capacity to absorb changes and shocks – to sustain the resilience of the systems. These services cannot be provided without interfering with various landscape components, such as both land and water pathways. There are also chemical influences originating from exhaust gases, solid refuse, wastewater and agricultural chemicals. It is an unavoidable fact that where there is human activity and socioeconomic development, there is waste production (Falkenmark and Lundqvist, 2000).

Due to the natural processes occuring in the landscape, all these human manipulations with landscape components, water flows and pathways will be reflected in unintended side effects. The processes referred to here include three that have serious consequences: water partitioning, the 'lift-up-carry-away' function, and the continuous water transport in the watercycle.

The result will be air quality deterioration – for example, acid rain, degradation of land productivity and fertility – and water quality degradation – for example, bacterial pollution, nutrient pollution and toxic pollution. When these phenomena change, ecological phenomena will be disturbed and various higher order effects develop, such as terrestrial and aquatic ecosystem degradation, and the loss of their capacity to cope with disturbances. Many of these side effects may result in undermining society's resource base and the development that builds on that resource base.

Human manipulations of the landscape are not a new phenomenon. They lead to large-scale and long-term impacts on soil, water animals and plants. As clearly shown by Redman (1999), overexploitation of natural resources in early civilisations has, through millennia, resulted in environmental degradation, sometimes so severe as to cause the downfall of whole societies.

Citizens of societies are frustrated when their needs are not satisfied or when side effects are considered unacceptable. Responses to this situation may be active or passive. Passive responses include morbidity and famine. Active responses include disputes, migration and altered expectation or behaviour (for example, leaving fields fallow or importing food). Landscape disturbances can, of course, also be natural. Environmental shocks, such as floods, droughts, storms and earthquakes, can cause complete shifts in ecosystems. For example, in Honduras after Hurricane Mitch in 1998, large areas of topsoil were completely removed by landslides. The result was a complete shift in soil composition and rainfall partitioning, which in turn brought a new type of vegetation.

BOX 1.2 LANDSCAPE DIVISIONS

Hydrologically, landscapes can be divided into geographical units in which all precipitation that falls within each unit flows downstream through the same outlet (for example, a river mouth). Large hydrological units are called drainage basins; smaller units are often defined as catchments. The boundary, or hydrological divide, is formed by the highest land, which directs runoff flow in different directions. Each catchment or river basin is enclosed by its own water divide. Therefore, all the rainwater that does not return to the atmosphere as green water forms blue water, and either feeds the river or passes underground as groundwater flow, seeping back to the surface in springs, hollows and valley bottoms. A slope is typically divided into uphill recharge areas where the rainwater moves downwards through the root zone, recharging the groundwater, and downhill discharge areas where groundwater returns back to the land surface. This movement is a useful tool to predict where groundwater pollution may first be detected (Falkenmark, 2000).

It is interesting to note that, within the matrix in Figure 1.4, different professional groups have tended to concentrate their interest in different compartments: engineers in the landscape sphere focus on manipulations of the natural resource base (Box 2); environmental professionals and ecologists, also in the landscape sphere, focus on environmental impact; business leaders in the social sphere focus on human needs and aspirations (Box 1); while social scientists and politicians focus on both the proactive and reactive sides of the social sphere (Boxes 1 and 4). This division into sectors probably explains the difficulties in dealing with the environmental side effects of human activities and the move towards sustainable development.

The great challenge in this complex situation is to find out how to balance human interests against secure and long-term functioning of the planet. Since water has to be shared among all those living in a catchment, a balancing of upstream interests against downstream interests is necessary. The catchment is an ideal unit for taking such an integrated approach. But that approach has to integrate not only all the different blue water uses, but also land use and related green water use. An integrated catchment approach also needs to include the uphill/downhill movement of water, and the flow from land to river. What is required, therefore, is an integrated approach to land, water and ecosystems. We will return to this challenge in the last chapter of this book.

Key functions and links in the new flow-based approach

Before we close this chapter, we would like to make some observations regarding policy directions. Table 1.2 gives an overview of various water functions and identifies crucial components in the major systems that support life.

Life-supporting flows. The life-supporting water flow is one of the most fundamental functions involved in plant production. Here water has multiple functions. As already mentioned, one function is to provide one of the two raw materials in plant production. Another is to give support for the structure of plants (without water a plant loses its turgor and wilts). Other functions of water are to act as a nutrient carrier to the different locations in a plant and function as a cooler because transforming water to

Table 1.2 *Parallel functions of water shown as a set of components of the systems that support life*

Function	Visible	Invisible
Life-supporting flows	Water supply	Plant production
Consequence producing functions		
Rainwater partitioning	Blue water flow	Green water flow
Lift-up-carry-away	Erosion/sedimentation	Dissolving/out-transport
Cycle-based cascading	Upstream/downstream	Along water cycle chain

vapour consumes heat. Huge amounts of water are consumed in the plant production process.

Three water processes that bring change to the landscape. Three different processes related to water are at work in the landscape (Falkenmark, 1999):

1   Incoming rainfall is being partitioned at the soil surface (see Chapter 2): first, between overland flow and infiltration into the soil, second, between evaporation and transpiration after uptake of plant water and groundwater recharge (see Figure 1.2).
2   Water picks up everything that is water soluble and carries it along, as it is a unique solvent continuously on the move above and below the ground.
3   Water moves continuously in the water cycle. This mobility produces continual chain effects of transport from the atmosphere to the ground and the terrestrial ecosystems, then to the groundwater and the rivers and lakes and aquatic ecosystems, and then again to the coastal waters and the coastal ecosystems.

We have already touched upon the first landscape process, and the rainwater partitioning in contact with the land. The second process above is related to the combined effect of water both as a solvent and as a substance involved in key chemical interactions between the infiltrating rainwater and the root zone system.

The third landscape process relates to the continental part of the water cycle where the three major components of the biosphere, the land, the ocean and the atmosphere, are interconnected. Water circulates in the solar-driven cycle from ocean to land using the atmosphere as transport medium. In this way oceans are linked to the atmosphere through rainfall and evaporation. The net evaporation from the sea turns into rainfall on land and its terrestrial ecosystems, and the waterbodies and their aquatic ecosystems. Freshwater flowing into coastal areas mixes with saline seawater, creating the unique brackish ecological habitats of coastal ecosystems. On the continents water moves above and below the ground under the influence of the law of gravity. This third process is illustrated in Figure 1.5. Human interventions in the water cycle here are distributed among the key compartments: atmosphere, land, groundwater and waterbodies. Waste gas goes into the atmosphere; soil and vegetation are manipulated physically and chemically; water is withdrawn from aquifers and waterbodies, and wastewater flow returns to the waterbodies.

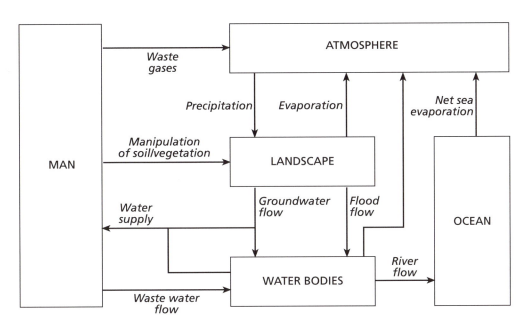

Note: The water cycle links evaporation from the sea, atmospheric water vapour flow, the moistening of continental landscapes, the recharge of aquifers and rivers, and the river discharge back to the sea. The human physical and chemical interventions influence the atmosphere, the landscape and the aquifers and rivers.

Figure 1.5 *The continuous water flow through the water cycle, linking sea evaporation, atmospheric vapour flow, moistening of continual landscapes, recharge of aquifers and rivers, and outflow to the ocean*

Lesson for the policy-maker: secure, avoid, foresee

The many parallel functions of water and our knowledge of the water cycle suggest that three policy perspectives have to be included in the integrated approach discussed above. The challenge is to bring together the main dimensions of water with its enormous complexity into three major categories for special attention (Table 1.3):

- What has to be *secured*? This question refers to what is necessary to secure – ie safe water to keep people healthy, water needed for income generation, and the water needed to produce the food.
- What has to be *avoided/minimized*? This question refers to avoidable activities and manipulations, in particular land-use activities causing erosion, and chemical manipulations and pollution resulting from human activities. These latter include bacterial pollution; toxic pollution, which poisons water users and degrades ecosystems; and the excess leaching of nutrients, which makes groundwater undrinkable and also degrades aquatic ecosystems in rivers, lakes and coastal waters.
- What has to be *foreseen* or *anticipated* and met by risk reduction? This question refers to floods and droughts and to the fact that a land-use decision is also a water

Table 1.3 *Fundamental policy directions*

Security dimension	Policy direction	Function	Phenomenon	Preparedness dimension
Human security	Secure	Necessity, life support	• Household water supply • Industrial water supply • Crop production	• Human health • Employment • Income generation • Food supply
Environmental damage security	Avoid	Mobile solvent	• Water pollution	• Ecosystem
		Eroding agent, silt carrier	• Land degradation • Silting	• Resilience degradation • Land productivity degradation • Silting of reservoirs
Human and environmental security	Foresee	Biosphere linkages	• Climate variability • Transport function • Rainwater partitioning	• Recurrent floods/droughts • Upstream/ downstream linkages • Green/blue flow linkages

decision. It also involves the effects of the continually ongoing transport in the water cycle. These create problems with upstream/downstream relations, making those downstream 'prisoners' of those upstream. In the same category are the upwind/downwind relations generating influences on downwind rainfall.

Summary

Human history is closely linked to the control of visible, or blue, water, in rivers, lakes and wells, but invisible, or green, water is even more important, since it is responsible for plant production, including food, and is involved in the generation of terrestrial ecological services. This makes an ecohydrological worldview essential as the new window through which both the water and environmental crises can be better understood, and thus properly addressed. Given the need to produce food for a growing humanity and the warnings from the ecological community that the margin for expanded irrigation has to remain limited, much more focus has to be put on rainfed crop production, the invisible water in the soil, and green water flow. If more water is used to produce plant mass, and precipitation over the catchment is a finite resource, then less water will remain to recharge aquifers and rivers. Producing more food therefore needs to be balanced against the consequences of using blue water.

The water cycle, with its essential balancing functions in terms of dissipating solar energy variations in time and space, can be seen as the most fundamental of all ecological services in the global systems that support life. The water cycle involves three sets of mutually balancing processes (Ripl, 1995): two physical (evaporation/ condensation), two chemical (crystallization/dissolution), and two biological processes (water molecule splitting/reassemblage). Through the primary functions of water, both in the biosphere and the anthroposphere, the water cycle links society and nature. Being able to bridge hydrology and ecology is therefore absolutely essential in order to reach a sustainable interaction between humans and the landscapes in which they live. Water/ecosystem linkages appear on all scales: the scale of the individual plant, the landscape ecosystems, and the global ecosystem.

The interactions are particularly complex in wetland ecosystems, a biological term that incorporates considerable hydrological complexity in view of the variety of water determinants. Wetlands are characterized by anoxia and low redox potential, but the water that keeps the wetland wet may have many possible origins. Wetlands are particularly abundant in regions where drainage systems are incompletely developed. Wetland vegetation exposes spectacular differences depending on whether the water feeding it is stagnant or slowly moving, nutrient-poor or nutrient-rich. Non-peaty wetlands are found in warmer and drier climates and take the form of swamps and marshes. Flood pulses are of fundamental importance for many wetlands; groundwater seepage is for others.

River and lake ecosystems are also critically dependent on the water constituting the habitat. Stream habitats tend to have a patchy structure due to variability in flow velocity and sediment distribution. The biological structure and metabolism of lake ecosystems are closely linked to the character of the water and chemical inflows from the catchment, as modified in the lake by the precipitation/evaporation balance. The habitat characteristics differ according to the relative dominance of the horizontal as opposed to the vertical water exchange.

Since the landscape and its ecosystems provide life support for humanity, there is a political imperative for leaders of society to secure/facilitate access to fundamental goods and services there. To this aim, humans tend to manipulate various landscape components by physical and chemical interferences. Such landscape manipulations are unavoidable measures in the efforts to satisfy societal needs for water, food, energy, minerals, etc, since the natural resources can only be made accessible in that manner.

In addition to the intended benefits, a number of environmental side effects tend to develop in response to these manipulations due to natural processes operating in the landscape. Three such processes that generate impact are involved here:

- Incoming rainfall is partitioned into green and blue flows. The partitioning changes when vegetation or soil characteristics change.
- Water picks up everything that is water-soluble and carries it along, as it is a unique solvent continuously on the move above and below the ground. The lift-up-carry-away functions are also linked to water's eroding capacity in combination with water mobility.

- Water moves continuously in the water cycle. This mobility produces continual chain effects of transport from the atmosphere to the ground and the terrestrial ecosystems, then to the groundwater and to rivers and lakes, and then to aquatic and coastal ecosystems.

Many of these side effects act as disturbances on the ecosystems and may threaten the resource base. This makes it essential from a policy-making aspect to find ways to reach an integrated land/water/ecosystem management that allows welfare without undermining the life support system on which that welfare is based.

Chapter 2

Water Availability – Expanding the Perspective

Rainfall over land is partitioned into two major flow branches: the blue branch of surface and sub-surface runoff and the green branch of evaporation or vapour flow

A Conceptual Shift to Incorporate Water for Ecosystems

In Chapter 1 we introduced the fundamental role of water for human survival. We showed our immense dependence on water and the multiple roles it plays in our health and material wealth. This dependence is both on direct blue water use for drinking, sanitation, washing and industry, and also on water that sustains ecological functions and values that directly support human well-being and survival.

Water is not only the 'bloodstream' of the biosphere. It is also a finite resource involved in complex and dynamic ecohydrological processes, which must be understood to enable the balancing of water needs for humans and nature.

During the last three to four decades there has been growing concern about the rapidly growing world population and the implications of increasing pressure on our finite freshwater resource. In the 1970s, the concern was primarily about the challenge of securing drinking water. This was manifested in the International Drinking Water Supply and Sanitation Decade (1981–1990) that followed the United Nations Water Conference in Mar de Plata, Argentina, in 1977.

Global and country level water resource assessments, based to a large extent on the work of researchers such as L'vovich (1974, 1979), and Budyko (1986), showed that human withdrawals of fresh water were high and directly proportional to population growth. In the preparatory work to the United Nations Conference on Environment and Development in Rio de Janeiro, Brazil, in 1992 (the Earth Summit), the Dublin principles on water pointed to the urgent need to safeguard scarce freshwater resources for future generations (ICWE, 1992). The UN Comprehensive Freshwater Assessment (CFWA) in 1997 (Raskin, 1997) confirmed earlier analyses, pointing out that at least 30 per cent of the world population would be facing physical water scarcity in 2025. At the second World Water Forum in 2000 in The Hague, a World Water Vision (Cosgrove and Rijsberman, 2000) vigorously supported the same theme: that humans

Photo: Johan Rockström

Note: The woman's only drinking water source is on an access road to one of Africa's most well-known wildlife attractions, the Ngorongoro Crater in Tanzania's Serengeti.

Plate 2.1 *A woman with her children scooping 'drinking water' from puddles on a roadside*

face serious water scarcity as a result of population pressure, water quality deterioration, and unsustainable water management.

The 'gloomy arithmetic of water' (Cosgrove and Rijsberman, 2000) presented at the World Water Forum in The Hague, pointed out that despite advancements in water supply and sanitation over the last two decades, 1 billion people still lack access to adequate drinking water and 2 billion people still do not have access to adequate sanitation. It is alarming as well as unacceptable in the 21st century that there are still large numbers of women and children in the developing world who are forced to collect untreated or impure drinking water from various sources, often having to travel great distances to reach them (see Plate 2.1).

We will argue later that the frustrations related to human water supply and sanitation are management failures and are not related to water scarcity.

It is now an accepted fact that the growing human use of fresh water has major impacts on ecosystems, and that water management has to include an integrated approach to water for socioeconomic development while at the same time safeguarding vital ecosystems. There is a growing understanding that managing water for the future can only be achieved by integrating water for humans and nature.

The systems perspective introduced in Chapter 1, which focuses on the multiple functions of water in the landscape, is useful for understanding the role of water for society and nature. A systems approach to ecohydrology begins by looking at the terrestrial part of the global hydrological cycle in order to reassess water availability and water use. The reassessment of the global hydrological cycle is not primarily required in order to adjust the quantitative flow estimates, but rather to contribute to a conceptual shift in the way we understand and value water flows in sustaining ecosystem goods and services vital for human life support.

From an ecohydrological perspective there are two central questions: What is meant by human pressure on freshwater resources? What is considered to be the water resource? Or, put in another way, does the freshwater resource considered in conventional water resource assessments include the water required to sustain vital ecosystem services? As will be shown below, the answer is no. This indicates a need for a new ecohydrological approach to water resource management.

Water resource management involves policy-making, social and economic issues, institutions and laws to support planning and decisions. It also involves methodologies and technologies to control and allocate water flows for different uses. For example, solutions to the food crisis in several regions of the world are found mainly by practising irrigated agriculture, which uses blue water. Additionally, it is not easy to convey the message that the world's largest biome, grasslands, consumes enormous volumes of water to indirectly sustain billions of humans. This amount corresponds to almost 10 m^3 or 10,000 litres of fresh water per person per day, if evenly distributed among all people on Earth. This is a green water flow that sustains the growth of fodder that generates meat from grazing livestock and wildlife. This water is not yet perceived as a water resource, even though it sustains ecosystem goods and services directly (meat) and by indirectly (biodiversity) supporting humans.

We will here present the global hydrological cycle and describe the determinants that influence rainfall partitioning into green and blue water flows, in order to explain the logic behind the conventional focus on water resources, and also to prepare the ground for an ecohydrological approach to these resources. In later chapters we will move the focus to present and future global water withdrawals and requirements, and the driving forces behind them, and introduce a broadened ecohydrological concept of water resources management.

Introducing Soil Water into the Water Balance Equation

Rainwater partitioning

As already stressed, the global water cycle is driven by solar energy and depends on thermal energy and gravity forces for its continued circulation of water. Evaporation from soil and foliage, and condensation of water vapour, all work under the influence of heat. The falling of raindrops, surface runoff, river flow, and movement of water in soil and groundwater are all affected by gravity. For the purpose of this book we can assume that the global water cycle is closed in the sense that the same volume of water

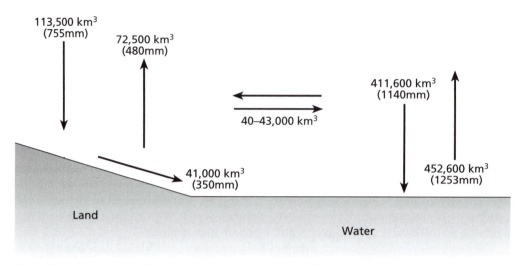

113,500 km³
(755mm)

72,500 km³
(480mm)

411,600 km³
(1140mm)

40–43,000 km³

41,000 km³
(350mm)

452,600 km³
(1253mm)

Land

Water

Note: The land and ocean link is shown by the cycle of runoff from land to sea that is returned from sea to land as vapour flow (from L'vovich, 1979).

Figure 2.1 *The global hydrological cycle showing average annual flow estimates*

that falls on land and water also returns to the atmosphere. Figure 2.1 shows the global hydrological cycle with water flows indicated as average annual volumes (in km³/year).

Precipitation over land surfaces amounts to an average of 113,500 km³/year, which is partitioned into two major flow branches. The blue flow branch, which consists of surface and sub-surface flow in rivers, lakes, and aquifers, carries an estimated 41,000 km³ of water per year from land towards the oceans. Not all of it reaches the oceans, the difference being the consumptive use of water by humans, which will be discussed further below. The second major flow branch is the return flow of evaporation, or water vapour, to the atmosphere, which we have defined as green water flow. From terrestrial surfaces the annual green water flow to the atmosphere is estimated at 72,500 km³/year. Exchange of moisture between the oceans and land plays a critical role for water resource availability. The volume of runoff drained to the oceans from land is returned to land as moisture generated from evaporation of ocean water. Therefore, the oceans have a fundamental role in generating precipitation over land. However, as the focus in this book is on terrestrial ecosystems, we will primarily discuss the terrestrial part of the global water cycle despite the important role of the oceans.

For instructive reasons we have chosen to base the presentation on L'vovich's data on the global hydrological cycle, which date back to 1974 (L'vovich, 1974). Our justification is that his data give the best opportunities to conceptualize rainfall partitioning into its different flows. Many more recent assessments limit their focus primarily on the blue water flow branches. However, with improvements in gauging techniques and hydrological monitoring, there have been some adjustments of L'vovich's flow estimates. For example, Shiklomanov (1993) estimated average rainfall of 119,000 km³/year, partitioned into 47,000 km³/year of blue water flow and 72,000 km³/year of green water flow. However, in a more recent adjustment, he estimated average blue water flow to be 42,650 km³/year, attributed to better data from Africa and a 20-year trend of reduced runoff in parts of Africa, Asia and Europe (Shiklomanov, 1996). These are likely to be the most reliable figures at present. Therefore, despite using L'vovich's data from the 1970s in our basic discussions on global water flow partitioning, we will consider Shiklomanov's (1996) data on blue water flow (42,650 km³/year) as the average annual flow in our analyses of water resources availability and use.

Root zone partitioning of water flows

In Chapter 1 we introduced the basic concept of partitioning precipitation into a vapour (evaporation) flow branch, which we defined as green water flow, and a runoff water branch, which we defined as blue water flow (see Figure 1.2). Partitioning of rainfall into evaporation and runoff is a common way to present the water cycle over land at scales exceeding the catchment scale (for example, river basins, regions, the world). However, this omits the important soil and vegetation links in the hydrological cycle. The consequence of this simplified partitioning is that we are not able to understand what determines the portion of rainfall for a given biotope that will turn into green or blue water flow. Two partitioning points, instead of only one, are critical in determining how rainfall is divided into different water flows.

ⅢⅢWhile showing the two partitioning points in the hydrological cycle, Figure 2.2 does not show the important soil–water link. Water in the soil, generally defined as soil moisture or soil water, sustains all terrestrial biomass growth with water for plant transpiration. Although generally presented as a stock, soil moisture (see Table 2.2) is a flow.

However, this does not generally appear in annual overviews of the water cycle because the annual soil moisture changes are normally approximated to even out. Thus, the soil moisture added over a year equals the moisture flowing out from the soil over the same time period. This easily gives the impression of a direct link between water and human water use, and between water, vegetation and atmosphere. Instead, rain falling on land always starts by passing on or through the soil before it can sustain ecosystems or benefit humans.

The two partitioning points are critical determinants of both the water flow available for downstream use in a catchment or river basin and the potential use of water for biomass growth. By visualizing the complexity of the partitioning of water in the hydrological cycle, two fundamental issues are highlighted:

- The first is that the availability of blue water flow is influenced by soil surface conditions, which determine partitioning between surface runoff and infiltration; soil properties determining water-holding capacity; vegetation characteristics determining capacity to take up soil moisture; and climatic conditions, which determine the atmospheric thirst for green water.
- Second, human land use directly affects partitioning of rainfall at the land surface.

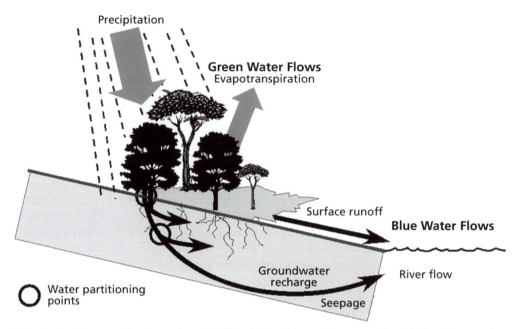

Note: At the first partitioning point rainfall is divided into surface runoff and infiltration. At the second partitioning point soil moisture is divided into evaporation from soil, transpiration from plants, and groundwater recharge. Evaporation and transpiration together constitute the green flow branch. Surface runoff and groundwater recharge together constitute the blue flow branch.

Figure 2.2 The hydrological cycle for an ecosystem showing the partitioning of rainfall[1]

Two return flows to the atmosphere

The distinction between productive and non-productive green water flow is fundamental in ecohydrology. Productive green water flow is the water transpired by plants and trees. It is a non-negotiable part of biomass growth (see the section on water productivity in Chapter 7). Non-productive green water flow is the water that evaporates from moist soil surfaces between plants, from open water surfaces from the soil profile or from interception.

Until recently it has been very cumbersome to distinguish between productive transpiration and non-productive evaporation. This has led to the combining of two thermodynamically similar but ecologically very different processes into the awkward notion of evapotranspiration. The processes are both driven by atmospheric thirst for water and wetness of soil. This awkward combination of productive and non-productive water flows into one term for consumptive vapour flow from the land has resulted in erroneous interpretations of the water implications when biomass growth increases. One component of evaporation sustains biomass growth while the other does not. Vapour flow to the atmosphere is presented only as total evapotranspiration on a river basin, country or global scale. In order to avoid this difficult and partly confusing term we will use the term 'total evaporation' throughout this book. This is the green water flow branch in the water cycle, and we will differentiate, as indicated in Chapter 1, between evaporation and transpiration by referring to non-productive and productive green water flows, respectively. This further strengthens the argument to avoid the term evapotranspiration, and instead to focus as far as possible on the two components of green water flow.

In Figure 2.3 the partitioning of rainfall is shown on a global scale, again with data from L'vovich (1979). At the first partitioning point rainfall is divided into surface runoff feeding rivers and infiltration feeding soil moisture storage. Additionally, at the first partitioning point, water is also returned to the atmosphere as interception from the canopy and direct evaporation from open water surfaces such as lakes. Approximately 80,000 km^3/year of water infiltrates and forms soil moisture. Soil moisture is then divided at the second partitioning point into groundwater recharge amounting to 7500 km^3/year (this is the freshwater sub-surface branch that returns to the river as stable river flow further downstream) and 72,500 km^3/year of green water flow to the atmosphere. This green water consists of a productive flow of transpiration estimated at roughly 30,000–35,000 km^3/year and a non-productive evaporation flow of 35,000–40,000 km^3/year (L'vovich, 1979).[2] It is important to note that all sub-surface flow of blue water does not reach a river, but a substantial portion (estimated by L'vovich to 2200 km^3/year) bypasses rivers and discharges directly into the ocean. Evaporation is also a major flow from open water surfaces, dams and wetlands. For example, the inflow of surface blue water flow from the Sudan to Egypt is estimated at an average of 65.5 km^3/year. At the Aswan High Dam, located not far downstream from the Sudan border, the evaporation losses have been estimated at 10 km^3/year, giving a real outflow potential from the reservoir of only 55.5 km^3/year (FAO, 1997).

Several interacting biophysical and human factors influence the partitioning of rainfall into the above-mentioned flow components. This affects the volumes of green and blue water flows. In order to understand the linkages between flow partitioning and land use it is convenient to start by assessing rainfall partitioning for different ecosystems as affected by biophysical factors, such as soil, climate, and biota. We will illustrate this by taking the savanna zone in Africa as an example.

The example of the savanna zone

The partitioning of rainfall in savanna ecosystems is shown in Figure 2.4a and Figure 2.4b. Figure 2.4a shows the first partitioning of rainfall into surface runoff and infiltration for natural savannas in different hydro-climatic zones, from dry semi-arid to sub-humid savannas. The rainfall range illustrates different savanna types. Infiltrated rainfall is then partitioned between green water flow (evaporation + transpiration) and groundwater recharge, as shown in Figure 2.4b. As shown in this example, on a wet semi-arid savanna receiving 1000 mm of annual rainfall, 100 mm will flow as surface runoff at the first partitioning point. Soil water flow of 900 mm (rain minus runoff) will be partitioned in the second partitioning point almost entirely into return flow of green water (875 mm) with a minimum of groundwater flow (25 mm). Increased rainfall indicates a gradual shift towards different ecosystems, from arid steppe savanna (<300 mm) to parkland savanna (<1000 mm) to wet savanna (<1800 mm). Rainfall in the tropics is thus a fundamental determinant of ecosystem type, as will be discussed in

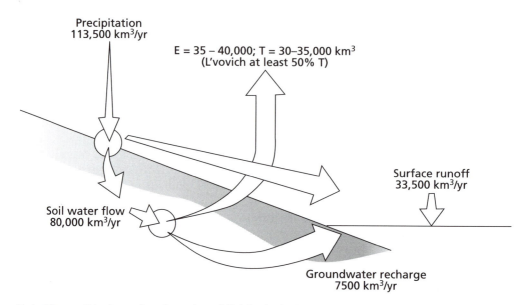

Precipitation
113,500 km³/yr

E = 35 – 40,000; T = 30–35,000 km³
(L'vovich at least 50% T)

Surface runoff
33,500 km³/yr

Soil water flow
80,000 km³/yr

Groundwater recharge
7500 km³/yr

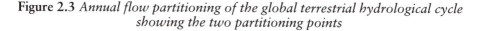

Note: The partitioning points show the soil link in the hydrological cycle and the distinction between productive and non-productive green water flow. Total green water flow amounts to 72,500 km³/year, of which at least 50 per cent is productive green water flow as transpiration (based on data from L'vovich, 1979).

Figure 2.3 *Annual flow partitioning of the global terrestrial hydrological cycle showing the two partitioning points*

more detail in Chapter 6. Increased rainfall also results in a larger proportion of soil water recharging the groundwater. As seen in Figure 2.4b, there is a sharp increase in groundwater recharge when annual rainfall exceeds 1000 mm, attaining up to 15 per cent of soil moisture in a wet savanna receiving 1500 mm of annual rainfall.

It is important to note that the generic relations of rainfall partitioning presented in figures 2.4a and 2.4b for the world's savannas show large local variation and, perhaps more importantly, are strongly affected by human influence. Water is a much stronger biophysical determinant of ecosystems in tropical than in temperate hydroclimates. In temperate regions temperature, solar radiation and light hours help shape the biological landscape. In the tropics, water is generally the fundamental limiting factor, creating the enormous variety of biomes we find today, such as rainforests, dense tree savannas, parklands, bush savanna, tiger bush savannas, and thorny arid steppes. Ecosystems also affect rainfall partitioning through various structures. Tiger bush formations, for example, create natural water harvesting zones for runoff concentration in bands of bush, which look like patterns on a tiger. Through its soil properties and vegetation cover, each ecosystem at its soil surface will affect the partitioning of rainfall between runoff and infiltration. The soil structure, which is influenced by the flora and fauna in the ecosystem, will then affect the partitioning of soil moisture in green and blue sub-surface water flows.

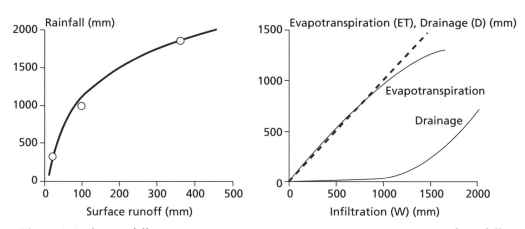

Figure 2.4a–b *Rainfall partitioning in savanna ecosystems. a: Partitioning of rainfall into surface runoff and infiltration. b: Further partitioning of the infiltrated water between green water flow and groundwater recharge* (adapted from L'vovich, 1979)

Influence of evaporative demand and soil characteristics

Table 2.1 shows the main biophysical determinants of how rainfall is partitioned over land. At the first partitioning point, surface runoff is biophysically influenced by the impact on soil surface conditions. The permeability is a result of crusting and compaction, by soil properties and by vegetation type. Several vegetation factors affect the amount of runoff generated from a land surface. Among these are root length and density, canopy cover, degree of litter fall, seasonality of vegetation and the impact of vegetation on the soil microbiology. All these factors together affect the infiltration capacity of the soil. The structure and wetness of the soil determines the velocity of water movement through it. The structure of the soil also determines the environment for the plant roots as well as the capacity of the soil to hold water.

At the second partitioning point, soil, climatic and vegetation factors interact to control the partitioning between green water flow and sub-surface blue water flow. Groundwater flow is driven by gravity and the hydraulic conductivity of the soil. Biophysically, the actual rate of evaporation is a result of the evaporative demand of the atmosphere and frequency of soil wetting. The number of rainfall events, combined with the soil structure, control the rate of the capillary rise of water. But the canopy cover also affects evaporation. Increased shading of the soil surface maintains higher air humidity and will reduce evaporation more than a surface without plants or trees. The transpiration rate is determined by plant water availability in the soil and plant water uptake capacity. Uptake capacity is a result of the root length and density, and the vigour of the above-ground canopy, which is primarily determined by leaf area. Hydraulic properties of the soil, and the competition for soil moisture from roots, determine ground water recharge.

Parallel to the biophysical determinants, land management has a primary influence on rainfall partitioning. Soil surface management, such as tillage practices, mulching, crop rotations and soil conservation, will affect the partitioning of rainfall between infiltration and surface runoff. Two important but invisible factors affecting surface runoff are soil compaction and soil wetness. Inappropriate tillage, such as repeated ploughing under wet conditions and with heavy machinery, can result in soil compaction. For animal-drawn tropical farming such compaction occurs at a very shallow soil depth, around 10–15 cm. Roots often cannot penetrate compacted layers, the so-called hard pans or plough pans, and water infiltrates at a very low rate. The effect is that the topsoil rapidly becomes saturated during rainfall. Wet soil generates a much higher runoff than dry soil, which means that compacted soils create crop water scarcity due to a thin soil layer, and also cause crop water stress due to a lower infiltration rate. As will be discussed in more detail in Chapter 8, there are several interesting tillage options, generally defined as conservation farming systems, that aim specifically at reducing the effects of soil compaction caused by conventional ploughing.

The second partitioning of water in the soil, between root uptake, soil evaporation and groundwater recharge, is strongly influenced by crop and soil fertility management, and the timing of field operations. The type of crop and timing of operations such as planting and weeding will influence root and leaf development, and in turn these directly affect crop transpiration. Organic and inorganic fertilization will also directly affect crop growth, and thereby change the proportion of soil water taking the productive path of green water flow path.

Non-productive green water flow as evaporation from soil is often the largest flow component of the tropical water balance. It often accounts for at least 50 per cent of rainfall. Evaporation from the soil is driven by atmospheric demand for water and the capacity of the soil to deliver water to the soil–air interface through diffusion and capillary rise. Management can affect these factors. Covering the soil surface with growing vegetation or dead crop residue, so-called mulch, creates a shaded and humid microclimate close to the soil surface and this reduces evaporation from the soil. Tillage can also be used to reduce the capillary rise from the soil. Growth of vigorous, groundcovering plants is one of the most effective ways of reducing non-productive green water flow.

We want to point out the dangers of seeing quantitative data on rainfall partitioning as fixed flows, irrespective of scale. Man and nature influence flow partitioning on all scales, from the individual plant to the river basin. This has often significant impacts on water availability. An extreme illustration of this is from the region of Cherrapunji in India. This humid tropical landscape is generally referred to as the world's wettest 'desert'. It receives an annual rainfall of over 10 m, and still suffers from severe water scarcity. The causes are the large variability of rainfall over the year and the huge local losses of water due to land degradation (Agarwal, 2000). Deforestation and exposure of the bare soil to intensive tropical rainstorms dramatically change the first partitioning point from a high proportion of soil infiltration to a dominance of storm surface runoff flow. This flow creates land degradation through water erosion. In the virgin state of the ecosystem the blue water flow branch is balanced between surface runoff in streams and a slow sub-surface branch of soil water recharging groundwater. This flow has been completely redirected in favour of flash floods in streams. Perhaps the present blue water flow is not far from the volumes in the past. However, the duration of the flow has decreased from months to days. Instead of resulting in a secure access to slow blue water flow recharging

Table 2.1 *Biophysical and human factors that determine the partitioning of water flows in the hydrological cycle*

Flow	Biophysical determinant	Human determinant
1st Partitioning point		
Surface runoff	Vegetation/Biome	Land use
	Soil surface conditions	Tillage practices
	Rainfall intensity	
	Soil wetness	Soil management
Soil moisture	Water holding capacity in soil	Soil management
2nd Partitioning point		
Evaporation	Atmospheric demand (potential evaporation)	Canopy cover
	Micro-meteorology	Mulching
	Wetness of soil	Timing of planting
Transpiration	Photosynthetic pathway	Crop management
	Plant available soil moisture	Forest management
	Atmospheric demand	
Groundwater recharge	Soil hydraulic conditions	Compaction
	Geological conditions	

groundwater, the stormwater flushes through the landscape as erosive flash floods and exits without being accessible for use within the basin.

Water Resource Estimates

Conventional water resource assessments

In ecohydrology it is essential to understand not only the quantitative partitioning of rainfall at different scales for ecosystems, but also the source of the flow estimates in water resource assessments. It is also necessary to remember that, even though the global water cycle as a whole can be considered as a closed circuit,[3] (what falls down as rain evaporates back to the atmosphere) there are large annual fluctuations. Average global rainfall fluctuates with 12,500 km³/year, while rainfall over land surfaces fluctuates with 9500 km³/year (Jaeger, 1983). This fluctuation over land corresponds to more than twice the total annual direct human withdrawal of blue water (estimated at 4000 km³/year, see below). It is equal to the total amount of blue water flow accessible to humans (estimated at 12,500 km³/year). Estimates of water flows in the global hydrological cycle are primarily based on the observed runoff flow from hydrographs measured at hydrological gauging stations along major perennial rivers of the world. Groundwater recharge is estimated from theoretical and empirical functions. Green water flow is estimated by subtracting observed surface runoff and estimated ground water flow, from raingauge observations of rainfall extrapolated spatially.[4]

In developing countries runoff observations are not available, so a meteorological approach is often used. Runoff is estimated by subtracting total evaporation from observations of rainfall (Shiklomanov, 1996). Total evaporation is calculated from meteorological data – often only temperature. However, compared to runoff observations, there are only limited observations on actual evaporation. This explains the approach of using two reasonably well-observed parameters, rainfall and runoff, to calculate evaporation as the difference between rainfall and runoff. Another advantage of runoff observations is that runoff generally is more precisely measurable than rainfall on large areas (Nemec, 1983).

A problem with water balance estimates at the regional or river basin scale is the lack of data for flow partitioning in different land areas along a stretch from upstream to downstream. For upstream areas, therefore, rainfall partitioning is generally measured by estimating the percentage of rainfall partitioned into surface runoff flow (P) and groundwater recharge (R). P and R are called runoff coefficients. The residual between P and estimates of R is the estimated green water flow. So, in a general sense, it is only at positions along a river where discharge measurements are available that actual observations of stream flow and rainfall can be used to calculate the partitioning into green and blue water flows. This is often the case only for downstream positions in a river basin.[5]

Upstream blue water resource

Why is the approach to water resource estimates important in order to understand the basis of ecohydrology? One reason is that the conventional approach of focusing on runoff observations and estimating green water flow as the residual of rainfall minus runoff directs our attention downstream and to the point of runoff measurement. We thus neglect the complex journey of water flowing from upstream to downstream. In this sense, stream flow observations only reflect the net end product of a journey that has often been long, spatially and temporally, and not necessarily straightforward.

For example, if we compare blue water runoff flows from downstream observations with estimates of runoff generation from basic land units along the river, the stream flow observations are generally lower than the land unit-based estimates. The reason is that runoff generated at a point upstream in a river basin does not necessarily reach the gauging station downstream where the stream flow observations are made. Instead, the locally generated runoff may take various complex routes: recharging wetland areas and returning as green water to the atmosphere; as direct soil evaporation at lower positions in the landscape; or crop transpiration from irrigation in midstream locations. Partitioning of rainfall in green and blue water flows at different positions in a basins is shown in Figure 2.5. We define the portion of this local runoff that evaporates and does not reach the river as upstream blue (we will return to this untapped resource in Chapter 8).

The point made here is that the seemingly unused residual green water flow back to the atmosphere may have started its journey as runoff generated upstream but then

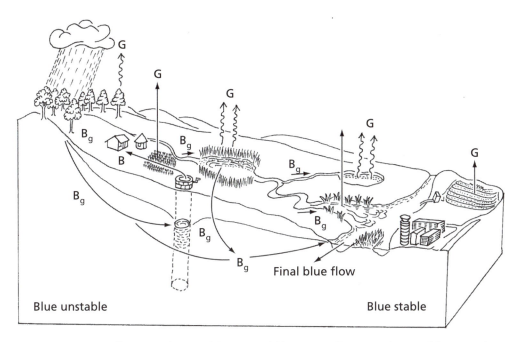

Note: Green water flows are shown with a 'G' and blue water flows are shown with a 'B', where subscript 'g' is groundwater flow and 's' is surface flow. Blue water flow that reaches a perennial river downstream is defined as stable runoff flow (BLUE STABLE). Local blue water flow that is on its way to evaporate is defined as upstream blue water flow (BLUE UNSTABLE). Local extraction of blue water from local water tables in, for example, upstream wells, is not documented as a blue water resource.

Figure 2.5 *The complex green and blue water flow flips that occur during the journey of water through the landscape*

turned into green water flow before reaching the outlet of the catchment or basin. This water has most likely carried out one, or perhaps several, ecological functions, such as blue water functions in a wetland habitat. It may have been involved in supporting ecosystem services and generating biomass before returning to the atmosphere as green water flow. A major limitation of the conventional methodology for analysis of water flow partitioning is thus the exclusion of the role of green water flow, and of the complex flow changes between temporary green and blue states when water carries out its journey from raindrop to river flow.

Water flows, stocks and residence time

Management of water resources requires not only an understanding of water flows, but also of water stored in stocks (dams, lakes, wells, etc), and the interactions between flowing water and water stocks. The water cycle provides humans and nature with renewable fresh water, thereby determining the sustainable volumes of water that can be used. Freshwater stocks, on the other hand, can be compared to storage of goods.

The stock is depleted by non-sustainable use when the water is not replenished. Human and ecosystem dependence on fresh water is correctly analysed as far as the annual freshwater flow is concerned. But the analysis often leaves out the fact that flowing water interacts with all components of freshwater stocks, adding and releasing water on a both seasonal and annual basis, much as food stocks in a supermarket are replenished with new goods when stocks run out.

Table 2.2 shows the major stocks of water in the hydrosphere compared to the flow of water occurring within each stock. Even though Earth is often called the Blue Planet, the concept is deceptive if associated with fresh water. Only 2.5 per cent, or 35 million km³ of the total 1.4 billion km³ of water on Earth is fresh. The remaining 97.5 per cent of the world's water is salty or saline, stored in oceans, as saline/brackish groundwater or in saline lakes. Furthermore, only a small fraction of fresh water is available to humans, as the bulk is locked into permanent ice and snow in Antarctica and Greenland, or in deep groundwater aquifers.

The freshwater stocks on which humans primarily depend are soil moisture, lakes, rivers and accessible groundwater. It has been estimated that the overall potentially usable portion of freshwater stocks amount to 200,000 km³ (Gleick, 2000). According to Shiklomanov (1997) there is a stock of soil moisture of 16,500 km³, which corresponds more to the real situation in a soil, where soil moisture normally is renewed several times per year (a flow of 80,000 km³/year suggests a residence time of around ten weeks).

It is critically important to understand the link between stocks and flows in ecohydrology, as this link determines the movement of water through the stocks. The time required to renew a stock is generally defined as the residence or renewal time, and is shown in the last column in Table 2.2. It takes several thousands of years to renew all water in oceans and groundwater, while the renewal time for moisture in the air is extremely quick: a water molecule stays an average of only eight days in the atmosphere, and reappears as vapour almost 46 times during a year. These characteristics of stock-flow interactions are important hydrological determinants of ecosystem functions and characteristics.

Another advantage of analysing both water flows and stocks is that crucial water flows appear more clearly. Analyses of flows in the water cycle using long time-units, such as months or years, do not have that advantage. This is particularly the case for water that has a short renewal time due to rapid changes of state.

Difference between major biomes

Global estimates of water flow partitioning in the hydrological cycle give us an understanding of the broader underlying picture of the availability of water resources. However, this has little value in understanding the availability of water in different regions of the world, as water resources are very unevenly distributed. On a global scale, average rainfall over land amounts to 755 mm/year. This suggests ample water. However, the extremely uneven distribution of water in different regions drastically changes that picture. Some parts of the world receive more than 10,000 mm of annual rainfall, while other parts receive less than 100 mm of water per year.

Again, the water balance between blue and green flows is the key to assessing water resources in different regions. As mentioned previously, both biophysical and human

Table 2.2 *Major world water stocks*

Component of hydrosphere	Stock volume (1000 km³)[a]	Flow volume per year (1000 km³/year)[b]	Residence time
Salt water stocks/flows			
Oceans	1,338,000	452	2500 years
Saline/brackish groundwater	12,870		
Saltwater lakes	85		
Freshwater stocks/flows			
Glaciers, permanent snow cover	24,064		
Fresh groundwater	10,530	?	1400 years
Ground ice, permafrost	300		
Freshwater lakes	91		17 years
Soil moisture	80	80[b]	1 year
Atmospheric water vapour	12.9	525	8 days[c]
Marshes, wetlands	11.5		5 years
Rivers	2.12	39	16 days
Incorporated in biota	1.12		Several hours
Total water on Earth (1000 km³)	1,386,000	525	2600 years
Total fresh water on Earth (1000 km³)	35,029		

a Adapted from Shiklomanov, 1997
b Annual soil moisture flow from L'vovich (1979). Shiklomanov (1997), focusing only on soil moisture as a stock of water in the soil, estimated the stock at 16,500 km³, indicating that fact that soil moisture is actually replenished at a much faster rate than annually, on certain soils even after each rainfall event
c Adapted from L'vovich, 1979

factors determine partitioning of rainfall into the different water flows of the water balance equation. Characteristic values for partitioning of rainfall in some of the major biomes of the world are shown in Table 2.3. These are synthesized values from different parts of the world and give an indication of partitioning trends for biotopes in different hydroclimates. Obviously, the variation is high within the same ecological zone located in different geographical regions. However, each zone has clear common traits. The existence of a certain type of ecosystem is generally strongly determined by factors directly related to rainfall partitioning but is also influenced by soil properties.

The fundamental water resource is rainfall. Figure 2.6 shows a map of global distribution of rainfall, which is the basic indicator for the availability of water resources. Atmospheric demand for water strongly affects the actual availability of water. Therefore, water resources are rarely presented in terms of rainfall only. But the basic fact remains that rainfall is the water that falls on land, and this is the water that is then partitioned into different flows, which are all involved in sustaining biological life on Earth. Maps showing only runoff data, for example, can easily give the impression that evaporation is an unavoidable flow that cannot be influenced – like a non-negotiable loss. But this is not the case. Both natural and human-managed ecosystems have developed principles to minimize evaporation flow. Tropical rainforests have such a dense canopy that most evaporation is in the form of productive green water flow as transpiration. Evaporation from soil is minimized thanks to a high

Table 2.3 *Typical partitioning of rainfall in blue and green flow components for some localities in major biomes of the world (annual averages in mm)* (adapted from L'vovich, 1979)

Hydroclimate	Zone	Rain (mm/year)	BLUE FLOW		GREEN FLOW	
			Surface flow (mm/year)	Ground water flow (mm/year)	Total Evaporation (mm/year)	Annual growth of phytomass (t/ha)
Subtropical and tropical	Desert savanna	300	18	2	280	2–6
	Dry sub-humid savanna	1000	100	30	870	4–12
	Wet savanna	1850	360	240	1200	8-20
Subarctic temperate	Tundra	370	70	40	260	1–2
	Taiga	700	160	140	400	10–15
	Mixed forests	750	150	100	500	10–15
	Wooded steppes	650	90	30	530	8–12
Equatorial	Wet evergreen equatorial forest	2000	600	600	800	30–50

humidity in the air and low solar radiation at the soil surface. Good examples of managed systems that minimize evaporation flow are drip irrigation methods in which actual non-productive evaporation is virtually non-existent.

The commonly used indicator of water availability is the total volume of blue water flow in the hydrological cycle. This should be distinguished from water accessibility, which is normally perceived as the portion of the blue water flow that is appropriated for use. In Figure 2.7 the global distribution of water availability at country level is shown. Water availability is expressed as m³ of blue water available per person.

An adequate analysis of the distribution of world water resources should also include maps showing the partitioning of water into runoff, groundwater recharge, evaporation and transpiration. We will focus more on the different flow components in the following chapters, when we introduce the wider ecohydrological concepts of water resources assessment and management. At this point it is enough to say that knowledge of the entire water balance is required to enable a full understanding of the role played by different water flows in the landscape.

Inter-annual fluctuations

Freshwater resources are not only unevenly distributed in space, among small catchments, river basins, countries and regions, but they also present large fluctuations over time. Temporal fluctuations of rainfall can be divided in between-year and within-year fluctuations. Between-year fluctuations are defined as inter-annual fluctuations,

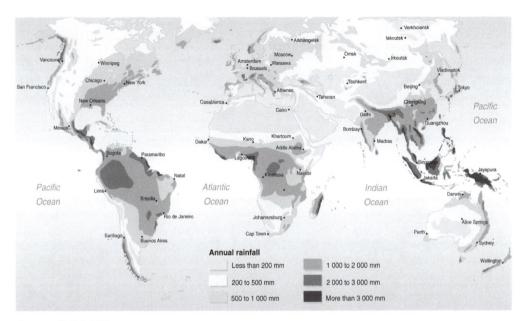

Source: GRID/UNEP

Figure 2.6 *World average annual rainfall distribution*

while within-year fluctuations are defined as intra-annual or intra-seasonal fluctuations. We will deal in more detail with intra-annual fluctuations in Chapter 6, as these determine the occurrence and severity of short periods of water shortage affecting plant growth, the so-called dry spells.

Between-year fluctuations of rainfall can be very high. Furthermore, the year-to-year variability occurs along a long-term climatic rhythm that is believed to have cycles of different lengths, from decades to millennia. The irregular variation of rainfall over short periods tends to be small compared to the long-period variations, with much greater variations. Christer Morales (1977) describes the short-term random variability along a long-term periodicity of rainfall fluctuations: '...we can consider the waves [long term rhythm], and swells [short term variability] of all sizes which travel more or less independently on the ocean surface.'

An example of long-term fluctuations is the dramatic shift in precipitation in several parts of the temperate and tropical regions following the end of the last glaciation during the early to mid-Holocene Epoch. It has been shown, for example, that Lake Victoria reached a peak lake level around 10,000 BP. Since then it has progressively shrunk because of increased aridity and the seasonal variation of rainfall (Stager and Mayewski, 1997). Complex changes in global weather systems linked to exchange of moisture and energy between oceans and the atmosphere affect such cycles. An example of a well-known climate periodicity is the El Niño phenomenon believed to occur in cycles of 3–7 years, when the easterly trade winds in the Pacific weaken and are unable to keep the warm water from the Western Pacific away from the coastal zones of the Americas. The result is large rainfall anomalies such as droughts and floods in different parts of the world.

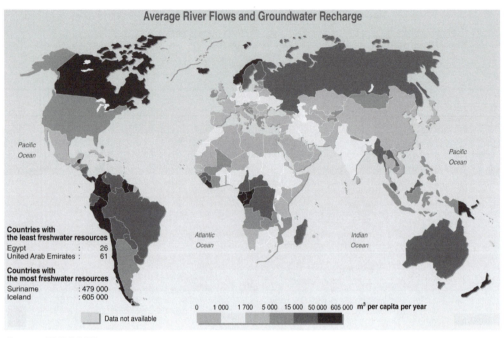

Source: GRID/UNEP

Figure 2.7 *World blue water resources, expressed as cubic metres available per person and year*

The inter-annual variability of rainfall increases with decreased average annual rainfall. This means that arid and semi-arid ecosystems experience not only lower rainfall than many temperate ecosystems, but also a very high inter-annual fluctuation of rainfall between years. For large parts of tropical Africa, rainfall deviates on average by more than 25 per cent from the long-term average rainfall. The world map in Figure 2.8 shows the rainfall variability for different regions of the world, given as the average deviation in annual rainfall. As indicated by the map, variability of rainfall is very high in the tropical and sub-tropical belts. Two important implications of this are that average rainfall, (or what is often referred to as normal rainfall), never occurs and that the concept has very little relevance for management of water resources and that environment. Variability of rainfall is so high that the only thing we can be absolutely sure of is that we will never experience normal rainfall! Yet researchers still base decisions largely on assumptions of average rainfall. This could be a result of temperate bias in our way of defining scientific and development questions. While science and development seem so attached to average and normal rainfall, everyday life seems to have a more humble attitude to the large variability of rainfall. As Professor Ignacio Rodriguez-Iturbe, the 2002 Stockholm Water Prize Laureate, said: '...we talk a lot about the average weather [like] rainfall for example, but we seem also to be always talking about conditions that are far from average' (Rodriguez-Iturbe, 2002).

Rainfall variability is a natural phenomenon, which plays a dominant role in determining living conditions for all biological life, especially in tropical climates. Cornerstones in the analysis of water requirements to sustain ecosystem goods and

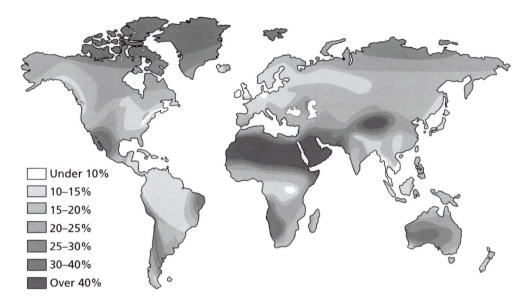

Under 10%
10–15%
15–20%
20–25%
25–30%
30–40%
Over 40%

Note: The average deviation in annual rainfall is shown as a percentage of long-term average (modified from Morales, 1977).

Figure 2.8 *World rainfall variability*

services are to accept hydro-climatic variability, and to understand the interactions between climatically induced fluctuations in water flows. A first step is to accept rainfall fluctuations as a natural and integral part of the ecohydrological processes occurring in an ecosystem or catchment.

Summary

An entry point to ecohydrology is the understanding of rainfall partitioning into green and blue water flows. Green water flow is the vapour flow in the water cycle over land, or total evaporation, consisting of non-productive vapour flow from foliage, open water or soil, and productive vapour flow as transpiration from vegetation. Blue water flow is the liquid water flow in the water cycle, consisting of surface flood flow and sub-surface recharge of groundwater. A useful way to analyse the factors determining partitioning of rainfall is to distinguish between two partitioning points in the water cycle. The first partitioning point is at the soil surface, where rainfall is divided into infiltration into the soil and surface runoff on top of the soil. An infiltrated rainfall forms soil moisture and then reaches the second partitioning point. At the second point water either forms green water or it continues to percolate through the soil to form groundwater recharge. Soil moisture forming green water returns to the atmosphere either as non-productive soil evaporation or is taken up by roots and returned as productive green water flow, plant transpiration.

The partitioning of rainfall demonstrates the critical water–soil relationship in the water cycle, and the fundamental role of soil moisture as the source of water that sustains biomass growth. The partitioning of rainfall is affected by both biophysical and human factors. Natural factors such as wetness of soil and slope, vegetation cover and soil structure, will affect the amount of floodwater generated at the first partitioning point. The content of organic matter in the soil, which strongly affects its water-holding capacity, and root vigour of plants influence the partitioning at the second point between plant water uptake and groundwater recharge. Human factors, such as agriculture and artificial surfaces in urban areas, strongly affect partitioning of rainfall in green and blue water flows. On a catchment scale, land use upstream will affect water availability downstream.

From an ecohydrological perspective, land use changes in a catchment will directly affect water flow availability to sustain ecosystems. The link between land use and water for ecosystems is found in the partitioning points of the water cycle. Every land use will generate a specific partitioning of rainfall, which in turn is strongly affected by the links between soil, water, plant and atmosphere.

The spatial link is important. Conventionally the water resource focus is on blue water. Moreover, the so-called available water resource is directly associated with stable blue water flow in rivers and aquifers downstream in river basins, neglecting the fact that this water resource is generated from rainfall partitioning upstream. Green water sustains all biomass growth, and local blue water flows sustain wetlands and human water use in small catchments before the water reaches downstream areas. Rainfall, not stable blue water flow, is the fundamental water resource, and, in a new approach to ecohydrology, the conceptual entry point is the raindrop and not the blue water flowing in rivers, lakes or aquifers.

Chapter 3

Human Water Requirements

When attempting to balance water for humans and nature it is essential to understand general human water requirements. As water for food constitutes the bulk of these, it is necessary to distinguish between consumptive and non-consumptive water use.

Household and Industrial Water Needs

Balancing the water needs of humans and nature requires knowledge of the actual water requirements necessary to sustain goods and services in society and in ecosystems. The biggest threat to secure availability of water for ecosystems is the pressure exercised by humans on finite fresh water. We need to understand the compelling forces that alter that availability. These powerful forces are linked to human water demand and to water-dependent land use in agriculture.

According to the latest estimates, global blue water withdrawals in 1995 amounted altogether to approximately 3800 km^3/year, out of which 2270 km^3/year were consumptive use, that is for green water (Shiklomanov, 2000). Figure 3.1 shows the development of withdrawals over the last century. Irrigation is by far the dominating sector, for which the withdrawals increased from an estimated 580 km3/year in 1900 to approximately 2500 km^3/year in 2000.

Domestic water for drinking, sanitation, washing and municipal uses represents a blue water withdrawal for direct use. Population growth, urbanization and economic development have created a rapid increase in domestic water use over the past century, especially in industrialized countries of the Northern Hemisphere.

Domestic water use shows large variations between different regions of the world. In Figure 3.2, the relative size of the water tankers illustrates the magnitude of difference between industrialized countries and developing countries. There is a large span between the world's largest domestic water users (USA with some 366 m^3/person/year) compared to the world's lowest users (Africa with some 25 m^3/person/year). Europe holds an intermediate level. These figures clearly show the close interdependence between economic development and direct human blue water use. The large difference in water use between industrialized and developing countries reflects the step from a society in which people still collect their domestic water manually from wells, boreholes, springs and dams, to one where households have

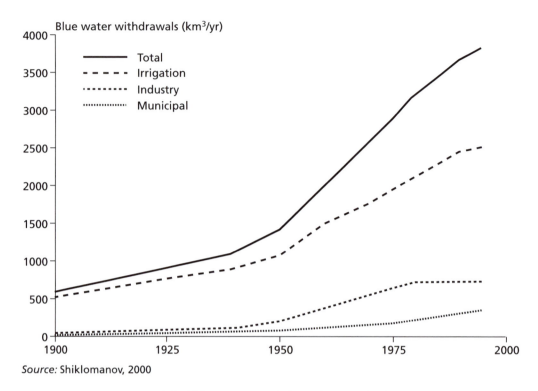

Source: Shiklomanov, 2000

Figure 3.1 *Global blue water withdrawals over the last century*

water connections inside their houses. The difference in use, in other words, is from a 'non-piped' society to a 'fully piped' one.

After irrigation for food production, industry is the sector withdrawing the biggest amounts of blue water, but industry is still a relatively small water user. Industrial use is very unevenly distributed over the world, with only 10 m^3/person/year used in sub-Saharan African countries while 140 m^3/person/year are used in European countries. Certain industrial sectors require large volumes of water, such as the wood pulp and paper industry. One tonne of cellulose pulp normally requires 400–500 m^3 of water. Ferrous metallurgy uses some 40–50 m^3 per 1 tonne of cast iron, and it takes up to 500 m^3 to produce 1 tonne of copper. Synthetic rubbers, fibres and plastics require large volumes in the range of 2000–5000 m^3/tonne (Shiklomanov, 2000), which is closer to the consumptive water use needs for food. The electronic high-tech industry also continues to grow, demanding sizable amounts of water. While industrial demand increases rapidly, new industrial water management techniques for recirculation of water and for dry production may reduce the pressure on withdrawals of fresh water for industrial use.

A reason for concern is the rapid increase of blue water withdrawals. As seen in Figure 3.3, water withdrawals have increased more than twice as fast as population growth over the last century.

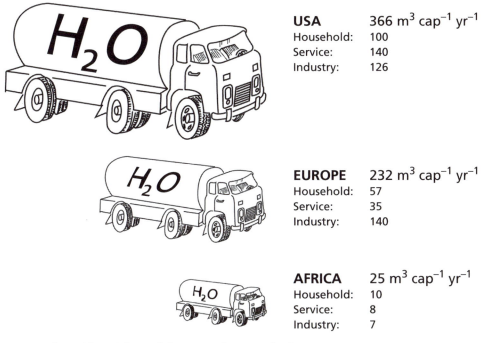

USA   366 m³ cap⁻¹ yr⁻¹
Household: 100
Service: 140
Industry: 126

EUROPE   232 m³ cap⁻¹ yr⁻¹
Household: 57
Service: 35
Industry: 140

AFRICA   25 m³ cap⁻¹ yr⁻¹
Household: 10
Service: 8
Industry: 7

Source: Adapted from Schertenleib, personal communication

Figure 3.2 *Domestic water use for different regions of the world (m³/person/year)*

As shown by these figures, meeting direct blue water needs for domestic and industrial purposes is not and will not cause any real water scarcity problem. The proportion of direct human needs of blue water is so small compared to the total human water need, that there is no region in the world where the most basic water needs cannot be secured. In other words, the reason why millions of rural and urban poor still lack proper drinking water and sanitation is purely a question of undermanagement, not a question of water scarcity.

Distinguishing Between Water Use and Consumptive Water Use

In this book we apply the most commonly understood terminology for water withdrawals, water use, water needs and water demand. As pointed out by Gleick (2000), there is a substantial level of confusion over terms even among water professionals. In the commonly used terminology, water withdrawal refers to the direct human extraction of blue water flow for societal use in irrigated agriculture, industry and municipal use. In practice, this means that water withdrawals refer to water

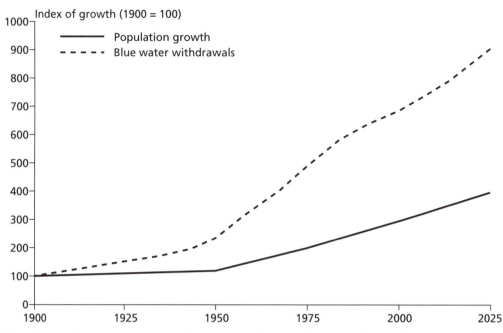

Note: To enable comparison of trends, world population and water withdrawals are set to 100 in year 1900.

Figure 3.3 *Relative development of population growth versus blue water withdrawals over the last century*

sources exploited by society (in dams, wells, boreholes and diversions from freshwater lakes) and distributed for human use as piped water.

Water withdrawal is not equal to true water use, as only a certain proportion of withdrawn water goes to a literally consumptive use while the rest returns to rivers or groundwater. In irrigation, for example, a certain proportion of the water withdrawn is consumed by the crops and turns into green water flow as total evaporation, while a significant proportion infiltrates into the soil and percolates below the root zone, recharging groundwater. Both the consumptive water flow and the return flow of drainage water are included in the water withdrawn but only the consumptive part can be considered as true water use. Water recharging groundwater may evidently be withdrawn again further downstream and reused. Alternatively, it may be involved in supporting an aquatic habitat in a river or wetland. However, the risk is high that the return flow will carry with it leached nutrients, salts, and perhaps also traces of pesticides, making the quality too poor for reuse.

Consumptive water use refers to water withdrawn from a source and made unsuitable for reuse in the same basin (Gleick, 2000). Green water flow from vegetation is by far the largest consumptive use of water, but not the only one. When use results in contamination of water it then has to be considered as consumed water. Thus, the term consumptive water use is applied also to evaporation flow from reservoirs, seepage of water to a saline sink, or contamination of water.

The effect of distinguishing between consumptive use (mainly green water flow) and non-consumptive use (mainly blue water flow) of water in agriculture is substantial. In most irrigation schemes at least 10,000 m^3 of water is generally applied per hectare per person and is normally considered as being 'used'. This corresponds to 1000 mm/hectare/season. Comparing this volume with the produced crop is generally seen as an indicator of water productivity, which gives the impression of a highly inefficient water use. Often only half of the applied volume supports crop growth and returns as consumptive green water flow to the atmosphere. But in reality the other half, the non-consumptive part of the applied water, can at least partly be reused. Focusing only on water withdrawals gives the impression of large losses of water, while in reality all water that is not consumptive can benefit other water uses downstream. This distinction between consumptive and non-consumptive use of water is extremely important in modern water resource assessments, as it substantially reduces the estimates of actual water used by humanity, as will be shown below.

Current Green Water Requirements for Food Production

We will now focus on the water requirements for food production, whether met by blue or green water. As projections of future water withdrawals are by necessity based on predictions of human water demand,[1] it is important to quantify these needs and demands on a per capita basis. Human water requirements are reasonably similar around the world. Irrespective of geographical location, we require roughly the same volume of water to meet our needs for food, drinking, sanitation, municipalities and industry. Human water needs to produce food vary with nutritional status, contents of diet, the hydroclimate where food is produced, and the management of water and land in agriculture. Management influences the amount of green water flow required to produce a certain crop or to produce a unit of food. At this stage though, we will not investigate the role of management. Instead, our focus here is primarily to develop a generic and synthesized indicator of human water requirements for food. Water for food is by far the largest human water use at the local, regional and global scale, and it thereby has strong relevance for the balancing of water for humans and nature, which is the focus later in the book.

However, the way in which that water requirement of approximately 1500 m^3/person/year is met varies from location to location, and there is a wide spectrum of water strategies to secure the volumes needed. At one extreme are the countries depending almost exclusively on green water to meet human water requirements, for example, countries in Europe and sub-Saharan Africa. At the other extreme are the countries in the Middle East with an exclusive dependence on blue water.

Water and diets

All the food we eat (except fish) requires a productive green water flow as transpiration through plants. For dairy products, meat and poultry, the green water is indirectly linked through the pasture, fodder and grain eaten by animals. As stated earlier, most data on water for food includes both productive and non-productive green water flow (evaporation and transpiration). In the following we will, therefore, use green water flow (total evaporation) to denote consumptive use of water to produce food. Later we will discuss the importance of distinguishing between productive and non-productive green water flow in efforts to improve water productivity and the amount of crop produced per drop of consumptive water use.

An approach to estimate actual water use and future water needs and desires for food is to calculate the water required to produce human diets. Currently, there are an estimated 800 million undernourished people in the world, with a calorie intake below the minimum required for a healthy life (UNESCO-WWAP, 2003).[2] This corresponds to 18 per cent of the population in developing countries. On a global scale, the number of undernourished people has remained at this high level for over 30 years, reaching a peak of 960 million people in 1969/70. However, over the same period, the population in developing countries has increased from 2.6 billion to 4.4 billion, indicating a substantial relative decline in the number of undernourished people. The challenge is still daunting, however, especially in sub-Saharan Africa, and in South and East Asia, where 33 per cent, 23 per cent and 13 per cent, respectively, of the populations are undernourished. Sub-Saharan Africa is worst off, with a constant low average calorie intake per person, which has not moved from the 2000–2100 kcal/person/day range since the 1960s (FAO, 2001). Population growth adds to the challenge of addressing current malnourishment, with a current estimated world growth of 77 million people per year, and an expected 3 billion more world inhabitants by 2050 (2000–2050) (UN, 2003).From the above it is clear that there are two challenges to securing water for food: the challenge of lifting almost 1 billion people from unacceptably low nutritional levels and the challenge of feeding an additional 3 billion people over the next 50 years (UNFPA, 2002; UN, 2003).

The principal question, then, is how much water is required to produce an adequate diet? The FAO, in discussions leading up to the World Food Summit in 1996 (Klohn, personal communication, 1996), carried out a very simple calculation on water requirements to produce a balanced diet of 2700 kcal/person/day. This estimate included 2300 kcal of plant foods and 400 kcal of meat foods, suggesting that meat would constitute 15 per cent of the diet, which is a rather low figure. According to the FAO, a European or North American diet includes around 35 per cent of meat, while an African or Asian diet includes between 1 and 15 per cent of meat (Gleick, 2000). In this estimate, it was assumed that 1 m^3 of green water flow was required to produce 1000 kcal of vegetarian foods, and a corresponding 5 m^3 of water to produce 1000 kcal of meat. The reason for this large difference between meat and vegetarian food is essentially based on water use in intensive industrialized meat production, where large amounts of grain feed are used. As the conversion rate from grain to meat is equal to about 20 per cent, meat production will end up consuming five times more water to produce the same calorie equivalents as plant food production. These assumptions give a daily water requirement to produce a balanced diet of 4300 litres per person per day, or 1600 m^3/year per person per year. This is a very simple and generalized figure, which does not reflect the huge differences in both diet contents and water requirements to produce food in different hydroclimates. However, it gives an indication of the order of magnitude involved.

In the following, we will scrutinize the water for diet requirements for different hydroclimates in the world, but first let us look at present diets and current estimates of water needed to generate them. Based on data from the FAO concerning average diets for different regions of the World, Gleick (2000) estimated water requirements for regional diets in the late 1980s. In these estimates, a European or North American annual average diet requires 1700–1800 m³/year to produce, while an African or Asian diet only required between 600–900 m³/year. The large difference in water requirements between industrialized and developing countries originates partly in the large difference in calorie intake, and partly from the very low proportion of water intensive meat production in developing countries.

Rockström et al (1999) recently estimated that in the mid-1990s, as a global average, 1200 m³/person/year was used to produce food. Similarly, Gleick's estimate from different regions of the world shows a global average of 1220 m³/person/year. These figures probably reflect rather well the actual global average of water required for the present levels of food production.

Productive green water requirements for most cereals

According to Gleick (2000), hydroclimate, technology and farming practices have an effect on the inter-regional differences in the amount of water required to produce present diets. It is taken as a general rule that more water (green water) is required to produce food in tropical ecosystems than in temperate ecosystems. This would imply that more water is required to produce an African and Asian diet, as compared to a European diet. However, the role of climate as a major cause of differences in the amount of water required to produce food may be exaggerated. The situation is less straightforward than is generally assumed.

The water used to produce food is generally considered to include the whole green water flow – both non-productive evaporation and productive transpiration. Crop water use includes two completely different water flows. Both flows are driven by atmospheric thirst for water but they involve completely different processes: transpiration is directly related and proportional to plant growth and evaporation is directly related to the conversion of water to vapour from soil, water and canopy surfaces.

As a rule, crop transpiration is directly related to crop growth, so more transpiration equals more crop growth. This relationship is linear, very conservative and physiologically determined. As long as water is a non-limiting factor it is difficult to influence the amount of transpiration required per unit of crop growth with management. Different crops require different amounts of productive water (transpiration) to reach maturity. If soil conditions such as soil fertility and aeration, as well as water availability for the crop, are non-limiting, then the amount of transpiration for a certain plant, crop or tree is determined only by climate and the physiological characteristics of the plant.

The climatic factors that drive transpiration are solar radiation, air temperature, wind speed, and the vapour pressure difference between the interior spaces of leaves (where vapour pressure is always near to saturation)[3] and the air surrounding the leaves. In simple terms, high solar radiation, high air temperature and a dry air will increase the atmospheric thirst, thereby increasing potential transpiration. The dryness of the air, or deficit of vapour between the air adjacent to the canopy and inside the leaves, is a key factor driving transpiration. This gradient of vapour deficit between leaf and air adjacent to the leaf, defined as the vapour pressure deficit, sucks water from the stomata to the atmosphere in an effort to equalize pressure between air and leaf. In a sparsely vegetated biotope (for example, a savanna), vapour released from leaves will rapidly be blown away by wind, leaving a dry air layer near the leaves. Wind speed thus contributes to maintain the pressure deficit and keeps the transpiration process running at a higher rate.

From a thermodynamic perspective, a plant in a dry and hot tropical ecosystem will transpire more than a plant in a cool and temperate ecosystem, because all the driving forces of the vapour flow are geared for higher flow: high solar radiation, high temperature, and large vapour pressure deficit. More water will therefore be needed to produce the same amount of carbon, since carbon concentrations in the form of CO_2 in the air will not differ between hydroclimatic zones. The implication would be that more water for transpiration is needed per unit of plant growth in the tropics compared to the temperate zone. This would hold for the same plant species, for example for wheat or a bougainvillea grown in Europe and in Asia.

However, plants in tropical regions often have a different physiology compared to temperate plants. For example, temperate grains (wheat, barley, rye, oats) have a photosynthetic pathway in which CO_2 has to be taken up continuously to maintain photosynthesis. This means that transpiration flow is also continuous, because transpiration flow occurs only when stomata are open for uptake of CO_2. These temperate crops are defined as C3 crops. Many tropical food crops, on the other hand, have developed a different photosynthetic pathway with an intermediary storage of CO_2 in the leaf, which enables them to carry out a more water-efficient photosynthesis. Less water is lost per unit of carbon assimilation. Crops with this photosynthetic pathway are called C4 crops.

It has been shown that C4 crops have roughly double the carbon assimilation per unit of transpiration compared to C3 crops, and interestingly, this assimilation rate, for a given vapour pressure deficit, is rather conservative for different crops. This means that for temperate food crops a moister atmosphere compensates for a less efficient photosynthetic pathway – that a lower pressure gradient is driving transpiration. Conversely, in the dry tropics a more efficient photosynthetic pathway compensates for a thirsty, dry atmosphere.

There are, of course, substantial variations in crop growth per unit transpiration between crop species, and there are fluctuations in reported transpiration efficiencies among the same species. But in a general sense, the implication of these facts is that a wheat crop in Europe and a maize crop in India will produce roughly similar biomass or grain per unit of transpiration. This rate of plant growth per unit of productive green water flow is in the order of 2–3 kg biomass per mm and hectare (or 300–500 m^3/tonne biomass) (Loomis and Connor, 1992; Ong et al, 1996).

To put it in a very simplified manner, the requirement of productive green water as plant transpiration to produce one unit of food does not differ significantly for most cereals on Earth. This is important. It corrects the common misunderstanding that food production in hot tropical regions requires more water per unit of food produced. This misconception led to the conclusion that hot and dry tropical regions are less efficient and therefore less appropriate for food production than cool and wet temperate regions. Instead, the implication of the above is that one cannot rule out semi-arid tropical regions as potential breadbaskets.

Non-productive green water flow in tropical regions

While tropical crops are efficient productive green water users, non-productive water flow as evaporation tends to be much higher in tropical regions. In most statistics about water requirements for different crops of the world, water requirement is defined as total green water flow, including evaporation. Such figures are generally used to explain that tropical crops require more water, but if we focus on the water that really counts, namely the productive flow contributing to biomass growth, requirements are not that different. The rate of evaporation, on the other hand, is directly proportional to evaporative demand of the atmosphere – the demand from moist soil is higher in the tropics than in temperate regions. Evaporation losses can, however, be reduced through management by using various systems of mulching, inter-cropping, and probably most importantly, by increasing the canopy of the crop grown by improving crop productivity.

Plant-related water productivity and locality-related water requirements

Even if evaporation is included in the consumptive water use, the differences for various crops between hydroclimatic zones still remain surprisingly low. It is often stated that tropical grains, especially rice, are very large water consumers compared to temperate crops such as wheat. Again, because of the efficient way in which tropical crops accumulate carbon, the amount of biomass produced per unit of green water flow is not that different between hydro-climatic zones. Table 3.1 shows water productivity data for a range of temperate and tropical crops. Interestingly, the range for most cereal crops is between 1000 and 2000 m^3 of green water flow to produce 1 tonne of grain. Many systems in the world, even rice, operate at this range. Tubers such as potatoes are generally more efficient, and often less than 1000 m^3 is required per tonne of potato. Tomatoes are another example of a highly water productive crop. The conclusion is that, in generic terms and disregarding the impact of management, it is possible to talk of a relatively universal average of some 1500 m^3 of green water to produce 1 tonne of terrestrial, plant-based of food, which is equivalent to 150 mm/tonne/ha.

However, there are many management opportunities that could influence these figures. The range of actual green water use in a farmer's field is huge, often between 1000 and 6000 m^3/tonne (or 100–600 mm/tonne/ha) for a given crop within a given hydroclimate. This range, for one crop within a certain hydroclimate, is larger than the average ranges for various crops between different hydroclimates shown in Table 3.1.

This suggests that the negotiable part of crop water needs – the portion that can be influenced by management – induces a larger variation in crop water requirements than the non-negotiable biophysical parameters, which are related to hydroclimate and crop physiology and which cannot be influenced by the farmer. For the ecohydrologist, this is an encouragement for the search for strategies to produce more food with minimum impact on water availability for the ecosystems. It shows that appropriate management can offer abundant opportunities to change the current water use in agriculture. Win–win situations in which more food is produced per unit of consumed water contrast with the common notion that extensive water requirements in hot tropical agro-ecosystems are a fixed factor that cannot be influenced.

A fundamental issue here is that water productivity only shows the relative efficiency of a plant in a certain environment, but it says nothing of the environmental conditions under which that plant can occur. Soil type, temperature regime, distribution and length of growing seasons, and above all cumulative water requirements, will determine where a certain plant can occur. As shown in Table 3.1, the water requirements for different crops vary widely, while water productivity shows a smaller range. Sugar cane is a good example of this. It appears in the table to be one of the world's most water-productive crops, requiring only 200 m³, or 20 mm per hectare, to produce 1 tonne dry matter of cane! Still, sugar cane can only be cultivated in humid tropical locations with the right temperature and radiation requirements, and where there are ample volumes of water accessible for agriculture. The reason is that seasonal crop water requirements amount to 1500–2500 mm per hectare. The yields are tremendous, up to 150 tonnes/hectare, and water productivity is impressive. Still, huge volumes of water are required. The implication is that while water productivity is important in ecohydrology, for a farmer, water productivity makes little sense, while crop water requirements make a lot of sense.

Generic Human Water Requirements

We can now draw the following conclusions:

The present global average use of water for food amounts to approximately 1200 m³/person/year. There is a range from 600 m³ for the most malnourished and vegetarian diets in the poorest developing countries, to 1800 m³ for the richest, most meat-based diets in industrialized countries. Past estimates of water to sustain an adequate diet of 2700 kcal/person/year amount to 1600 m³/person/year (Falkenmark, 1997).

Per capita water needs for food will vary with diet composition and nutritional level, and as a result of farm management. However, climate has a lesser role to play in explaining differences in water needs per unit of food output. The explanation is that in atmospherically thirsty environments, an effective photosynthetic pathway balances the influence of the climate. In other environments, where the atmosphere has a smaller evaporative demand, less effective pathways are adequate.

Calorie-based estimate

To enable assessments of future water requirements to feed a growing population and to relieve hunger, we need to identify a desired volume of water for food requirement. We will do this by revisiting the calorie-based estimate of 1600 m³/person/year, based on the assumption of 1 m³/1000 kcal for plant foods, and 5 m³/1000 kcal for animal

Table 3.1 *Water productivity (m³ of green water flow per tonne grain) and crop water requirements (mm) for major food crops of the world*

Crop	Hydroclimate	Type of Crop	Water productivity Range		Average	Source	Yield range (t/ha)	Water requirement (mm)[1]
Wheat	Temperate	C3	780	2640	1480	Rockström et al, 1999	4-6	450-650
Wheat	Temperate	C3	900	2000	1000	Gleick, 2000		
Barley	Temperate	C3	540	1580	1270	Rockström et al, 1999		
Rye	Temperate	C3	540	2640	1370	Rockström et al, 1999		
Oats	Temperate	C3	540	2640		Rockström et al, 1999		
Rapeseed	Temperate	C3	1530	2030	1780	Rockström et al, 1999		
Temperate cereals	Temperate	C3	660	2300	1250	Rockström at al, 1999		
Beans, green	Temperate	C3	500	670	580	Rockström et al, 1999	0.6-0.8	350-500
Peas, green	Temperate	C3	1430	2000	1720	Rockström et al, 1999		350-625
Potatoes	Temperate	C3	200	400	250	Rockström et al, 1999	25-35	
Rice	Tropical	C3			1900	Pimentel et al, and Houser, 1997		
Rice	Tropical	C3	900	1400	1150	Doorenbos and Kassam 1979	3-8	500-950
Maize	Tropical	C4	940	1460	1150	Rockström et al, 1999	6-9	400-750
Millet	Tropical	C4	590	4370	1630	Rockström et al, 1999		
Sorghum	Tropical	C4	1100	1800		Gleick, 2000	3-5	300-650
Tropical cereals	Tropical	C4	500	2480	1400	Rockström et al, 1999		
Sugarcane	Tropical	C4	100	200	150	Rockström et al, 1999	50-150	1500-2500
Cotton seed	Tropical	C4	2080	2230	2160	Rockström et al, 1999	4-5	550-950
Sunflower seed	Tropical	C4	1530	3500	2370	Rockström et al, 1999		
Beans, dry	Tropical		1730	2500	2120	Rockström et al, 1999	1,5-2	250-500
Soya beans	Tropical		1250	1960	1610	Rockström et al, 1999		450-825
Banana, plantain	Tropical		230	320	280	Rockström et al, 1999		
Bananas	Tropical		230	320	280	Rockström et al, 1999	40-60	700-1700
Oranges	Tropical		200	500	350	Rockström et al, 1999	25-40	600-950

Note: 1 Doorenbos and Kassam 1986; Doorenbos and Pruitt 1992

Table 3.2 *Volumes of water (consumptive use of green water) needed to produce plant foods in developing countries*

Food type	m^3/kg	$m^3/1000\ kcal$
Cereals	1.5	0.47
Starchy roots	0.7	0.78
Sugarcrops	0.15	0.49
Pulses	1.9	0.55
Oilcrops	2.0	0.73
Vegetable oils	2.0	0.23
Vegetables	0.5	2.07
Average		0.53

foods, and a diet of 2700 kcal/person/day. For plant-based foods we have used crop water requirement data from Rockström et al (1999) shown in Table 3.1 and combined them with nutritional data on calorie contents per crop from FAOSTAT (2002). For developing countries with primarily tropical crops, the weighted average green water requirements necessary to produce food of plant origin amounts to 0.53 $m^3/1000$ kcal. The weighted average is based on the relative proportion of each plant type in present diets in developing countries. For developed countries, the corresponding figure at present is 0.41 $m^3/1000$ kcal. For tropical environments, the green water requirements (m^3) to produce edible dry matter (kg) and calories (1000 kcal) are shown in Table 3.2. Based on these estimates and the fact that almost all additional food produced in the world in the future will be consumed by people in developing countries (as 95 per cent of population growth and the totality of malnourishment occurs here), we assume a generic volume of 0.5 m^3 of green water flow to produce 1000 kcal of plant foods.

For animal food, the estimate of green water requirements is more complicated. The reason is that animals use water both directly for drinking, and indirectly through green water that generates animal feed, such as fodder, pasture grass, concentrates and cereals. For intensive meat-producing systems in industrialized countries where cereal-based feeding plays an important role, 5 $m^3/1000$ kcal of meat may be an adequate figure. Almost all animals in large parts of the developing world, but also in semi-arid regions of the Americas and Australia, are raised primarily on free grazing. Therefore, the water requirement to generate meat is tied to the green water to generate grass. However, as grasslands and woodlands used for grazing also generate other ecosystem services, it seems incorrect to attribute the full water requirement to sustain grazing lands. That requirement is estimated to be 20,400 km^3/year on a global scale. This corresponds to 3400 m^3/person/year globally, which is almost three times higher than current average water requirements for total diets (1200 m^3/person/year) This is a very large proportion of global green water flow. Therefore, it seems reasonable to assume that free-grazing animals should be regarded as having a lower green water requirement than cereal-fed animals. We have therefore assumed a value of 4 $m^3/1000$ kcal for meat foods.

We assume a desired diet in 2050 of 3000 kcal/person/day, the same level that FAO predicts as a global average in 2030. We assume that 20 per cent of this is meat. This may be a low figure compared to the present meat consumption of 30–35 per cent in developed countries, but slightly higher compared to the present average of 10–15 per cent in developing countries. With this assumption, we arrive at a desired water requirement of 1300 m³/person/year to generate a desired diet of 3000 kcal/person/day. We can thereby conclude that to achieve a desired diet, 1300 m³ of consumptive water is required per person per year. Based on the limited differences in water productivity between food plants in different hydroclimates, we can also, in general terms, speak of this 'desired' volume as a 'generic' volume for all human beings. It is generic also in the sense that the water needed to generate the diet can originate from both direct green water use in rainfed agriculture for growing grass for fodder on pastures, or from blue water withdrawals in irrigation.

The desired volume of 1300 m³/person/year is close to the present global average of 1200 m³/person/year. This affirms two essential points. First, that we are already very close to a desired dietary balance in terms of water on a global scale – that is, there is enough water used for food production in the world today to feed everyone at desired levels. Second, it shows how distorted the calculations of the present average dietary water volume are. The global average dietary water requirement is relatively high –1200 m³/capita/year only because a relatively small proportion of the world population or 13 per cent 'eat' 23 per cent of present estimated green water flow in the form of food. This refers to Europe and North America, which use 1600 m³/person/year and 1800 m³/person/year, respectively.

The desired requirement of water for food thus primarily indicates the need to improve diets in developing countries, where presently the average water-for-food intake is 850 m³/person/year. This suggests that developed countries in Europe and North America should reduce their diets in the future. Most indications suggest that this will be the case, not only in terms of cumulative calorie intake, but also in terms of a lower dietary proportion of animal foods as reflected by the growing concern over the health problems caused by overly large and unbalanced diets. However, we do not expect the water for food requirements to drop from the present 1700 m³/person/year to the desired 1300 m³. In the continued analyses in this book we therefore apply a differentiated range of desired diets in our estimates, where 1300 m³/person/year is used for developing countries and 1600 m³/person/year is used for developed countries.

Adding domestic and industrial water requirements

Apart from water for food, direct human water requirements also include domestic and industrial needs. Gleick (1996) recommended a basic water need of 50 litres/capita/day or 18 m³/capita/year for human domestic purposes, including drinking, sanitation and food preparation. This is lower than the present range of domestic use, from a low of 25 m³/person/year for Africa to a high of almost 240 m³/person/year for North America (see below). Falkenmark (1989) used a domestic average of 100 litres/person/day, which, in addition to drinking and sanitation, also included washing. This corresponds to 36 m³/person/year for domestic purposes. We can conclude here that the range of domestic water needs range in the order of 20–40 m³/capita/year.

For industry it is difficult to assess the water needs. It therefore makes more sense to consider present withdrawals. These range from less than 10 m³/person/year in developing countries to 140 m³/person/year for industrialized countries.

Table 3.3 *Indices of actual and desired human direct water use*

	Human direct water needs (m³/person/year) ACTUAL		DESIRED			% of total need	
	Range	Average	Developing	Developed	Global average[1]	Actual	Desired
Diet	600–1800	1200	1300	1600	1350	88	90
Domestic	20–40	30	30	30	30	2	2
Industry	10–140	1302	130	130	130	10	8
Total	630–1980	1360	1460	1760	1510	100	100
		~1400	~1500	~1800	~1500		

1 The average is weighted in relation to the relative proportion of population in developed (13.6%) and developing (86.4 %) countries in 2050.
2 The global average withdrawal for industrial purposes according to Shiklomanov's prediction for 2000 (780 km3/year) divided by a world population of 6 billion people.
Sources: Gleick, 2000; Rockström et al, 1999; Shiklomanov, 2000

Table 3.3 summarizes the actual and desired water requirements to satisfy direct human water needs – whether blue or green – for food, in industry and for domestic purposes. For domestic and industrial water needs, we assume the same desired volumes for developed and developing countries. The desired total volume of direct human water requirements amount to 1500 m³/person/year in developing countries (1470 m³) and 1800 m³/person/year in developed countries (1760 m³). The global average is 1510 m³/person/year, when weighting for population in developing and developed countries. This average is almost equal to the desired average for developing countries, which underlines the fact that almost all population growth will occur here (UNFPA, 2002; UN, 2003).

In summary, therefore, the desired direct human water requirement for food, industry and domestic purposes is 1500 m³/person/year, which applies both as a global average and as an average for developing countries.

It is important to note that the figures in Table 3.3 show human needs for industry, domestic uses and for food at actual and desired nutritional levels, irrespective of the source of water. It is a generic measure of human water needs to generate industrial, domestic, and dietary goods and services. For food, the water can be consumed in both irrigated agriculture, after withdrawals of blue water flow, and in rainfed agriculture through direct consumption of green water flow from infiltrated soil moisture. While both ways of consumption involve green water flow, the implications for the hydrological cycle, and therefore for water resources management, will differ. The green water flow consumed in irrigation originates from the blue water flow branch, while that consumed in rainfed agriculture is an integral part of the green water flow branch. This distinction is perhaps obvious, but, as will be seen shortly, it is crucial for assessing future regional and global water requirements. Therefore, it is useful to think of water for food in terms of blue use in irrigation and green use in rainfed agriculture.

The reason is that the generic human water need is a major force behind increased pressure on future freshwater resources. It can, however, be derived from both green and blue water flows. Therefore, it is not possible to project future withdrawals of blue water based on human water demands, as major parts of the demand can be met from green water flow in rainfed agriculture.

To this we may add two points of importance for management:

First, human water requirements for domestic and industrial purposes constitute a very small proportion of direct human water needs. Domestic water needs are only 2 per cent of total human water demands, which again indicates that the crisis experienced in many parts of the world to secure direct blue water uses for drinking, washing and sanitation is really an issue of management and not an issue of water scarcity.

Second, an important point to reiterate is that water requirements for food, as expressed here, include both evaporation and transpiration. While transpiration is difficult to influence because an incremental increase in food will always equal an incremental increase in water use, land management directly influences evaporation flow. A critical starting point in balancing water for food and nature is to identify the management options available to reduce the amount of consumptive water required to produce one unit of food.

Ultimate water requirements – a function of diets and water losses

The generic measure of 1300 m^3 per year for human food production provides a tool for assessments of future water needs. However, it is important to understand that even though this volume is biophysically generic in the sense that a similar volume applies for a person whether living on the semi-arid savanna or in the temperate taiga, it will still vary considerably as a result of other factors that humans can influence: what we eat and how we manage land.

To begin with, we can change our diets. A more vegetarian diet would result in reduced water requirements in societies where meat production is based on grain feeding. Theoretically, a purely vegetarian diet of 3000 kcal/person/day could be achieved with only 1.5 m^3 of green water per day, or 550 m^3 per year. This is 750 m^3 less than a balanced meat-based diet.

Furthermore, it could be seen as a sign of a 'temperate bias' to assume that meat production consumes eight times more water (4 m^3 as compared to 0.5 m^3 per 1000 kcal) than plant foods. That assumption remains largely based on a temperate/industrialized society where there is a dominance of grain-fed animals. According to Pimentel and Houser (1997), 15–17 m^3 of water is needed to produce 1 kg of beef (7–8 m^3/1000 kcal), while chicken requires less, in the order of 3.5–7 m^3/kg (2–4 m^3/1000 kcal). In large parts of the tropics, and especially in developing countries, animal husbandry is carried out without grain feeding, and often even without stall-feeding. Instead, meat is produced through extensive grazing systems, in which animals convert energy from grass and other plants into usable energy in the form of meat, milk and eggs. This raises the question of whether it is relevant to consider water needs to sustain pastures in estimates of human dietary water requirements. As earlier stressed, grasslands and woodlands used as permanent grazing areas generate many other ecosystem services besides pasture, which makes it very difficult to assign specific water requirements to sustain livestock.

The final factor affecting human water needs is management. There are opportunities to produce more water per unit of green water flow and per unit of rainfall – more 'crop per drop' of evaporated water – which would reduce the volume of water required to produce a diet. Since water for food constitutes 90 per cent of direct human water needs, one of the most promising avenues to reduce future pressure on finite freshwater resources, and thereby secure more water for ecological functions, may be to reduce water needs to produce adequate human diets by improving 'crop per drop' ratios.

Additional Water Requirements to Feed Humanity by 2050

The central question in the 21st century is how to balance water for humans and nature. How much green and blue water will be required to supply humans with food, and where will this water come from? In other words, what ecosystem services will have to sacrifice water flow in order to secure water for humans? In order to answer these questions, we first need to assess how much more water will be required to secure food for a growing world population

There are two future challenges in relation to water and food. The first is to elevate to an adequate diet the populations suffering from malnutrition. The second is to produce food for the additional world population. To achieve this, the total water use to produce food in 2050 would amount to 12,600 km^3/year, as shown in Table 3.4. Part of the first challenge is to eradicate current malnutrition. It would require an additional 2200 km^3/year of water to raise the populations suffering from malnutrition to the desired level of 1300 m^3/person/year. In this analysis we have assumed that Europe and North America, where current diets exceed the desired volume, will stay at present volumes.

The second challenge is to feed the additional population. Population growth is projected to increase from 6 billion people at present to 9.3 billion in 2050 (FAOSTAT 2002). The volume of consumptive water use for that purpose would amount to 3400 km^3/year. Feeding an additional 3.3 billion people[4] in 2050 and at the same time eradicating malnutrition would require an estimated additional 5600 km^3/year (12,600 km^3/year – 7000 km^3/year) in consumptive water use. Where will this water come from?[5]

Where will the additional water come from?

Conventionally, the first source that comes to mind is to use more blue water through expansion of irrigation. Shiklomanov (2000) estimated an increase in irrigated land from 253 million hectares (ha) in 1995 to 330 million ha in 2025, with an increase of approximately 500 km^3/year of consumptive water use. FAO, in its latest study on agriculture until 2015/30 (FAO, 2002), estimates a lower irrigated surface in 2025 (271 million ha) based on an annual growth rate of 0.6 per cent (1997–2025), primarily in developing countries. This is where the bulk of the modest irrigation expansion is expected to occur, with an estimated increase of some 300 km^3/year of consumptive water use (FAO, 2002).

If we assume a continued modest irrigation expansion of 0.6 per cent per year during the period 2025–2050, we estimate the increased consumptive blue water use

Table 3.4 *Total water requirements for food in 2050 assuming a global situation where malnutrition is eradicated and water for food is secured for a growing population*

Water for food challenge	Water requirement 2050 (km³/yr)
Current food from crop land (year 2000)	7000
Eradicate current malnutrition to desired (1300 m³/cap/yr)	2222
Food for additional population 2050 UN medium (9.3 billion)	3364
Total	12,586

Note: Current water for food is taken from Table 4.3 (year 2000). The desired water for food volume of 1300 m³/person/year refers to Table 3.3. For regions of the world (Europe and North America) where present water for diets exceeds 1300 m³/person/year, we assume that current dietary levels will persist.

in irrigation by 2050 to be 600 km³/year.[6] This is consumptive water use only as a result of expansion of land under irrigation. That is to say it considers all bue water 'losses' through seepage in conveyance channels and drainage from cropland as re-usable downstream of an irrigation system. It is a high figure and we therefore assume that we are unlikely to arrive at a higher blue water use in irrigation. This volume would generate diets for 0.6 billion people, or roughly a fifth of the expected population over the next 50 years.

Irrigation development until 2050 will certainly result in water productivity improvements, which will enable the production of more food per unit of water consumed. As our estimate of the total additional water for food requirement in 2050 of 5600 km³/year is based on current water productivity levels, we need to consider the additional contribution to future food production of water productivity improvements in irrigation. Present estimates of green water productivity in irrigation range from 1500 to 2500 m³/tonne (FAO, 2002; Shiklomanov, 2000). With an estimated average green water productivity of 1700 m³/tonne in 2050, the total contribution from irrigation to food production in 2050 as a result of water productivity increase will amount to 200 km³/year.

This results in a total contribution of 800 km³/year to the deficit of 5600 km³/year in 2050. Of this flow, 600 km³/year originates from an increase in consumptive use (more irrigated land and larger production), and 200 km³/year originates from higher water productivity (reduction of non-productive losses).

Subtracting the projected contribution from irrigation (averaged to 800 km³/year) leaves us with a water deficit to cover global food needs in 2050 of 4800 km/year (subtracting 800 km³/year from the estimated 5600 km³/year required). This is higher than the current cumulative blue water withdrawals, of approximately 4000 km³/year. This water can only come from food production in rainfed agriculture. It would result in an increase of the share of rainfed agriculture in the total terrestrial green water flow from the present 4500 km³/year to 9300 km³/year. This corresponds to slightly more than a 100 per cent increase in green water requirement for food production over the next 50 years.

This shifts our focus from the conventional predictions of a global water scarcity crisis related to human pressure on blue water resources, to a new global water scarcity crisis, related to human pressure on green water resources. About 90 per cent of the current green water flow from land is used to sustain ecosystem services in agriculture, forests, woodlands, grasslands, wetlands and arid lands. It seems that any attempt to substantially increase green water flow in agriculture will have to result in reduced green water available for other ecosystems. We will be forced to accept trade-offs between ecosystems dependent on green water. There are three ways to attain the increased green water requirements in rainfed agriculture:

- expanding rainfed agriculture into non-agricultural land;
- increasing water use in present rainfed agriculture by diverting local rainfall from adjacent ecosystems;
- improving water productivity in rainfed agriculture through vapour shift.

Expansion of rainfed agriculture into non-agricultural land is a direct green water trade-off, in which ecosystem services sustained by green water flows in a wetland, forest or grassland are lost in favour of other ecosystem needs, such as food production. The option of increasing water use in current rainfed agriculture may increase water productivity but will divert water from adjacent ecosystems, either by using runoff generated upstream, or by reducing flows for ecosystems downstream.

However, several studies have shown that there are only limited possibilities of expanding agriculture into 'virgin' lands (Leach, 1995; possible in Africa and South and Central America). Arable land is very limited in Asia and agricultural expansion is unlikely in Europe and Russia, North America or Oceania. Moreover, about half the cultivable land in Africa and Latin America is concentrated in just seven countries – Angola, the Democratic Republic of Congo, the Sudan, Argentina, Bolivia, Brazil and Colombia. The IIASA study (Fischer et al, 2002) also concluded that the expansion of agricultural land is limited by several other constraints, including ecological fragility, degradation of resources, toxicity, incidences of diseases, lack of infrastructure or markets, and limited financial resources. It therefore seems reasonable to conclude that expansion of agricultural land to produce more rainfed food is difficult as land is not available, and in many cases expansion is not desirable because it will always mean social and ecological trade-offs. Where it is possible it is still often hazardous and expensive.

The primary challenge is therefore to pursue all avenues possible to increase the amount of food per unit water. There is also the possibility to increase productive green water use in present agriculture by either adding more local water through supplemental irrigation, using runoff generated from adjacent non-agricultural land, or by reducing non-productive flows of water from present crop land. Improved soil, crop and water management could achieve this by reducing groundwater recharge or evaporation and surface runoff. This would help to produce more food per unit green water flow by shifting vapour from non-productive evaporation to productive transpiration.

The water required to feed the world population in 2050 can be estimated at 4800 km^3/year of additional green water flow in rainfed agriculture. This is based on the assumption that water productivity in agriculture will stay constant at present levels. Today, an average of 1500 m^3 to 3000 m^3 of green water is needed to produce 1 tonne of grain food.

Summary

In this chapter we have focused primarily on human water requirements to cover direct uses for food, industry and domestic purposes. By far the world's largest direct water user is for food to support humans. At present 1200 m^3 of green water is required to produce food for one person during a year. Behind this average is hidden a huge range – from the most malnourished regions in the world using only 600 m^3/person/year, to the most well-fed regions, with diets requiring some 1800 m^3/person/year.

It is an enormous challenge to feed a growing world population and lift the current population from malnutrition. We calculated a 'desired' human water need of 1500 m^3/person/year, which includes 1300 m^3/person/year for food, with the remaining 200 m^3/person/year to cater for industrial and domestic water needs. Importantly, we found that this desired human water requirement to provide for direct needs is 'generic'. It is similar for all people irrespective of hydroclimate; it includes both plant foods and meat; and it can be filled from both green and blue water flows. Water for drinking and sanitation constitutes such a small portion of human water needs, around 2–3 per cent, that there will always be enough water on Earth to enable us to secure domestic water for all, irrespective of population size.

It was shown that management caused a larger variation in green water requirements for food than the hydroclimate. This is encouraging for our efforts of minimizing the human pressure on water resources that presently sustain ecosystems. If management can reduce green water needs to produce food, then more water can be secured to sustain ecosystems.

Due to the large water requirements to produce food, regions that depend strongly on irrigation face, and will increasingly be facing, blue water scarcity problems. This affects primarily the arid regions of the world in North Africa, the Middle East and South and East Asia. Adding the fact that a large portion of the accessible blue water flow has to remain uncommitted to human direct use in order to sustain aquatic ecosystems, puts further pressure on blue water resources. In order to lift the current 800 million people from malnutrition and secure a desired diet for a future population, we must add an additional amount of consumptive green water for rainfed agriculture. In 2050 this amount will be 4800 km^3/year, according to our estimate. This estimate assumes that irrigated agriculture will continue to expand according to current projections and contribute 800 km^3/year of additional consumptive water use in 2050 (600 km^3/year from consumptive water use and 200 km^3/year from water productivity improvements).

When analysing the challenges of balancing water for humans and nature in the following chapters we will return to these generic human water requirements and use them as indicators in analysing present and future pressure on freshwater resources.

Chapter 4

Incorporating Water for Ecosystem 'Services'

A new approach to ecohydrology requires adequate focus on both green and blue water. Green water flow sustains ecological functions in terrestrial ecosystems, where biomass production is a major ecosystem service. This means that human water dependence is much greater than previously thought.

Expanding the Water Paradigm

Direct and indirect water use

Water resource management tends to focus on irrigated agriculture, industry and the domestic and municipal sectors. These are the sectors that directly use blue water flow. For our discussion below we will call these sectors 'direct' water uses. The current perception is that this is the water use that directly benefits society. As mentioned previously, water availability is conventionally seen as the total volume of blue water flow, and often as the renewable freshwater resource. This is an oversimplification and an extremely narrow approach taken by conventional water resource management.

L'vovich touched on this narrow attitude in his monumental work on quantifying the freshwater resources in the world:

> *The water consumed in the production of vegetation on fields, which are not irrigated, is not given attention in practical water management at the present time. There is no basis whatsoever for such an approach except perhaps that this expenditure of water takes place imperceptibly (water is not actually pumped from streams and aquifers, as is the case in irrigated agriculture).*
>
> L'vovich, 1974, p316.

In Chapter 3 we showed that 1500 m³/person/year, or 4100 litres/person/day, can be seen as an average human water need. The question is: are direct human water needs really covering the full spectrum of water-dependent activities supporting human livelihood? Can we humans do with 'only' 4000 litres per person per day (already an enormous volume of water!), or do we depend on additional goods and services that require water? Yes, we do. Humans depend on even larger volumes of additional freshwater flow. This is the water touched upon in Chapter 1 and needed to sustain numerous ecosystem services and goods, which directly and indirectly support human livelihoods. These include a wide range of goods and services, from the most obvious, such as sustaining growth of the world's forests, to the less obvious, such as supporting plant pollination and maintaining humidity levels within rainforest habitats. In ecohydrology, therefore, we use an integrated approach to include all water flows in the hydrological cycle, as well as the ecological functions of water.

The beneficial role of green water flow

The water resources concept has to be broadened and given an ecohydrological foundation. What we call fresh water should include both green and blue water flows, and the ecohydrological functions performed by these flows in both nature and society have to be understood as part of our entire life support base. We therefore suggest a new ecohydrological paradigm based on the following principles:

- Rainfall, not runoff, constitutes the basic freshwater resource, which means that assessments of access to water, water needs and water uses begins with rainfall, and include the analysis of how water is partitioned between green and blue water flows in terrestrial ecosystems, ultimately benefiting aquatic ecosystems.
- Both vapour and runoff support ecological functions such as photosynthesis and nutrient cycles, and ecosystem services such as biodiversity and pollination. They generate ecosystem goods such as food, timber, fibre, and fuel wood, which are crucial for our survival and which directly support societal well-being and development.
- An ecohydrological approach to freshwater resources includes a multiscale approach in which the functions of water flowing through the landscape are analysed from the micro-scale – for example, a crop field or pasture – to the macro-scale – for example, a river basin or a river from upstream to downstream – in order to capture the multitude of water transformations from raindrop to river flow.
- Water quantity and quality are considered together and attention is given to the dynamics of water in time and in space. Seasonality and extreme events, as well as variability in the landscape space, are more important than average flow volumes.

Four water flow domains

The basic conceptual cornerstone in an integrated ecohydrological model is to understand the implications of integrating green and blue water flows. An integrated approach involves a widened scope covering four main domains of water-dependent uses and functions that directly or indirectly benefit humans. These four domains are shown in the matrix in Table 4.1. We distinguish between functions generated by green and blue water flows, and we distinguish between direct and indirect uses of water.

The conventional focus is found in the direct blue withdrawals for economic use in society (shaded with grey in Table 4.1). With 'direct water use' we mean water withdrawn or used, and which is conceived at present in society to directly benefit humans.

'Indirect water use' denotes ecological water functions that benefit humans in an indirect way, such as green water flow supporting biomass growth that forms the

Table 4.1 *The four domains of freshwater functions*

Use Domain	Water flow domain	
	Green	Blue
Direct	ECONOMIC BIOMASS GROWTH Rainfed food, timber, fibres, fuel wood, pastures, etc	ECONOMIC USE IN SOCIETY Irrigation, industry, domestic/municipal
Indirect	ECOSYSTEM BIOMASS GROWTH Plants and trees in wetlands, grasslands, forests and other biotopes Biodiversity, resilience	ECOSYSTEM FUNCTIONS Aquatic freshwater habitats Biodiversity, resilience

habitat for flora and fauna. Indirect water use can also include some other functions, such as ensuring that an adequate volume of river water reaches a river mouth to sustain fish populations in estuaries.

We have chosen to use the word 'withdrawal' when discussing appropriation of blue water. The reason is that this is the normal term used by irrigation engineers and water resource managers. For the other three freshwater domains we recommend the term 'use', to reduce confusion in relation to available water resources information. For example, if we analyse data on freshwater resources for any country of the world, it is without exception that renewable freshwater and annual water withdrawals only include 'direct blue', and for this water the term 'withdrawal' is used. Another reason for retaining the term withdrawal when talking of direct blue water use refers back to our discussions in Chapter 3 on the consumptive and non-consumptive use of water. Only a fraction of the withdrawn blue water is actually 'used' in the sense that the water is consumed. It is worth remembering that green water uses are always consumptive, since they consist of evaporation and transpiration flow.

The purpose of widening the idea of the 'freshwater resource' to include indirect blue uses, direct green uses and indirect green uses is twofold. The first is to enable an integration of ecological, hydrological and economical perspectives in water resource management. The second is to demonstrate explicitly the value of fresh water in all its forms, both liquid and vapour, in sustaining functions that are indispensable for human survival.

A critical consequence of this widened approach is that our focus shifts from runoff flow in rivers, lakes and aquifers, to the source of water, the rainfall, and especially to the point where the raindrop hits the soil and is partitioned into green and blue water flow paths. This shift in hydrological focus is illustrated in Figure 4.1, where rain is conceptually partitioned into the four water domains.

The first challenge in the framework presented in Figure 4.1 is to quantify our dependence on direct and indirect blue and green water flows. This is not easy, however, as there have been very few attempts to quantify the volumes of direct and indirect green flows and the indirect blue flows that are necessary to sustain ecosystem services at all levels, including the regional and global level.

Hydrological functions

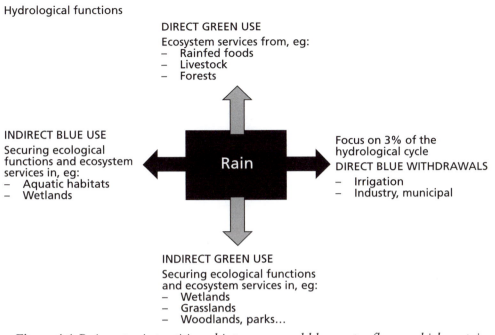

DIRECT GREEN USE
Ecosystem services from, eg:
  – Rainfed foods
  – Livestock
  – Forests

INDIRECT BLUE USE
Securing ecological
functions and ecosystem
services in, eg:
  – Aquatic habitats
  – Wetlands

Rain

Focus on 3% of the
hydrological cycle
DIRECT BLUE WITHDRAWALS
  – Irrigation
  – Industry, municipal

INDIRECT GREEN USE
Securing ecological functions
and ecosystem services in, eg:
  – Wetlands
  – Grasslands
  – Woodlands, parks...

Figure 4.1 *Rainwater is partitioned into green and blue water flows, which sustain freshwater functions in four ecohydrological domains*

Water Flows to Sustain Food Production

Relative role of food produced by irrigation

We begin by analysing water use in agriculture, which is the sector generally considered to be the largest in the world dependent on fresh water. It is normally claimed that agriculture accounts for 70 per cent of the annual withdrawal of renewable freshwater resources (Cosgrove and Rijsberman, 2000). Even though it is normally not specified, this only concerns the annual withdrawal of blue water for irrigation. This focus on large agricultural water withdrawal based only on blue water flows would be justifiable if food production was exclusively a result of irrigation. This is, however, not the case. As earlier indicated, on a global scale, 80 per cent of crop land is rainfed, and rainfed agriculture is estimated to contribute to 60–70 % of world food crops. The lower contribution to production of rainfed agriculture is due to the higher yields generally experienced in irrigation systems.

Half the world's irrigation is used in paddy rice production, primarily in Asia. In sub-Saharan Africa and in most European countries over 95 per cent of the agriculture is rainfed. There are, therefore, large regional differences in dependence on blue withdrawals or direct green water use in rainfed agriculture to sustain food production.

The relative role of blue water withdrawals and direct green water use to sustain food production in different countries of the world is shown in Figure 4.2. Here we

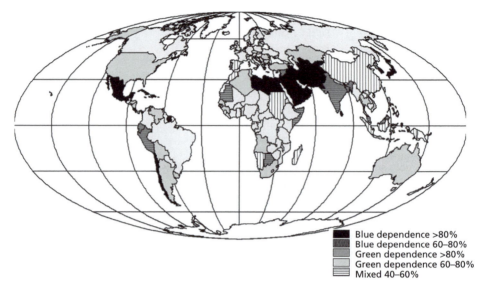

Figure 4.2 *The predominant sources of green or blue water to produce food*

have calculated at country level the predominant water source (green or blue), used to produce grain foods, which are the largest agricultural crops. The estimates of volumes of green and blue water use in agriculture are based on actual data on grain yields, land areas under irrigated and rainfed crop production, blue water withdrawals for irrigation, and water productivity in rainfed agriculture.[1,2] Countries where green water flow from rainfed agriculture accounts for over 80 per cent of the water for food production are shown in light grey; countries with a green water dependence of 60–80 per cent are shown in white; countries depending on over 80 per cent for blue water withdrawals in conventional irrigation systems are shown in black; and countries in a blue water range of 60–80 per cent are shown in dark grey. Intermittent countries, with a blend of green and blue water dependence (a green water range of 40–60per cent) are shown with horizontal lines. Countries where data are lacking are shown with vertical lines.

Most food originates from natural green water flow

As seen in Figure 4.2, the world is largely 'green', in the sense that food production is predominantly produced in green water-dependent rainfed agriculture. Approximately 70 per cent of countries depend up to 60 per cent or more on green water flow to sustain food production. It is interesting to note that the 'blue' countries (those that predominantly use blue water withdrawals to produce food) are almost the same as the countries that withdraw more than 40 per cent from the available resource. These countries are primarily found in North Africa, the Middle East and Central Asia. This is not surprising, as conventional assessments (such as the UN Comprehensive Freshwater Assessment) focus only on withdrawals from the blue water resource. Such assessments can only be performed in a correct way when comparing countries where blue water is used to produce food. For countries generating their food with green water in rainfed agriculture the analysis is flawed. In these countries a blue water resource is compared to a water requirement (for food), which is met by green water.

The reason why the source of water (blue or green) plays such a fundamental role in water resources assessments is that 90 per cent of the direct water needs are used to produce food. Blue water uses in industry and for domestic purposes are so small that they do not significantly affect the analysis. However, as we showed in Chapter 3, human direct water requirements are generic in two ways: they are relatively similar across hydroclimatic zones, and they constitute a need that can be met, at least for food, from both green and blue water flows. In all the countries shown in Figure 4.2 where green water flow is used to sustain food, the bulk of the present water use for food of 1200 m³/person/year originates from green water flow in rainfed food production. In other words, in 70 per cent of countries it is not relevant to compare blue water availability with indices of human water need or demands. Only a small fraction of the present human water use has to be supplied from the blue water resource. Rainfall returned as beneficial green water flow in agriculture satisfies almost the total direct human need. This dramatically reduces the pressure on blue water.

The dominating role of rainfed agriculture to sustain world food production thus makes it impossible to maintain that agriculture is the world's largest withdrawer of freshwater. Instead, the correct statement is that irrigated agriculture is the world's largest withdrawer of blue water for direct human use (World Water Council, 2000). The surprising truth is perhaps that we do not know how much water, or what form of water, green or blue, sustains present food production. Nor do we know what water will be needed to sustain future production. However, what we do know is that rainfed agriculture will continue to be the major source of food security in the world in the foreseeable future.

We should also emphasize that the analysis above focuses only on grain foods. We have omitted until now the water needed to sustain livestock, vegetables, fruits, legumes, and forests. These depend for their generation on even larger volumes of beneficial green water flows.

Relative contributions to present diets

Let us now return to the human diets discussed in Chapter 3. There we showed that on average, 1200 m³/person/year of water is required to produce present diets. We also calculated that 1300 m³/person/year is required for a desired diet. Here we want to know how much green or blue water is presently used to sustain diets in different regions. We estimated water requirements to sustain current diets for different regions using information on the composition of diets from the FAO (FAOSTAT, 2002) and we combined this data with water requirements necessary to produce the different components (for example, grains, legumes, meat, diary, fruit, tubers and vegetables). Table 4.2 shows such an attempt based on data adapted from Gleick (2000). As seen in the table, the actual human water use for food varies from less than 700 m³/person/year in sub-Saharan Africa to 1800 m³/person/year in North America. This is explained by the differences in calorie intake.

Table 4.2 *Water requirements to sustain present diets in different regions*

Region	Water to sustain present diets (m³/person/year)
Sub-Saharan Africa	690
North Africa and Middle East	1113
Central America	1030
North America	1830
South America	1108
Asia	823
Europe	1637

Source: Adapted from Gleick, 2000

Understanding the relative human pressure on green and blue water flows, in terms of water for food, will enable a more complete understanding of the needs and options available to secure water for ecosystems dependent on green and blue water.

The question then is what proportion of the water required to sustain present food consumption originates from green water use in rainfed agriculture, and what proportion originates from blue water withdrawals in irrigation? At the country level there are data on blue water withdrawals for irrigation. This enables us to estimate the portion of the human water use for food that originates from blue water flows in irrigation. The remaining volume of water to produce present diets must originate from green water use in rainfed systems. A complication is trade. Import of food contributes so-called virtual water (the water consumed in producing that particular food) (Allan, 1995), to a country's diet, while export is an outflow of virtual water. We have taken this into consideration, but only for cereals, which are the largest agricultural commodities in international trade.

In Figure 4.3 we present the relative contribution of green and blue water to present diets (from Table 4.2) for the different regions of the world. The relative size of the block arrows represents the present total volume of water flow behind each type of diet. Sub-Saharan Africa is used as the reference unit. The relative arrow sizes reflect the large variability in calorie intake between regions. North America and Europe are the world's net virtual water exporters in terms of grain. Sub-Saharan Africa, South America and Europe are the regions with the largest contribution from green water flow in rainfed systems. The arid countries in North Africa and the Middle East are one region where blue water flow is the dominant contributor to present diets. At present this region is also strongly dependent on the influx of virtual water. For exporting regions, the actual per person volume of water used to produce food is higher than the water consumed in diets. Subsequently, importing regions use less in production than in consumption.

On the global level, direct green water in rainfed systems (including rainfed crop production, vegetable gardening, livestock and dairy production) contributes 70 per cent of the water in the average global diet, while direct blue water in irrigation covers 30 per cent of the diet.

As in all regional and global analyses, here, too, there are sources of error. First, there is always an uncertainty related to the country level estimates of actual diets or

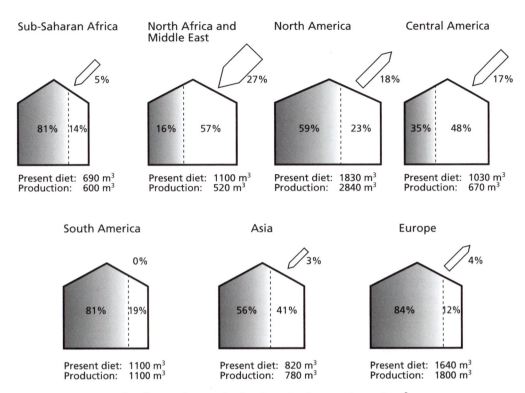

Note: Present water for diets and water for food production are shown in m³ per person per year. The small arrows show import and export of food in terms of water (virtual water). The water for production is higher than the diet in countries that are net exporters of food, while the production is lower than the diet in countries, depending on food imports of virtual water. In the large arrows, the relative blue (white) and green (shaded) water contribution refers to food produced in exporting countries and food consumed in importing countries. The size of the arrows are scaled in relation to sub-Saharan Africa.

Figure 4.3 *Green, blue and total water to sustain present diets in different regions of the world*

blue water withdrawals in irrigation. Second, there is in reality a large variability in the volumes of water required to produce each dietary component. Moreover, there is a tendency for only formal irrigation to be included in statistics at the country level, whereas informal, small-scale irrigation may play a very important role in certain regions. Therefore, the regional and global estimates are only indicators of water for food production and relative partitioning between green and blue water flows. However, an advantage with this approach is that it is a simple way of clarifying the relative contribution of blue and green water for food production, as the focus is on total human diets irrespective of type of food (meat, grain, tubers, vegetables and fruits).

Green Water Flows Are Sustaining Major Biomes

Water flows in direct and indirect use

We have discussed the green and blue water flows in supporting direct uses for food, industry and domestic purposes. We will now take a wider ecohydrological step and incorporate the indirect uses of water to sustain ecosystem goods and services. In doing so we are focusing on the green water flows to sustain the major biomes of the world. As clarified in Chapter 1, productive green water flow in the form of transpiration is a fundamental process in all plant growth, where the stomata release vapour to the atmosphere simultaneously with the uptake of CO_2 during photosynthesis. Essentially, transpiration is a prerequisite for the existence of all terrestrial ecosystems on Earth, and therefore a prerequisite for all life. Vapour flow, both evaporation and transpiration, also influences microclimates by regulating humidity. As discussed in Chapter 1, the magnitude of green water flow impacts on regional climate by feeding the atmosphere with water vapour flow, which generates rainfall. As there is only limited data available on vapour flows, divided into non-productive evaporation and productive transpiration, we will consider the total volume of green water flow.

Among the major biomes, we include crop land, permanent grazing land, forests and woodlands, grasslands, wetlands and arid lands. The annual green water flows to sustain these systems on a global scale are shown in Table 4.3. These estimates of green water flows originate in the work of Rockström et al (1999) and are based on data on water productivity for all major food crops measured in m^3/tonne and from estimates of green water requirements to sustain other ecosystems in mm/year. These green water estimates for each biome are multiplied by production in the case of systems with water productivity data and by area coverage (1995) for systems with data on green water requirements.

In Table 4.3, the volume of direct withdrawal of water for irrigation, defined as 'blue food', originates from Shiklomanov's estimates of consumptive use or green water flow (Shiklomanov, 2000). Even though the focus here is only on green water to sustain goods and services, we have included direct blue water withdrawals for industry and domestic purposes. This is done to enable a comparison of an ecohydrological assessment of water to sustain beneficial ecosystem goods and services with the conventional assessment of freshwater use to sustain society. Direct green uses include all main foods[3] and green water flow to sustain permanent grazing areas, which in turn generate meat and dairy products. Indirect green water use includes green water to sustain grasslands, forests and woodlands, wetlands and arid ecosystems. In order to estimate the relative size of permanent grazing areas, forests and woodlands, data from Rockström et al (1999) and FAOSTAT (1999) have been correlated to estimate the annual use for the three categories.[4]

Relative proportions between blue and green water use

The column in Table 4.3 that is the easiest to compare with conventional water resources assessments is the percentage of direct human withdrawals/use (far right in

Table 4.3 *Assessment of water withdrawals and water uses to sustain direct and indirect human water-dependent activities*

Flow domain	System	Annual freshwater withdrawals/use (km³/yr)	% of rainfall
Direct blue	Blue food	1800 [1]	2
	Domestic + industry	1300 [2]	1
Indirect blue	Instream ecology		
	remaining time-stable runoff	9400 [3]	8
	flood runoff	30,150 [4]	27
	Sub-total blue flow	**42,650**	
Direct green	Green food	5000 [5]	4
	Permanent grazing	20,400 [6]	18
Indirect green	Grasslands	12,100 [7]	11
	Forests and woodlands	19,700 [7]	17
	Arid lands	5700 [8]	5
	Wetlands	1400 [7]	1
	Lake evaporation	600 [4]	1
	Evaporation from reservoirs	160 [9]	0.1
	Green areas in urban settlements	100 [10]	0.1
	Unaccounted green flow	5690 [5]	
	Sub-total green flow	**70,850**	
Total		113,500	100

Notes:
1 Irrigated food from Shiklomanov (2000), estimated for year 2000.
2 Industry and municipal withdrawals, from Shiklomanov (2000), estimated for year 2000.
3 Accessible blue water flow consists of the time-stable portion of the total runoff branch in the hydrological cycle, and is estimated by Postel et al (1996) to 12,5000 km³/year; the remaining portion of this flow is calculated by subtracting present blue water withdrawals (3800 km³/year) from this threshold.
4 Flood runoff to the sea.
5 Total annual green water flow to sustain crop foods (rainfed and irrigated crops) was estimated by Rockström et al (1999) at 6,800 km³/year (average production 1992–1996). This volume minus consumptive water use in irrigation (1800 km³/year) gives 5000 km³/year of consumptive water use to sustain rainfed crop production.
6 Green water flow to sustain permanent grazing areas. There are 34 million km² of permanent grazing area in the world (FAOSTAT, 1999). The average annual evapotranspiration for grazing land is taken from the average weighted (against land surface) green water requirements to sustain grasslands and woodlands calculated from Rockström et al (1999), which amounts to 600 mm/year. 34 million km² x 600 mm/year = 20,400 km³/year.
7 Green water flows to sustain grasslands, forests and woodlands, forests and wetlands (Rockström et al, 1999).
8 Green water flows from arid lands (Rockström et al, 1999).
9 L'vovich and White (1990) and Rockström et al (1999).
10 Postel et al (1996).

Note: Withdrawals are systems depending on direct use of blue water flow, while water uses are systems depending on direct and indirect use of green water flow. Direct human water-dependent activities consist of crop and livestock production, while indirect human activities supply ecosystem services (grasslands, forests and wetlands).

the table). Here only direct human withdrawals for food, industry and society are considered. The annual cumulative withdrawal amounts to 31,600 km^3/year compared to conventional estimates of 4000–5000 km^3/year. Here, irrigated agriculture accounts for only 9 per cent of annual withdrawals, compared to 70 per cent as estimated in most studies (for example, Gleick, 1993; Shiklomanov, 2000). Green food in rainfed agriculture accounts for roughly twice the blue food (16 per cent of annual water withdrawals) and it appears that animal husbandry is by far the largest sector depending on direct green water use. This large water dependence to raise livestock should, if anything, be a strong argument for more vegetarian diets.

However, it is highly questionable if one can blame animal husbandry for inefficient use of water. The opportunity cost of the rainfall used to sustain permanent grazing land may in most cases be zero. The land is used for permanent grazing simply because it cannot sustain other land uses. In addition, pastures around the world used as permanent grazing lands generate other ecosystem services than just fodder. These services, such as biodiversity, depend on ecological functions – for example, the conditions for competition between flora and fauna, which in turn are a result of the land use, in this case to the degree of grazing. It is therefore difficult to attribute the totality of green water flow from pastures to fodder for cattle. In summary, grazing may in many cases be the most effective use of rainfall, which otherwise, to a large extent, would only flow as evaporation and transpiration back to the atmosphere anyway.

Plant food production accounts for only 11 per cent of total withdrawals and uses, of which 4 per cent is for 'blue foods' and 7 per cent for 'green foods'. This fact can be explained by the green water use of vast areas of forests, grasslands and – which may be surprising – green water flow from arid lands. Food accounts for only 6 per cent of the total rainfall over land areas, which strongly indicates opportunities to do something wise, in balance with nature, to sustain humans with the remaining 94 per cent of the fresh water.

However, the degrees of freedom to exploit green water flows are limited. On a global scale, the annual flow of green water amounts on average to 70,850 km^3/year (taking the latest and probably the most precise estimate from Shiklomanov, 2000). The estimates presented in Table 4.3 suggest that, on average, 90 per cent or 63,900 km^3/year of this vapour flow is presently used to sustain ecosystem services in the major biomes.

Committed and Uncommitted Water Flows

The ecohydrological assessment of green water dependence to sustain ecosystem goods and services from major biomes of the world places the conventional blue water focus in a new perspective. Sustaining irrigated agriculture from blue water withdrawals forms a very small component of the global water use to sustain humans and nature (only 2 per cent of rainfall and 3 per cent of total water use).

What about the looming water crisis about which water professionals and policy-makers around the world are warning? It is definitely a reality within the relatively narrow boundary of blue water supply, use and demand (see Chapter 5). Figure 4.4

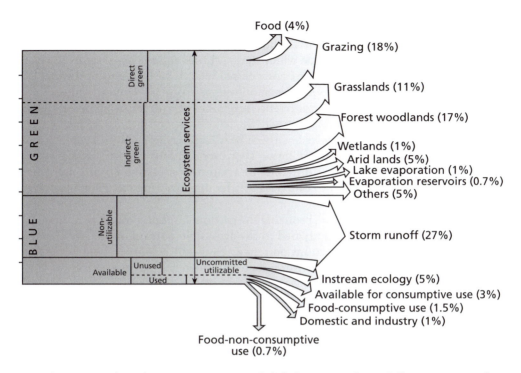

Figure 4.4 *The relative partitioning of global terrestrial rainfall into green and blue water flow components*

places the blue water resource in the perspective of global-scale water flows to sustain direct and indirect green and blue water-dependent activities, and ecosystem goods and services.

Accessible blue water constitutes 11 per cent (12,500 km³/year) of the terrestrial freshwater flow. Humans withdraw 3.5 per cent of the rainfall on land, of which 45 per cent is non-consumptive use and returns to the river afterwards. Our water resource focus has been, and largely still is, in the lower right hand corner in Figure 4.4. The remaining part of the blue water flow can be divided in two flow components: the 'potentially accessible' but presently uncommitted flow, and the 'non-utilizable' flow. The uncommitted but potentially utilizable blue water flow amounts to 9 per cent of the total freshwater cycle, while the non-utilizable blue water flow represents 26 per cent of global freshwater resources.

The Blue Water Bias Is Unwarranted

The value of green and blue water flows

As shown in this chapter, in one way or another we use all water flows to sustain our life-support system. To illustrate the significant implications of this basically common-sense approach, we have calculated that humans currently depend on approximately 10,000 m³/person/year to sustain direct and indirect green and blue ecosystem services. This excludes the large flow of blue water that sustains aquatic ecosystems in rivers and lakes. This is in contrast with the conventional view, where present freshwater use amounts to approximately 500–600 m³/person/year to sustain irrigation, industry and municipal water use. The dramatic difference is linked to the dominating perception of the value of water.

The question that arises is why has there been, and largely still is, such a strong emphasis on groundwater and stream flow? There are certainly several answers to this question. One may be the relative difficulty of accurately assessing green water flows and local runoff, compared to the relative simplicity of measuring perennial blue water flow in streams.

The primary cause is, however, probably the predominant perception that the social and economic value of water is only tied to the accessible portion of blue fresh water. In all assessments and data collections on renewable water resources, blue water flow is the only flow considered. There are two factors influencing the perceptions of value related to blue water flow. First, blue water is the visible liquid associated with drinking and health. Second, blue water is strongly manipulated by humans to serve our purposes. The last century has been called the water development century, characterized by an unprecedented development of water resources for human purposes. Dams, river diversion, groundwater extraction and large-scale river control schemes are examples of human investments in blue water development. Empires have been built based on large-scale water engineering. Blue water is, in other words, engineered water flow. It is the water flowing in pipes, the water stored in dams, and the metered water that is given a price in many countries.

But blue water is also the water that counts among economists. It is the water considered as an economic good. In the principles for sustainable water resource management adopted as an input to the UN Conference on Environment and Development (UNCED) in 1992, it was agreed that water should be considered as an economic good (see Chapter 10). Considering developed blue water flow as the only water with economic value sends an important signal to politicians, managers and policy-makers.

Blue water is the water that policy-makers and decision-makers understand. This is the water that the media has normally focused upon. It is the only component of the hydrological cycle that has been associated with money and socioeconomic development. The dominating role played by economics and engineering in industrial and post-industrial societies has therefore had a direct bearing on professional disciplines dealing with water – the water flow that has been directly linked to these societal domains or professions has also received the main attention.

It should be noted that the water resources biases highlighted in this book are not to be interpreted as a scornful critique of scientific ignorance. There is of course a wide and competent knowledge of direct green uses (the domain of agronomists and agricultural engineers), indirect blue uses (the domain of aquatic ecologists), and indirect green uses (the domain of biologists). Processes driving water flows in the hydrological cycle are studied in the fields of climatology, meteorology and hydrology.

In modern history and science there has been a profound understanding of the fundamental role that is played by soil moisture, evaporation and transpiration flow to sustain both human needs (for example, food, timber, fibres, fruit, etc) and ecosystem needs (such as biota). L'vovich, in his groundbreaking work on global water resources in the 1970s pointed out that:

> *As is frequently done in hydrology, the losses (referring to the difference between rainfall and observed surface runoff) include the water that goes to infiltration, evaporation from the soil, and the feeding of groundwater; this conforms with the conception that regards only river water as useful. In actuality, if we assess the importance of all the elements of the water balance and do not regard river water as the most important link in the water cycle, though indeed an important one, the losses should consist of surface runoff, which represents a loss of water for the given area. At the same time, soil moisture, as one of the components of soil fertility from the standpoint of human interest, is a more important element than river water.*
>
> L'vovich, 1974, p36.

The point is not that the soil link and the green water link in, for example, hydrology, are not understood. The problem is that they are not taken properly into consideration in conventional water resource assessments, and hence not in mainstream water policy. This is a question of perceptions where visible and extractable water flowing in rivers and lakes is considered as a 'resource' for society, while invisible soil moisture, vapour flow and to some extent also groundwater, are not fully appreciated as beneficial. Falkenmark pointed out (2001): 'Facts are facts, but perceptions are reality', a truth that also affects the way in which science, policy and development deals with water resource management.

Policy implications of blue water bias

The major problem with the common blue water-oriented approach is the consequences it has on management. A blue water focus, in terms of resources and risks, leads undoubtedly to a blue water policy orientation. Putting it simply, if the problem is blue, we seek a blue solution. If the analysis is based on an integrated approach to green and blue water, chances are higher that solutions are integrated. A new broadened approach to analysing and managing fresh water is therefore needed. This approach can be based on the ecohydrological framework presented in this chapter, which takes rainfall as its starting point, and incorporates green and blue water functions for both nature and society.

A final and somewhat different question with water policy implications is the following: When does rainfall turn into water? This is possibly the core question in a new approach to ecohydrology. Rain is evidently not water from a conventional perspective. Rain generates runoff and turns into water flow that can be withdrawn from rivers and aquifers. Before it has stabilized in perennial rivers, it is not documented as a water resource. However, most upland farming communities depend on this non-documented water for their living. This is a critical misconception, which locks our thinking into a narrow blue water-oriented view in both hydrology and ecology. In a broadened approach to ecohydrology and water resource management, every raindrop is already water, which is involved in dynamic and complex ecological functions in different places in the landscape as it moves on its gravity-driven journey from upstream to downstream.

Summary

In this chapter we have introduced a new ecohydrological paradigm, which integrates green and blue water flows and their direct and indirect ecological functions. Based on this model, we have shown that human dependence on freshwater resources is more complex than conventionally perceived.

There is no doubt that the largest direct water use on earth is for food production. Some 90 per cent of direct human requirement is to secure green water flow for biomass growth in agriculture. We have shown in this chapter (Figure 4.3 and Table 4.3) that with large regional variations, 70 per cent of the human diet is produced by green water flow in rainfed farming systems. The remaining 30 per cent originates from blue water withdrawals used for irrigation. This sheds new light on the predominant view that the extensive human demand for water (read water for food) is pushing mankind rapidly towards a global physical water crisis. There is very little evidence to suggest that this is the case, once the role of green water flow to sustain direct human water needs is properly sorted out. We presently depend on only 2 per cent of global rainfall for production of irrigated food. This is dramatically different from the conventional conclusion that agriculture uses 70 per cent of global freshwater resources. Through integrating green and blue water flows our attention has been to the crucial role played by direct flow of green water in rainfed biomes of the world. Humans already depend on 90 per cent of global vapour flow to sustain ecosystem goods and services from the major biomes of the world.

This in turn suggests that humans may be facing a biophysical water crisis after all, but a different one from the conventional blue water crisis. The fear of a physical blue water crisis is based on the fact that some regions of the world (especially in North Africa, the Middle East, South and East Asia) are withdrawing an unsustainable proportion of the accessible blue water resource. The estimated global ceiling of 12,500 km^3/year of extractable blue water flow definitely sets a very real limit to further blue water development in many water-scarce regions of the world. Integrating green and blue water flows into a wider freshwater concept, however, indicates that there is an enormous untapped freshwater resource. There are no 'free lunches', however, and the ecohydrological water resource analysis carried out here suggests that the major water resource challenge of the future is whether there is enough fresh water to sustain global food production while at the same time sustaining ecosystem services in the major biomes of the world. Our estimates in Chapter 3 show that we will need to secure an additional 4,800 km^3/year of consumptive green water flow in rainfed agriculture by 2050, in order to lift the current 800 million people from malnutrition and to secure a desired diet for future generations. This estimate assumes that irrigated agriculture will

Table 4.4 *The relative partitioning of global terrestrial rainfall into green and blue water flow components*

Water for food challenge	Water requirement 2050 (km³/yr)
Current food from crop land (year 2000)	7000
Eradicate current malnutrition to desired level (1300 m³/cap/yr)	2222
Food for additional population 2050 UN medium (9.3 billion)	3364
Total	12,586

continue to expand according to current projections, and will contribute 800 km³/year of additional water needs in 2050.

The implications of the 'new' water scarcity will be a growing pressure on water that is now used to secure ecological functions. The limited possibilities of expanding rainfed agriculture will result in a direct trade-off in terms of water between ecosystems and agriculture. Instead, more focus must be given to increasing water use on current rainfed lands and on producing more crop per unit green water flow – that is, shift non-productive evaporation in favour of productive transpiration. Both these options increase water productivity, but the former will affect water availability for ecosystems. Later we will investigate different avenues of producing more crops per drop of water.

Chapter 5

Regional Differences

The environmental conditions of the globe involve constraints on human activities. Past difficulties to adapt the activities of society to such constraints now cause a number of serious problems.

This book focuses on water as a determinant of human livelihood and for safeguarding environmental security. We have analysed water availability over the world's continents, in absolute terms and in relative terms in a per capita dimension. We also distinguished between the blue water flows available for direct withdrawal and use, and the green water flows linked to terrestrial ecosystems, including crop production and forestry. World maps highlighted fundamental differences in terms of per capita blue water flow, and clarified that certain regions are much more vulnerable than others.

In this chapter we will evaluate the remaining degrees of freedom available in a country or region to meet an increasing per capita demand and improve welfare and food security. This means that we will have to look closely at some intricate connections. We will deal with water, both green and blue, as a determinant of conditions for human livelihood. Blue water flows will be related to the current level of water demands in order to identify water use intensity and to clarify if increasing demands can easily be met. We will relate blue water flows to the size of the population in order to assess the degree of 'water crowding', or the number of people that have to share a finite amount of water. Dispute proneness and pollution risks are some of the multiple implications of human pressure on finite freshwater resources.

The Green Water Perspective

The environmental preconditions of water for human livelihoods are conventionally shown by using a precipitation map to demonstrate how mean annual rainfall differs over the different world regions. However, a closer analysis shows that most precipitation tends to fall in mountainous areas where livelihood conditions are constrained in other ways. Living conditions can therefore not be said to be better just because there is more rainfall. Other factors, such as steepness of the land, soil cover, soil permeability and temperature, are equally relevant.

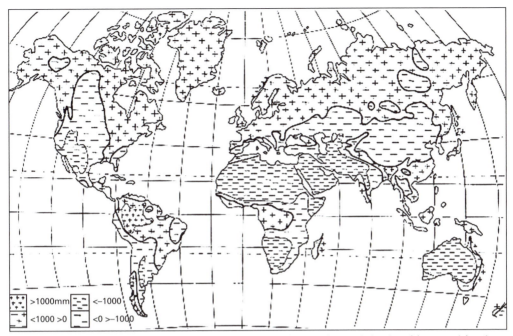

Note: A water deficiency exists if evaporative demand exceeds precipitation (shown with minus signs). In the reverse circumstances there is a water surplus, seen on an annual basis (shown with plus signs).

Figure 5.1 *Relationship between annual precipitation and annual evaporative demand of the atmosphere*

Living with differences in hydroclimate

In regions with limited rainfall, for example the semi-arid tropics, the thirstiness of the atmosphere or the evaporative demand (what hydrologists call potential evaporation) is of particular importance.[1] A world map illustrates this phenomenon by showing the difference between annual precipitation and annual evaporative demand (Figure 5.1). We will later return to the fact that rainfall in water-deficient zones is often concentrated during short periods of the year, resulting in a distinct seasonality of water flows and biomass growth.

In the surplus zones, there is more precipitation than the atmosphere is able to take back, or year-round vegetation would be able to consume. In the water-deficient zones, however, there is not enough water for undisturbed vegetation, and plant production would suffer from water deficiency. The map therefore shows some important differences in the preconditions for trees and plants in ecosystems and crop growth in agro-ecosystems. It is impossible, evidently, to ignore the evaporative demand of the atmosphere if we want to have an idea about the preconditions for plant growth.

The barrels in Figure 5.2 illustrate the relevance of the evaporative demand. They visualize the influence of that demand in three different localities that all get the same precipitation, 1000 mm/year (Falkenmark, 1999). Since the barrels – which are all 2 m

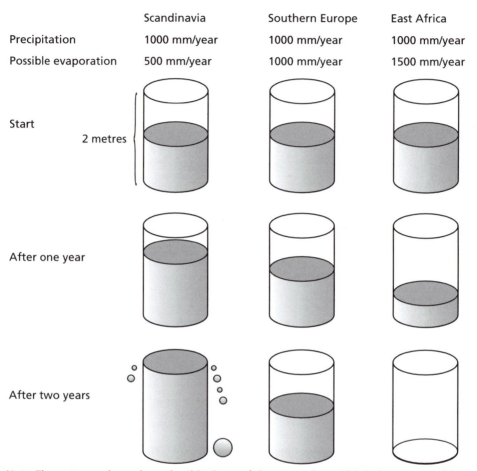

Note: The outcome depends on the thirstiness of the atmosphere. This is demonstrated here with three barrels, 2 m high and placed in different climatic surroundings: southern Scandinavia with an evaporative demand of 500 mm/year, Southern Europe with 1000 mm/year, and East Africa with 1500 mm/year. After two years the first overflows while the third is empty.

Source: From Falkenmark, 1999

Figure 5.2 *Is 1000 mm of rainfall a little or a lot?*

high and contain water up to the 1 m level when we start the experiment – are open to the air, the water is exposed to the evaporative demand and will evaporate at the potential rate. This example illustrates the importance of analysing evaporative demand and rainfall together in assessing water availability in an ecosystem. However, the rate of evaporation will obviously be different in a landscape where the rain rapidly disappears under the soil surface through infiltration, and thus partly escapes the evaporative demand of the atmosphere above it. As visualized in the figure, the barrel in Scandinavia that has an evaporative demand rate of only 500 mm/year is full and overflows after two years. The barrel in South Europe, which has a higher but still not excessive potential evaporation of 1000 mm/year, does not change, while the barrel in East Africa, with a high potential evaporation of 1500 mm/year, is empty.

Some observations may be made with reference to the world map in Figure 5.1. Most of the industrialized countries tend to be located in a region with a water surplus. There is one important exception: the western USA. This is a region where water deficiency has been compensated for by technical means. The European immigrants who settled the region were skilled in technical solutions and had the means to implement them. A rapidly growing economy opened for expensive investments in reservoirs, pipelines, canals and long-distance water transfers. It is also evident that the majority of less-developed countries, where we know that malnourishment is largest (Dyson, 1994), are located in the deficiency zone marked by minus signs. But we can also see from the map that Australia is located in the minus region. This is important and indicates that Australia is a country that should be able to provide guidance on how to secure improved living conditions and even a high level of income under such hydroclimatic preconditions.

It is a provoking thought to note that many industrialized countries, located in the temperate zone, tend to take water for granted. Many of the poorest countries are located in the arid, semi-arid and dry sub-humid tropical and sub-tropical climate zones where the main everyday question is where to find water for humans and animals and how to grow the food needed to survive. The fact that experts in the many colonial administrations in the tropical and sub-tropical regions based their understanding on the natural conditions of the temperate climate zones invites the question as to whether their decisions were environmentally damaging, and resulted in the introduction of environmental problems, rather than their elimination.

Understanding the role of seasonality

In tropical and sub-tropical regions, rainfall is subject to a definite seasonality. Certain parts of the year are rainy seasons, other are dry seasons. A crucial question for crop production is, of course, when is there enough rainfall for seeds to germinate and crops to grow and ripen? The presence of water available for plants is thus the factor determining the start of the growing season, which is often defined as the time of year when rainfall is greater than half the evaporative demand. Even if there is a certain water deficiency, plant production can proceed, but at a lower rate. The period of undisturbed growth is limited to the much shorter period when rainfall exceeds the evaporative demand. Planting may however start earlier, approximately when rainfall provides some 10 per cent of the evaporative demand and the soil is soft enough to be worked.

Differences in hydroclimate are reflected in large differences in terms of both human livelihood and dominating vegetation patterns (Falkenmark and Chapman, 1989). A visualization of basic hydroclimatic contrasts is provided for three different situations in Figure 5.3. The temperate region is the least complicated, as there is enough precipitation, moderate evaporative demand and, therefore, a precipitation surplus left to produce a moderate runoff.

In the semi-arid and dry sub-humid tropics, there is the same order of magnitude of rainfall as in the temperate case. However, the evaporative demand is massive and

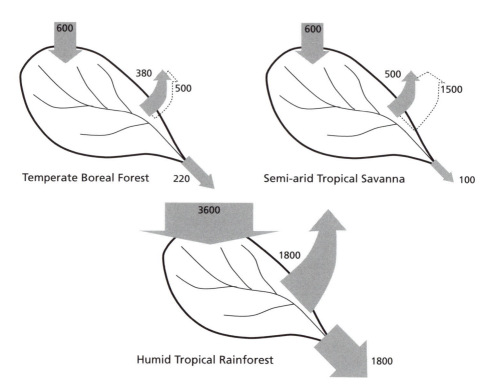

Figure 5.3 *Livelihood contrasts in terms of annual precipitation, potential and actual evaporation, and runoff*

the atmosphere takes back practically all rainfall. Only a very limited surplus is left to form runoff from water that was able to escape from evaporation. The result is that both blue and green water are scarce. A key management challenge is to get rainfall to infiltrate by avoiding easily produced soil crusts and soil compaction, and to sustain soil organic matter to secure the water-holding capacity of the soil. We will return to these issues in Chapter 7.

In the *humid tropics*, both rainfall and evaporative demand are very large. The green water flow is therefore huge and, in fact, provides an important input to the vapour flow over the continent, which in turn will form the basis for subsequent rainfall. This fact generated considerable interest among climate change researchers as early as the 1980s. In spite of the large return flow to the atmosphere, the runoff is also large. There is also plenty of water in the soil. This complicates agriculture in the humid tropics, which is difficult for several other reasons: high groundwater, diseases, leaching nutrients, and vulnerability to environmental consequences of deforestation.

The relation between rainfall and evaporative demand is essential for the vegetation. Figure 5.4 shows the biomass production of dry matter above soil set against the green water flow or total actual evaporation for the main biomes around the world (Falkenmark, 1986, based on data from L'vovich, 1979). The diagram reveals that the *natural ecosystems* in the humid tropics are highly productive and

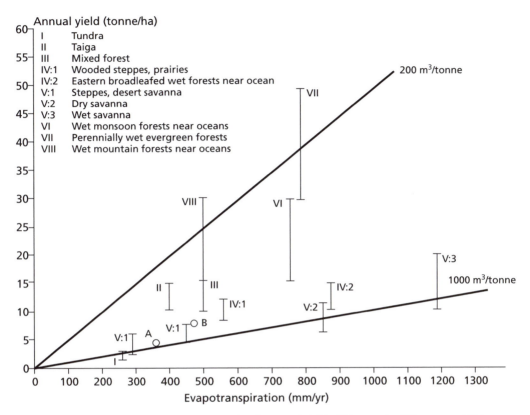

Note: The diagram shows characteristic data for the actual yield of biomass in different world biomes as a function of total evaporation (evaporation plus transpiration). Diagonal lines indicate amount of water consumed per tonne biomass produced. Points A, virgin steppe, and B, a barley field, represent field measurements in USSR.

Data from L'vovich, 1979 (from Falkenmark, 1986)

Figure 5.4 *Green water flow in biomass production in natural ecosystems*

produce much biomass per drop of evaporated water. Those systems consumed only about 200 m³ water /tonne biomass. In contrast, in the systems of the semi-arid climate zone 1000 m³/tonne is generally required. This is mainly due to the large evaporation losses from soil with sparsely distributed vegetation.

Hydrological reflections on plant-water strategies

In Chapter 2, we discussed rainwater partitioning as exemplified by the savanna zone situation, based on data from L'vovich (1979). He analysed hydrological data from all the continents, presenting them as generalized graphs showing the dependence of total evaporation and groundwater recharge on what he called the wetting of the soil or the infiltration of rainfall into the soil, forming soil moisture. Figure 5.5a shows the emerging curves indicating the partitioning of infiltrated rainfall into its different flow components.

In Figure 5.4 we could see the particular eco-hydrological preconditions of the drier biomes, including a gradient from desert to wet savannas (Code V). We could also see that these natural ecosystems have a low water productivity (1000 m³ of consumptive green water per tonne of above-ground biomass). Figure 5.5a also shows the gradient from dry to wetter conditions, where each set of curves is composed of three different wetting intervals, separating main intra-zonal differences (Widstrand, 1980):

- Conditions of low wetting where practically all infiltrated water returns as green water flow (E, total evaporation) to the atmosphere and only a very small part recharges the groundwater (U, groundwater recharge). In this interval, the flow is driven by high evaporative demand compared to rainfall, and neither evaporation nor groundwater recharge is affected by previous retention of moisture (wetness) in the soil.
- Above a certain level of wetting, the interdependence turns parabolic, expressing the dependence of both evaporation and groundwater recharge on the preceding moisture content in the soil. The larger the infiltration, the larger the percolating part.
- Above a certain level of wetting total evaporation has reached the potential level. Further surplus of water directly recharges groundwater.

The geographical distribution of major biomes of the world is shown in Figure 5.5b (developed from Hadley, 1975). The savanna zone, characterized by low water productivity of the natural ecosystems (covering zones with code 10 and 11 in Figure 5.5b), is evidently representative for large areas of the developing world. Therefore, this zone requires special attention. We will return to the special vulnerability of the savanna zone in chapters 6–8.

The Blue Water Perspective

Since human life and activities are water-dependent, much engineering effort has been devoted to finding out how to bring water to settlements, cities, industries and farmlands to facilitate easy access to water at the right time and the right place.

To bring water to the right place involves various technical measures, amply described in textbooks on water technology and management, and these will not be discussed here. Basically, these techniques involve intakes and pumps for water withdrawal from rivers, and well pumps to hoist groundwater from aquifers and as well structures for transport in canals, through pipelines and distribution systems. Since water is needed on a year-round basis, special challenges have to be faced, especially in monsoon climates with a distinct separation of a rainy season and a dry season. The typical situation in large parts of India is, for instance, that rainfall is limited to only some hundred hours per year, and the rest of the time there is no rain to rely on. To secure water supply during the dry season, arrangements are needed for a supply based

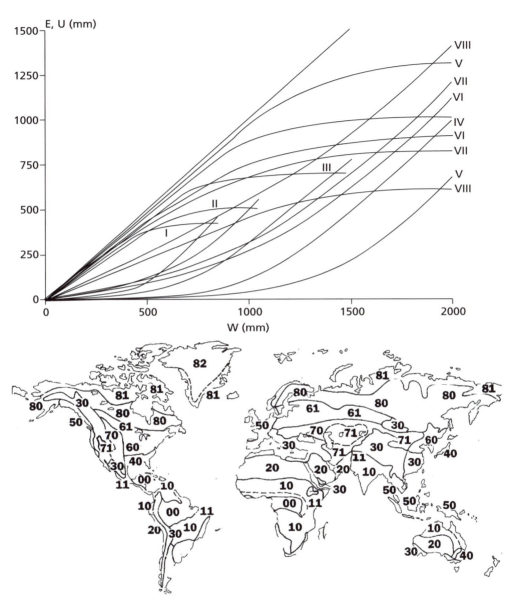

LEGEND

a Principal relationships

b World distribution of main biomes

I Tundra; II Taiga; III Mixed forest; IV Dry wooded steppe, prairies. Wet – Eastern broadleaved wet forests near ocean; V Dry – steppes, desert savannas. Intermediate – dry savanna. Wet – wet savanna; VI Wet monsoon forest near ocean; VII Perennially wet evergreen forest; VIII Wet mountain forest near oceans

Note: Principal relationships for different hydroecological zones between total evaporation E, and groundwater recharge U, as well as infiltrated rainfall W, for main biomes in the world, according to L'vovich, 1979.

Figure 5.5 *Main biomes of the world*

on water left over from the surplus generated during the wet season. This calls for storage arrangements of various types of which ancient history offers many ingenious examples.

Intensity of blue water utilization

Depending on differences in climate, population density, and socioeconomic development, countries have had to mobilize different relative amounts of their available blue water. The relation between total water availability and withdrawals has often been to indicate the degree of water mobilization (percentage) in comparison to the total resource available. The higher up on the availability percentage scale the country is, the larger are the costs in terms of necessary infrastructure. The experience in Europe has been that when a society reached a blue water withdrawal of 20 per cent of the available water, further development of water started to get problematic, in the sense that the costs for various types of infrastructure were getting high in relation to the national economy (Falkenmark and Lindh, 1976). In the studies leading up to the special session of the UN General Assembly in June 1997, referred to as the Rio + 5 Conference, water policy analysts used the term 'water stress' to express these technical/economic difficulties.

For instance, the UN study *Comprehensive Assessment of the World's Freshwater Resources* (CFWA, 1997) introduced the scale in Table 5.1 for relative amount of water use and characterization of what we may refer to as technical water stress.

The relation between gross water demand and use-to-availability level has been used in many international studies. For instance, the International Water Management Institute (IWMI) in Sri Lanka has tried to estimate how technical water stress is going to increase under the double pressure from continued population growth and the simultaneous increase in water for food needed in irrigated agriculture (Seckler et al, 1998). The underlying assumption was that crop production on lands already under irrigation should be maximized. In calculating the water need to achieve this, careful attention was paid to precipitation and crop water requirements. The outcome was used to identify four groups of countries with different circumstances in relation to the amount of blue water needed to achieve the required level of crop production, and their ability to mobilize that amount of water. For countries with physical water scarcity the ability to feed the growing population might already be limited by a high level of water stress. Even where water stress is low the ability may be limited by constraints of the general coping capability, such as lack of access to expertise, trained manpower and financing potential.

Water crowding and the social aspect of water stress

There is another water perspective that needs to be introduced besides the engineering view. The social side of water stress is critical in understanding implications of water crowding – the different types of social disputes among the population that may occur in a situation when a large number of people have to share the same limited amount of blue water. For a long time demographers have given special attention to the implications of population growth on socioeconomic development. In the late 18th

Table 5.1 *Characterization of technical water stress*

Percent withdrawal	Technical water stress characterization
< 10	Low water stress
10–20	Medium low water stress
20–40	Medium high water stress
> 40	High water stress

Source: CFWA, 1997

century, Thomas Robert Malthus, and in the 1960s Paul Ehrlich, were both concerned with food production difficulties. Owing to human ingenuity, the world has, however, continued to be able to produce enough food and the catastrophe that these two proponents were warning against has not yet materialized. Instead, in line with Esther Boserup's agrarian analyses (1965), agricultural development in the world has increased productivity, with production largely driven by necessity, arising primarily from population pressure.

Whether one has an optimistic or pessimistic view of the potential of agriculture to keep pace with population growth, it is important to remember that the high water consumption linked to crop growth will lead to limitations of water availability and, in the long run, constrain food production. In the mid-1980s attention was given for the first time to the limitations set by water on food production and human livelihood, caused by the increasing population pressure on water availability. For this new limitation to human development we will use the term 'water crowding' (Falkenmark, 1986; FAO, 2000). An empirical water competition scale is introduced that focuses on the number of people sharing one flow unit of (blue) water. The flow unit was taken as 1 million cubic meters per year of renewable water, corresponding to a cube with 100-meter sides. Moreover, to facilitate inter-country comparisons, a set of intervals on this scale was introduced (see Figure 5.6).

For the upper limit, the most water-crowded threshold with 2000 persons/flow unit, the term 'water barrier' was introduced, understood as the maximum level that an advanced, irrigation-dependent country can sustain without increasing groundwater salinization problems. The foremost example was Israel, which, at that time, was at this high level of water crowding. This term was inspired by an ongoing discussion in Poland, where concern was developing about future water scarcities (Z Mikulski, personal communication).

Falkenmark's aim was to bring the world's attention to the growing problem of relative water scarcity as the world population, which depends on a finite water resource, continued to expand. At this point, the proposed water-crowding intervals were altogether empirical and based on general impressions of the difficulties encountered by countries with different positions along this scale.

Engineers were, of course, also aware of the exacerbated technical problems that population growth generated. They were used to thinking in terms of the relation between water availability and population, and had for a long time been using the relative indicator of per capita water availability as a measure of (blue) water stress. They therefore inverted the scale of population per flow unit introduced by Falkenmark (Ashton, 2002), so that the water-crowding thresholds were read in terms of volume of

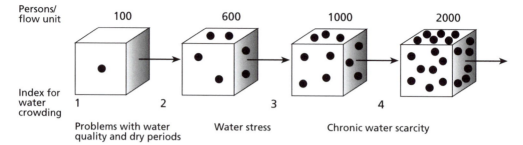

Persons/flow unit
100   600   1000   2000

Index for water crowding
1   2   3   4

Problems with water quality and dry periods   Water stress   Chronic water scarcity

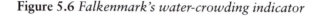

Note: Each cube indicates one flow unit of blue water (1 million cubic meters recharged per year), and each dot 100 persons.

Figure 5.6 *Falkenmark's water-crowding indicator*

freshwater per capita, instead of number of persons sharing a flow unit. These water-crowding indices were soon widely adopted, and the intervals were used primarily to indicate mounting problems of water limitations to development at the country level. These water scarcity indicators have since been referred to as the 'Falkenmark indicator', renamed later by Population Action International to 'standard indicator' (Engelman and LeRoy, 1995).

Population Action International published a graph of a large number of countries showing their positions in relation to the standard indicator, based on the inverted population pressure scale, or m³ of blue water availability per capita. The 600 person/flow unit would correspond to 1667 m³ per person, but this was rounded up to 1700 m³/person. The widely used scale is shown in Table 5.2.

It is important to realize that the original water-crowding indicators described a different dimension of water stress than the mobilization difficulties emphasized by the engineering community. The original focus was not on the technical challenges of making water accessible for use when and where needed – that is, on the *distribution challenges*. Instead, the focus was and remains on the social side of water competition and on the emerging social stresses that accompany a high level of competition for a limited and finite resource. Increased water crowding means that more and more people pollute each flow unit of water and raise pollution levels. There is an increasing risk for disputes, especially when trade-offs and re-allocations have to be made between competing water needs.

The Combined Perspective

The environmental preconditions of the globe place constraints on human activities. The inability of society to adapt its activities to such constraints is causing a number of serious problems. Instead of adaptation, the main tendency is still continued exploitation of ecosystems aimed at supplying goods and services to humans in the short term. Although our knowledge of ecosystems has increased dramatically in recent

Table 5.2 *Water crowding and annual per capita water availability*

Original Falkenmark indicator for water crowding (persons per flow unit)	Adapted water scarcity index 'The Falkenmark indicator' (m³/capita)	Water stress implication
> 600	< 1700	Water stress
> 1000	< 1000	Chronic water scarcity
> 2000	< 500	Beyond the water barrier

decades, the knowledge has not kept pace with our ability to alter them. This applies also for ecohydrology, where our knowledge of the dynamic and complex interactions between water and ecosystems has increased dramatically, but where the exploitation mode is still largely concerned with water development for the service of society.

Regional challenges

A first step towards an ecohydrological management of the landscape is to understand the regional differences in the hydroclimatic preconditions. As has been demonstrated so far, hydrological constraints will be very different in different climatic regions. The most urgent environmental problems are not the same, for example, in the Amazon region, Central Europe and Namibia.

Let us compare the three main regions illustrated in Figure 5.3. The present hydrological understanding is best developed for the temperate zone, both for slopelands and for flatlands (Falkenmark et al, 1999, Falkenmark and Ayebotele, 1992). The *temperate humid region* has considerable differences between summer and winter temperatures. The evaporative demand is moderate so that precipitation surplus is large enough to recharge aquifers and rivers. There is usually streamflow generated all year round, although limited during summer when the soil is not saturated but tends to absorb all rainfall. Studies on these processes indicate that the landscape is divided into recharge areas with infiltration surplus, and discharge areas where the precipitation surplus meets a rising groundwater. In this region, water shortage is seldom a concern. Instead, pollution is the most acute problem caused both by ongoing emissions as well as by pollutants inherited from industrial and domestic activities in the past.

In the *tropical humid regions* seasonal differences in temperature are rather low. Evaporative demand is lower than the precipitation and there is no water deficit. Due to the high temperature and the wet conditions, biological and chemical processes and the transport of pollutants or other substances from the soil to groundwater and rivers are very quick. A major concern in this region is the effect of deforestation, which is often followed by non-sustainable land use. Soil productivity tends to decrease due to soil compaction, erosion and nutrient leaching. Land degradation is followed by increased frequency of severe storm floods causing severe downstream damage. The forest canopy has a profound impact on local climate. When the canopy is removed over large areas, there is no protection of seedlings. The lowering of green water flow from a large-scale deforested area would result in decreased rainfall due to the moisture feedback processes in the atmosphere. Green water flows generated from tree and plant ecosystems upwind feed vapour flow to the atmosphere. This vapour is carried by wind, which in turn feeds downwind rainfall. Forests have deep roots and large canopies and therefore have a year-round productive green water flow to the atmosphere. They are in this sense climatic lungs, feeding vapour to the air today, which becomes the rain of tomorrow. Three driving forces tend to determine the rate of deforestation: slash-and-burn agriculture by shifting cultivators that need to grow food; the activities of landowners of large properties producing fodder for extensive cattle ranching; and the big timber industries. In this region the key to understanding hydrological phenomena is often outside hydrology, and land-surface processes are of major importance for the circulation of the atmosphere.

Finally, in the *arid, semi-arid and dry sub-humid tropical region* the evaporative demand exceeds rainfall so that rivers can only be fed with water during limited parts of the year. In many countries of the semi-arid and dry sub-humid tropical region, population growth is very high and the pressure to increase agricultural production is enormous. The primary challenge is how to secure a livelihood for the additional population. As will be discussed in Chapter 7, there is an alarming rate of decline in crop yields. At the same time, in order to keep pace with the population growth, food production has to increase by no less than 3 per cent annually, which is a faster growth rate than was achieved during the Green Revolution. This is a region of serious man-made environmental problems, due mainly to disturbances of the land surface. The disturbances have vast implications for rainfall infiltration into the soil, which is necessary for onwards transport to other water cycle components. Changes in intensity of biomass production would be expected to influence the water partitioning and hence also runoff production. Such changes may be considerable on an absolute scale, even if they are moderate on a relative scale. In the temperate zone, hydrologists tend to concentrate their interest on horizontal flows or blue water flow. In these regions vertical and horizontal flows, that is both green and blue water flows, will have to be studied in combination. In the largest river basin in Australia, the Murray-Darling, plant production has indeed been used as a way of mitigating the waterlogging and salinity problems suffered as a consequence of the European immigrants' way of life.

For future discussions of environmental problems in a global context it is vital to create a broad understanding among world leaders and researchers and students in the life sciences of the significant differences between world regions in terms of environmental opportunities and vulnerabilities. The cube in Figure 5.7 is a first effort to visualize some crucial differences that indicate the preconditions of a number of countries, most of them in Africa. The following indicators were selected for the cube axes:

- temperature, which controls potential evaporation during the rainy season and thus the 'efficiency of the rainfall';
- population pressure on available water (the degree of water crowding), which influences the possibility to compensate the lack of soil water available to plants in agriculture through small-scale or large-scale irrigation;
- climate aridity that defines the ecological zones or biomes.

The cube visually represents the incompatibility between environmental opportunities and vulnerabilities in the two temperate and humid innermost sub-cubes at the bottom,

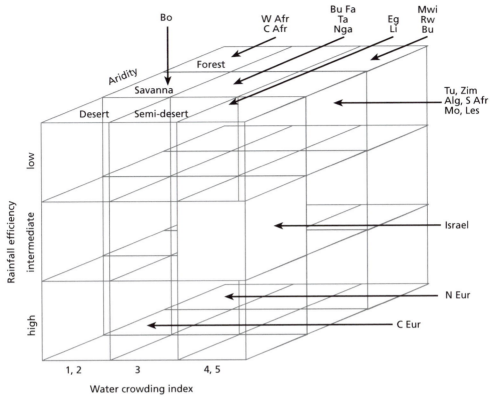

Water crowding index

Source: Modified from Falkenmark and Widstrand, 1992

Figure 5.7 *Regional differences in terms of environmental opportunities and vulnerabilities; evaporative demand as an index of rainfall efficiency; aridity as an index of ecological zones; water-crowding index*

where most industrialized countries are located, and the two hot and dry ecological zones in the uppermost layer, where the poverty-stricken countries tend to be concentrated. The most extreme water scarcity situation in industrialized countries is found in the intermediate layer.

Blue water scarcity clusters

Combining the technical stress distribution aspects and the social stress/crowding aspects creates an interesting global picture. Shiklomanov (1997) presented a comprehensive overview of blue water availability and use. He divided the world into 26 rather homogenous regions. Figure 5.8 exposes major regional differences in terms of water-use level (diagonal lines), water crowding/social stress (horizontal axis), and technical stress (the current mobilization ratio expressed as the use to resource ratio, vertical axis). One has to remember that according to the earlier reference in this chapter to Balcerski (Falkenmark and Lindh, 1976), the costs and efforts needed to

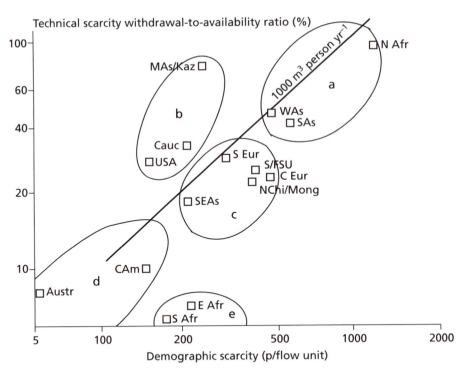

Note: Many regions are invisible at the lower end of the logarithmic scales. Diagonal line shows per capita water withdrawal of 1000 m³/person/ year.

Source: Data from Shiklomanov (modified from Falkenmark, 1999)

Figure 5.8 *Fundamental regional differences: social and technical water stress for Shiklomanov's 26 regions*

mobilize water resources begin to be high in the national economy at a withdrawal ratio of 20 per cent of available blue water on the vertical scale.

The diagram suggests that the 26 regions form five clusters with distinct differences in both water abundance/scarcity and water use levels. The latter basically reflects irrigation use. The five clusters can be characterized as follows:

a: Dry climate region with high population pressure on blue water and high dispute proneness. Use-to-resource ratio is high in spite of moderate to low per capita withdrawals. Potential in terms of unused water is low (North Africa, West and South Asia).

b: Temperate zone regions with low to moderate population pressure on blue water. Use-to-resource ratio is high due to highly wasteful water use. Potential in terms of unused water is low (USA, Middle Asia/Kazakhstan, the Caucasus).

c: A climatically mixed region with moderate levels in all respects: in population pressure on blue water, in per capita water withdrawal, and in use-to-resource ratio. Good potential in terms of unused water (Central and Southern Europe,

S/FSU [the southern part of the former Soviet Union], Southeast Asia and North China).

d: Water-rich regions with low water needs and therefore low use-to-resource ratio. High potential in terms of unused water (South America, Northern Europe, Northern North America and Central Africa).

e: Savanna climate regions with erratic rainfall and moderate population pressures. Use-to-resource ratio remains low due to lack of irrigation. Theoretically, a high potential in terms of unused water but the water is difficult to mobilize, see below (semi-arid savannas of Sub-Saharan Africa).

Adding capability to cope

As already indicated, climbing up the vertical use-to-availability axis in the diagram to mobilize a larger part of the available blue water resource and make it accessible for use depends not only on access to reservoirs, or energy, but also on coping capability and money to finance the structures involved. This makes coping capability crucial. Table 5.3 gives a final overview, summarizing three non-negotiable dimensions of water scarcity (green water scarcity referring to the aridity dimension discussed in the beginning of this chapter, and the two modes of blue water stress – the technical and the social). To represent the coping capability problems in the different clusters, GNP (gross national product) per capita was used as a proxy. Moreover, clusters b, c and d have been divided into two subgroups, number one containing the industrialized regions, number two the developing regions and regions in transition.

Particularly critical regions with social water stress or chronic water scarcity are those that (a) have more than a 20 per cent mobilization level, (because of the high investment needs required to make more water accessible for use), and (b) have more than 600 persons per flow unit. The table suggests a regional structure with the following combinations of parameters:

- Some *developing regions*, whether in the temperate or tropical/sub-tropical zone, tend to have at least two types of problems – green water scarcity and insufficient

Table 5.3 *Main water management problems in the different clusters*

Region	Green water scarcity	Blue water scarcity		Coping capability problems
		Technical stress	Social stress	
a	•	•	•	•
b1	•	•		
b2	•	•		•
c1	(•)	•		
c2	•	•		•
d1	(•)			
d2	(•)			•
e	•			•

Note: Parentheses indicate part of the region only (for explanation see text).

coping capability. Some of the regions suffer from both social and technical water stress (North Africa, South Asia). Population growth will also push many of the other regions into social water stress (South Africa, West and East Africa, North China and West Asia). However, other countries facing a similar development are located in the humid tropics (parts of South America, and Central Africa).

- *Countries in transition* generally have both green and blue water scarcity problems or technical water stress. There are, however, no water-crowding problems or social water stress.
- *Industrialized regions* tend to have a certain degree of technical water stress (central and south Europe, USA). They generally do not suffer from water crowding or low coping capability problems.

Summary

This chapter has focused on water as a determinant for conditions of human livelihood. Attention has been paid to both green and blue water situations, to differences in environmental vulnerability between different regions, and to the remaining degrees of freedom for coping with population growth and increasing per capita needs. Such constraints will influence future efforts to eradicate poverty and improve welfare and food security in line with the Millennium Declaration (see Chapter 10).

A major livelihood determinant is the relation between precipitation and the thirstiness of the atmosphere, or potential evaporation. This relation determines both the length of the growing season and biomass productivity. It was shown that most of the industrialized countries – except western USA and Australia – are located in a region with water surplus, while the poorest countries with massive problems of malnourishment are mainly located in the water deficiency zone. While water tends to be taken for granted in the former, it constitutes a main everyday question in the latter, and scarcity of both green and blue water is central to human endeavours. Large differences were demonstrated in water productivity of natural biomes; while the consumptive use in wet biomes with dense canopies is only 200 m^3/tonne, it is in the order of 1000 m^3/tonne in dry climate biomes with sparse canopies.

The blue water preconditions were analysed from different perspectives. Particular attention was paid to challenges related to population. Degrees of freedom were analysed with the focus on options and types of constraints that will meet efforts to satisfy rising water needs.

Several perspectives were introduced. First, the perspective as seen by the engineers: the technical–economical water stress is related to difficulties to mobilize more of the available water. Second, the perspective of social water stress that is related to water crowding and the increasing risk for social disputes when more people would be sharing every flow unit of water. Third, the perspective of the coping capability, which has deficiencies in terms of institutional preparedness, access to trained manpower, educational level, and sources of financing.

Finally, important regional differences were analysed from several different perspectives:

Blue water scarcity revealed five separate regional clusters. Green water and coping capability show systematic regional differences between developing regions, countries in transition, and industrialized regions.

A cube incorporating differences in aridity, evaporative demand and water crowding made it possible to visualize global environmental opportunities and problems. These showed systematic differences between groups of countries.

We pointed out that the level of hydrological understanding of water resources problems in the temperate zone concentrates the interest on blue water problems, whereas hydrological phenomena in the tropics and sub-tropics demand extended attention to both green and blue water perspectives.

The conflicts of interest between the demands for blue or green water will, however, look different in different hydroclimates and will culminate in the savanna regions with their rapidly rising food needs and restricted availability of blue water. The increasing change in land use must be implemented without threatening the production of major ecological services. Guidelines will be needed to find out how this can be done.

Part 2

Closing Up on the Vulnerable Savanna Zone

Chapter 6

Vulnerability of the Savanna Zone

Many developing countries facing major challenges related to water scarcity, poverty and population growth have a large proportion of their land area in savanna ecosystems.

Drylands – the Cradle of Mankind

The media and science often portray arid, semi-arid and dry sub-humid regions of the world as being regions of endemic poverty and economic and social disruptions. They are supposedly affected by serious land degradation such as the expansion of deserts from advancing sand dunes. People are said to be victims of the interconnected threats of drought and famine (Agnew and Andersson, 1992). In this book we prefer to identify challenges and opportunities instead of problems. It is important in this perspective to recall the critical evolutionary role played by open savanna ecosystems, which indicates an inherent potential for human development in balance with nature.

Early man probably lived and developed in a savanna ecosystem in East Africa. Charles Darwin suggested as early as 1871 that Africa was the cradle of mankind. Early settled agriculture and livestock herding probably took place in another dryland savanna in the Middle East 10,000–12,000 BP. Finds in the Negev Desert show that water management to bridge droughts and dry spells probably became important very early in the development of agrarian societies (Evenari et al, 1971). Here water-harvesting systems have been discovered that date back to the time of the Judean kings, some 2700 years ago.

It will be argued in this chapter that a broad set of water-related environmental and development challenges converge in semi-arid and dry sub-humid tropical savanna agro-ecosystems. Water in these ecosystems is the primary determinant of biological life. The challenges in the savanna zone are about ecological vulnerability, past and present degradation of natural resources, water scarcity, low productive farming systems, poverty and rapid population growth.

Are the 'drylands' really dry?

Generally, the term 'drylands' is used when referring to arid, semi-arid and dry sub-humid tropical savannas (UNESCO, 1979). This suggests the non-justifiable perception of notoriously dry ecosystems that are subject to persistent water scarcity. If you mention drylands to someone it will create a mental picture of sand storms, rolling dunes, cracking dry soils, deep wells, cacti and thorny shrubs. This perception of notorious dryness is exaggerated, however. To start with it is influenced by the inclusion of arid desert ecosystems among drylands. These are truly dry but host only a very limited number of human beings. We will therefore exclude the arid regions of the world's desert ecosystems, and instead focus on drylands and on landscapes where we find rainfed agriculture and sedentary rural societies.

In the semi-arid zone where such rural societies exist the annual rainfall normally exceeds 350 mm. Sedentary societies in winter rainfall areas, for example, in the Mediterranean, are often having a slightly lower annual rainfall.[1] The annual rainfall in the semi-arid and dry sub-humid zones is in the range 350–1500 mm, and is concentrated in growing seasons of 2–6 months. The rainfall can be either mono-modal, as in West Africa, with only one rainy (growing) season, or bi-modal, resulting in two rainy seasons, one major and one minor, as in East Africa, India and SE Asia.

In a semi-arid tropical savanna the annual potential evaporation may be in the order of 2000 mm and the annual rainfall in the order of 700 mm, giving a ration of rainfall to potential evaporation (P/PET), often defined as an aridity index, of almost 0.3, which indicates a very dry area. However, rain usually falls during a period of 120 days. The potential evaporation is lower during the rainy season than during the dry season, due to increased cloudiness, lower air temperature, and higher air humidity. Atmospheric demand for water during the rainy season may amount to only 5 mm per day, compared to almost 10 mm during the dry season. The result is a seasonal evaporative demand over the rainy season of 600 mm, which is lower than the seasonal rainfall. The aridity index during the rainy season, equal to the hydrologically active season is thus 1.2, indicating rather wet conditions, with an average runoff surplus potential. As a comparison, the annual aridity index for a temperate zone in mid-Sweden is drier than this, around 1 (an annual rainfall of 550 mm and an annual atmospheric demand of a similar size). Here the annual comparison makes sense, as rainfall is relatively evenly distributed over the year. The conclusion is that a hydroclimatic zone that may look very dry on an annual basis actually may be very wet during the rainy season.

Pronounced regional contrasts

The dry season is, on the other hand, very dry or completely dry, and constitutes a basic ecological factor that determines the life forms that have evolved in such ecosystems. The life forms have adapted, however, to the dry and wet season fluctuations, either by coping with the dry seasons (perennial shrubs, trees, migration of animals) or by not living during the dry seasons (annual plants). If potential evaporation rates exceed 10 mm/day during the dry season this tells us only that it is very hot and dry. Hydrologically it means nothing for terrestrial ecosystems. There is no actual evaporation because there is no water that can satisfy the atmospheric thirst. During the dry season atmospheric thirst is highly critical only for areas of ponded water, for example, wetlands, reservoirs, and lakes, where evaporation will attain potential evaporation levels and result in very high actual evaporation.

This sharp ecohydrological contrast between dry and wet periods in savannas has certainly inspired the idea of semi-arid tropical landscapes as marginal drylands. In ecology there is a tendency to focus on perennial plant life, such as bush and tree formations in savannas. Because of the prolonged dry periods of 5–9 months between rainy seasons, perennial life forms are more or less adapted to desert-like conditions. From an ecological perspective, therefore, it makes sense to perceive savannas as a form of dryland. For annual plants, whose life cycles start and end with the 3–7 months of rainy season, the savanna is largely wet. It is within this annual biological reality that we find agriculture. The ecological preconditions are very different between the perennial ecological plant formations adapted to drylands and the annual agricultural plant formations adapted to wetlands. This fact makes it impossible to transfer an ecological dryland label to the agricultural situation on the savanna.

We also believe an important perceptional step is to abandon the definition of drylands altogether when discussing ecohydrology in semi-arid and dry sub-humid tropical ecosystems. Therefore, we will instead use the ecological term 'savanna' when discussing semi-arid and dry sub-humid regions populated by sedentary rural societies. Because these savannas almost exclusively are inhabited by sedentary farming societies, we will also use the term 'savanna agro-ecosystems'. These include the same areas of the world that are covered by the Convention to Combat Desertification (which unfortunately uses the term drylands), but excluding the really arid areas.

Savannas are defined in the broadest sense as ecosystems that lie between the forests and deserts of tropical regions (Huntley and Walker, 1982). This is the definition we adopt in this book. Savannas are ecological adaptations to the following hydroclimatic characteristics:

- a pronounced climatic rhythm of wet and dry seasons;
- a rainfall range of 250–1500 mm of annual rainfall;
- high potential evaporation (>1000 mm) and an average annual temperature above 18°C;
- large rainfall variability.

The broad definition of savannas and the wide rainfall range indicate the vast diversity of vegetation that may be found in these areas. In a gradient from low to high rainfall, savannas include scrub savannas, low tree and scrub savanna, savanna grasslands, savanna parklands and savanna woodlands (Cole, 1986; Archibold, 1995). The global coverage of savannas was shown in Figure 5.5b as zones 10 and 11. As seen from that map, savannas cover large areas in sub-Saharan Africa, India, Southeast Asia, northeast Brazil and Australia. On a global scale, savannas cover some 5000 million hectares, which is 40 per cent of the total land area (UNEP, 1992).

Savanna Agro-ecosystems – A Most Difficult Challenge

From an ecohydrological and development perspective, the challenges to balance the needs of humans and nature converge in the savanna agro-ecosystems:

- A large proportion of the world's population inhabit savannas and, in many countries, these have the most rapidly growing populations of the world's biomes.
- Ecosystems of the semi-arid tropics are extremely sensitive to over-exploitation or inappropriate land use.
- The huge population and the high water requirement linked to agriculture in the semi-arid and dry sub-humid savannas present the major water-related environmental and development challenges of all ecosystems.
- Poverty and environmental degradation are serious problems in these landscapes.
- Food productivity is low at present and, in many regions (such as parts of the Sahel), even at a standstill.
- Most of the population make their living from agriculture, predominantly rainfed land use.

Drought-related land degradation

The concern over social, environmental and political implications of ecohydrological challenges in savanna agro-ecosystems is not new. Since 1977 this concern has emerged on the international scene as a global environment and development problem, but unfortunately under the term 'desertification'. Drought management had been an important part of local and national governance and land management throughout the whole century and has been an internal part of an indigenous coping mechanism, probably for millennia. The difference in the 1970s was that the rapid population growth, low agricultural per capita productivity and, among impoverished and incompetent governments, a weak preparedness to cope with drought-induced famines, then combined to create large-scale human suffering.

Over the years the term desertification[2] has suffered from the same perceptional bias as the term dryland. The fear of the 1970s and '80s was that of advancing sand dunes in the Sahara resulting in deserts engulfing productive farmland. Olsson proved this idea wrong (Olsson, 1993). Today, desertification is much more broadly defined as 'land degradation in arid, semi-arid and dry sub-humid areas resulting mainly from adverse human impact'. An area of debate is still the relative role of human-induced change at the hydrological partitioning points versus desertification induced by climate change (Rapp, 1974). At present the important point from an ecohydrological perspective is that savannas – where already from a purely climatic point of view water is a scarce resource – are extremely vulnerable to human-induced desiccation, which results in desert-like conditions. According to UNEP (1992), desertification affects the capacity for food production of savannas in every continent, involving people in almost 100 countries; 70 per cent of the world's arid, semi-arid and dry sub-humid agricultural lands are affected to some degree by land degradation, and one-sixth of the world population is threatened by the effects of desertification (UNEP, 1992).

Savanna vegetation is adapted to the availability of soil water

There are three major causes of human-induced land degradation: overgrazing, deforestation and land mismanagement in agriculture. All these affect partitioning of rainfall and result in a shift towards increased erosive surface runoff, reduced productive green water flow and lowered ground water recharge.

Water plays a determinant role in shaping the ecological climax of semi-arid and dry sub-humid savanna ecosystems. Eagleson and Segarra (1985) have shown that in ecosystems that are water-limited, such as tropical savannas, the ecological response to adapt to water scarcity is to minimize water demand from vegetation through adjustments of canopy density and plant species. This is done in order to maximize plant access to soil moisture. The competition for soil moisture can explain the hydroecological climax in parkland savannas, where *Acacia faidherbia* trees have a certain radial distance between each tree to minimize moisture competition.

Similarly, the tiger bush formations in dry savannas in the Sahel and Australia are adaptations to spatial and temporal soil moisture availability. In these systems, the bush vegetation forms bands separated by zones of bare soil, which look like tiger stripes in aerial photos. These lines of vegetation are an adaptation to the recurrent risk of water scarcity due to rainfall variability and seasonality. The rows of bare soil between the lines function as natural water harvesting zones, concentrating surface runoff from these rows to the lines of bush vegetation. In this way the vegetation receives soil moisture at levels several magnitudes larger that the rainfall. Research on the tiger bush formations in the Sahel showed that the bare soil bands in between vegetation bands are highly crusted with low infiltration capacity and low water-holding capacity (30 mm of soil moisture per meter of soil depth). The vegetation band, on the other hand, has high infiltration capacity and can store 300 mm of soil moisture per meter of soil. Diversity of vegetation species in the bands is high and permits the presence of species in drier climates than their normal habitats (Leprun and da Silveira, 1992). However, the hydroecological climax of the tiger bush system is sensitive to exploitation of the soil between the bands of vegetation and is sensitive to overgrazing.

Physical and perceived water scarcity

As indicated above, the degree of 'dryness' of a landscape is determined by a wide set of complex interacting processes. These relate to spatial and temporal variability of rainfall and to how rainfall is partitioned in green and blue water flows. Water scarcity can be both physical and perceived. Physical water scarcity is determined not only by hydroclimatic factors such as rainfall and potential evaporation, but also by soil and vegetation factors that determine partitioning of rainfall into blue and green water flows. Perceived water scarcity is related to human needs and demand for water. Population pressure and socioeconomic development increase the needs and demands for certain water flows such as blue water flow for urban bulk water supply. High human demand for water combined with environmental degradation will reduce access to time-stable blue water flow. For example, deforestation can result in more storm surface flow and less groundwater recharge, and may turn a relatively water-rich region into a region experiencing seasonal water scarcity.

This indicates that by classifying regions or countries in categories of 'dry' or 'wet' lands on the basis of rainfall and potential evaporation alone one does not capture the landscape reality. The catastrophic drought-related famines in 1984–85 in sub-Saharan Africa caused Falkenmark (1989) to carry out the first systematic analysis of the water

Table 6.1 *Understanding water scarcity: categorization of factors behind water scarcity according to the Falkenmark framework*

Water Scarcity Mode	Type		Water scarcity manifestation	Additional features
A	Aridity	Green	Short growing season determined by annual rainfall and potential evaporation	Sensitivity linked to crop choice
B	Drought	Green and blue	Recurrent interannual meteorological droughts	Linked to the El Niño phenomenon
C	Land degra- dation	Green	High vulnerability resulting in extensive land degradation	May lead to man-made drought – ie soil moisture deficit – without experiencing Type B drought
D	Water crowding	Blue	Very limited blue water surplus results in blue water scarcity, which is exacerbated by population growth	Blue water scarcity. In the Savanna zone < 100 mm/year of runoff surplus

predicament of African countries. In this analysis she noted that there was a close congruence between famine proneness, short growing seasons and low runoff production, all factors that converge in savanna agro-ecosystems. Similarly, the analysis also highlighted the importance of distinguishing between natural (meteorological) droughts and man-made (agricultural) droughts and their respective relation to the huge famine disaster then facing people of the African savannas.

Interestingly, Falkenmark's analysis brought forward the inconsistency of the views regarding availability of water in Africa. Here is a continent considered water-rich according to most conventional large-scale (basin) hydrological studies, starting with the work by Korzuon et al (1974), but subject to social suffering induced by recurrent drought. The idea of the water-rich continent can mainly be attributed to the few but large equatorial rivers on the continent. However, as already indicated, runoff production in semi-arid Africa is low and the level of dryness largely determined by rainfall seasonality. This shows that the water predicament of a landscape cannot be measured from blue water data alone, from runoff gauging, or from annual rainfall and comparisons of atmospheric thirst. A more sophisticated analytical framework is required for landscapes such as the savanna ecosystems, which have a reasonably high rainfall concentrated in short periods of the year and are subject to high evaporative demand, but which also experience major spatial and temporal variability of rainfall. All these observations were brought together under the idea of a multiple water scarcity framework with four different modes of water scarcity superimposed on each other (Falkenmark et al, 1989) (see Table 6.1).

As shown above, the definition of hydroclimatic zones is based only on the water scarcity mode A in Table 6.1. Water scarcity A, aridity, provides one basis for understanding the ecohydrology of a landscape. The degree of aridity or the relation

Table 6.2 *Estimated proportion of land affected by droughts*

Region	Land affected by meteorological droughts (%)
Southeast Asia	2
Europe (mainly Spain)	8
South America	17
East Asia	17
North America	20
Australia	28
Central America	32
South Asia	43
Africa	44

Source: Barrow, 1987

between rainfall and potential evaporation determines the length of the growing period and gives a theoretical indicator of the potential green water use of an ecosystem and thereby the potential to generate a surplus of blue water flow.

The high spatial and temporal variability of rainfall is expressed through water scarcity B. A more important factor to determine in tropical ecosystems is the ecological climax and agro-ecological productivity. Variability can be a more important biophysical parameter than aridity in determining biomass growth in a tropical ecosystem.

Water scarcity can also be man-made. For biomass growth, this refers to scarcity of soil moisture for green water use. This water scarcity mode may be caused by land-use changes leading to land degradation. Deforestation, intensive tilling of agricultural land and over-exploitation of grazing or cropland that leads to soil crusting and soil erosion, will result in altering of the rainfall partitioning. This is water scarcity C: a man-induced green water scarcity caused by land degradation and manifested in soil moisture and groundwater deficits.

Irrespective of the natural mode A and B or man-made water scarcity, mode C, humans may experience blue water scarcity in a landscape due to limited runoff generation and their increasing needs and demands for water. Water scarcity D easily causes the water crowding discussed in Chapter 5. This scarcity increases when more people demand more water per person and put pressure on a finite freshwater resource. Examples of water scarcity D can be found in several rapidly expanding and densely populated river basins such as the Yangtze River, the Indus and Krishna rivers in Asia, and the Limpopo in Africa.

Challenges are greatest in sub-Saharan Africa

One of the greatest water-related challenges in the world is to achieve sustainable development in the savannas in sub-Saharan Africa. Nowhere does the severity of land degradation, poverty and water scarcity emerge so clearly as in the crescent of savanna ecosystems from the Senegalese Sahel to the South African *veldt*. Africa has the largest proportion of people living in savanna ecosystems. An estimated 44 per cent of the land area in sub-Saharan Africa is prone to meteorological droughts, as shown in Table 6.2.

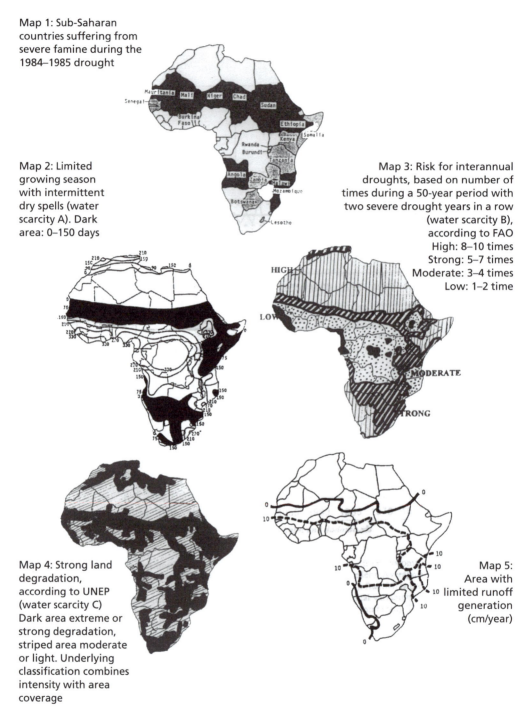

Map 1: Sub-Saharan countries suffering from severe famine during the 1984–1985 drought

Map 2: Limited growing season with intermittent dry spells (water scarcity A). Dark area: 0–150 days

Map 3: Risk for interannual droughts, based on number of times during a 50-year period with two severe drought years in a row (water scarcity B), according to FAO
High: 8–10 times
Strong: 5–7 times
Moderate: 3–4 times
Low: 1–2 time

Map 4: Strong land degradation, according to UNEP (water scarcity C) Dark area extreme or strong degradation, striped area moderate or light. Underlying classification combines intensity with area coverage

Map 5: Area with limited runoff generation (cm/year)

Source: Falkenmark and Rockström, 1993

Figure 6.1 *Links between sub-Saharan proneness to famine and complex water scarcity*

This is the highest figure on earth (Barrow, 1987).

The water-related challenges facing people living on the sub-Saharan African savannas are illustrated in the five maps in Figure 6.1. Map 1 shows the countries most critically affected by famines during the drought years of the 1970s and 1980s. These form the so-called 'hunger-crescent' of Africa (Falkenmark and Rockström, 1993). These countries coincide with the savanna ecosystems on the continent, illustrated in Map 2. These are regions with a growing period between 0 and 150 days, which is an indicator of high water scarcity, mode A in Table 6.1. The high interannual rainfall variability is reflected in Map 3 by showing the risk for recurrent meteorological droughts or high water scarcity, mode B. The savanna belt has a strong risk of meteorological droughts, defined as an area experiencing 5 to 7 drought years over a 50-year period – roughly one drought year per decade.

Savannas are both vulnerable and subject to severe land degradation (Map 4). Here dark areas are affected by extreme land degradation, while striped areas suffer from strong degradation and a high occurrence of water scarcity, mode C. The hydroclimatic challenge of high atmospheric thirst in relation to annual rainfall is given as recharge of blue water flow (cm/year) for the savanna area in Map 5, indicating the annual average surplus of blue water flow.

Hydroclimatic Challenges and Opportunities

The hydroclimate in savanna ecosystems is characterized by:

- concentration of rainfall during one or two rainy seasons of 3–5 months;
- extreme high spatial and temporal variability of rainfall;
- high risk for meteorological droughts and dry spells;
- high intensity rainstorms resulting in high risk for storm surface runoff;
- high atmospheric demand for water.

Short hydrologically active life cycles

The growing season for annual plants roughly starts when rainfall exceeds half the potential evaporation. The potential evaporation shows only small fluctuations over the year, while rainfall fluctuates enormously. The hydrologically active period of the year is short, concentrated to rainy seasons of 3–7 months in semi-arid savannas. When assessing the hydrological reality of savanna ecosystems it is important to focus on the short and intensive rainy season because during large parts of the year the savanna is completely dry.

Table 6.3 shows the hydroclimatic gradient zone from desert to rainforest, from the Sahara desert to the rainforest zone in West Africa. Seasonal rainfall is always below the potential evaporation in the desert and shrub steppe zone (hyper-arid to arid zones), resulting in water deficits (P – PET < 0). Moving south from the Sahara desert into the dry bush savanna means moving from a situation where even the rainy season is arid and ecosystems are subject to water deficit to a situation where the rainy season

Table 6.3 *The hydroclimatic gradient zone in the Sudano-Sahelian zone in sub-Saharan Africa*

	Desert	Desert shrub	Dry-bush savanna	Parkland savanna	Wooded savanna	Rainforest
Rainfall (mm)	0–150	150–250	250–600	600–900	900–1200	>1200
Rainfall variability	100%	50–100%	30–50%	20–30%	15–20%	<15%
No of wet season days	30	50	70–90	90–140	140–190	>190
Potential evapotranspiration (PET) during wet season (mm)	200	200–400	400–600	600–800	800–900	900
Water surplus/ deficit (mm)	−70– −200	−50– −150	−150– 0	0–+100	+100–+300	>+300

```
          ←——— Nomadism ———→
               ←———Transhumance ———→
                    ←——— Sedentary agriculture ———→
                         ←——— Agroforestry ———→
```

Source: Mageed, Vadstena Seminar, 1989, and L'vovich, 1979

is humid and ecosystems are generating a water surplus. When sedentary rural societies are present, and at the transition point from nomadic to sedentary living forms, they signal the location of the wet bush savanna or the parkland tree savanna. Here the rainy season usually generates a water surplus. The wetter end of the savanna zone receives 1200 mm of rain during 6–7 months (in some areas up to 1500 mm), which is a very substantial amount of water during a relatively short period.

Table 6.3 is a further indication that the so-called drylands are not that dry after all. Instead, during the rainy season there is a substantial water surplus in the wet savanna zone. If the rainfall during the growing season is considered, savannas exist in landscapes with at least 100 mm of rainfall per rainy month in the driest zone, and up to 250 mm per month on average in the wettest zone. This is substantially more rainfall than in most so-called wet temperate areas.

Highly erratic and variable rainfalls

Average rainfall in savannas is an illusion. Rainfall variability is so high that the only certainty is that there will never be an average rainfall year (Gustafsson, 1977). Rainfall in savannas is very unreliable, manifested in high coefficients of variation,[3] which vary between 15 and 50 per cent (Table 6.3). Moreover, rainfall becomes more unreliable with reduced seasonal rainfall. In other words, the variability of rainfall thus increases when moving from the wet to the dry savanna zone.

Rainfall is highly erratic, and most rain falls as intensive, often convective storms, with very high rainfall intensity often exceeding 75 mm/hr, and extreme spatial and temporal variability. The combined effect of high temporal variability and high-intensity rainfall events is that a large proportion of the annual rainfall can fall during

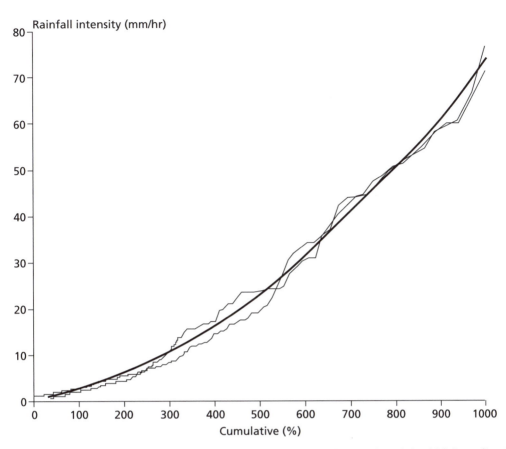

Note: Thin lines are observed data from 1994 (595 mm) and 1995 (517 mm), and the thick line a fitted regression. Average rainfall is 550 mm for the location. Rainfall intensity is in mm/hr taken from 15-minute time steps.

Figure 6.2 *Rainfall intensities and their contribution to cumulative seasonal rainfall: example from a semi-arid savanna in the Sahel (Niger)*

very few showers during the rainy season. This is illustrated in Figure 6.2, with an example of the 1994–95 rainy seasons in a parkland savanna in the Sahel (Niger) that, on average, receives 550 mm of rainfall during a short four-month rainy season (from May/June to September/October). One-fifth of the total seasonal rainfall consists of events with intensities exceeding 50 mm/hr (measured at 15-minute time steps) while half the total rainfall has an intensity exceeding 20 mm/hr. During these two rainy seasons three to four rainfall events ranging from 30 to 70 mm contributed 25 per cent of the cumulative annual rainfall.

The information on rainfall intensities is critical for understanding ecosystem dynamics and for land management in semi-arid savannas. Large rainfall events with high intensity generate high volumes of storm surface runoff. This runoff flows rapidly in ephemeral gullies over a short time span, often only a couple of hours. The hydrological dynamics of the savanna form the basis for water functions in seasonal wetlands that are inundated through surface runoff generated from large tropical rainstorms. For farmers, timing of operations such as planting, in order to get maximum benefit of the few but critical rainfall events, is a fundamental challenge that often determines the outcome of the whole cultivation season.

It is clear from the previous section that there are a number of the hydroclimatic challenges in savanna ecosystems, such as high atmospheric thirst for water, high risk of droughts and dry spells, concentrated rainfall over a short period of time, high-intensity storms, and high vulnerability to water-induced land degradation. At the same time the hydroclimate opportunities need to be understood in order to identify sustainable paths of savanna management, as they are surprisingly abundant:

- adequate volumes of rainfall for agriculture during most years;
- large volumes of unused local surface runoff at catchment scale (as opposed to small volumes of annual generation of blue water flow at the basin scale);
- relatively lower potential evaporation during rainy seasons (compared to dry seasons);
- no actual water losses during dry season;
- good opportunities to reduce evaporation losses during rainy season;
- excellent agro-meteorological conditions (high temperature, solar radiation and low relative humidity).

Large rainfall volumes

Even the dry savanna receives rainfall volumes that, on average, exceed the water requirements of agricultural and natural growing vegetation. This is illustrated in Table 6.4 for a semi-arid 'dry' savanna receiving 600 mm of annual rainfall, and a sub-humid 'wet' savanna with 1000 mm of annual rainfall. Statistically, the natural fluctuation of rainfall will give a departure from the average of between 20 and 25 per cent, indicated in Table 6.3 as the coefficient of variation. One can get an idea of the annual rainfall fluctuations in these examples by comparing a dry and a wet year. Here, this range is defined simply by the average rainfall minus 1 standard deviation for a dry year, and plus 1 standard deviation for a wet year. The rainfall will range from 400 to 750 mm in the drier savanna, and 800–1200 mm in the wetter savanna. This range excludes meteorological drought years, however, which occur on average one to two years out of ten, and which result in rainfall totals below the minimum volumes required to develop a fruit-setting plant or harvestable crop. The rainfall range discussed here can thus be seen as representative for 80–90 per cent of the years.

Considering that 50–60 per cent of the actual rainfall is 'lost' to a plant community or agricultural crop as evaporation and surface and sub-surface runoff, one can get a measure of actual soil moisture stored in the root zone. This effective soil moisture range will amount to 180–300 mm in the dry savanna and 400–600 mm in the wet savanna. This amount is assumed to be available for plant water uptake. A further assumption is a productive green water productivity of 300 m^3 of transpiration required to produce one tonne of biomass (30 mm/tonne/ha). This is a reasonable range for natural savanna vegetation and tropical grain crops grown on the savanna. The

Table 6.4 *Example of rainfall, actual plant water availability and biomass potential in a dry and wet savanna during dry and wet rainfall years*

Flow and growth	Dry savannah		Wet savannah	
	Dry year	Wet year	Dry year	Wet year
Average rainfall (mm)	600	600	1000	1000
Variability				
CV (%)	25	25	20	20
SD (mm)	150	150	200	200
Actual rainfall (mm)	450	750	800	1200
Partitioning of rainfall (% of rainfall)				
Evaporation + runoff	60	60	50	50
Effective soil moisture for plant growth (mm)	300	300	400	600
Water productivity (m³ of transpiration/tonne biomass)	300	300	300	300
Biomass potential (tonnes/ha)	6	10	13	20

resulting biomass production will range from 6 to 10 tonnes/ha/year in the dry savanna and 13–20 in the wet savanna. These are large figures, which show that even in a dry year in the dry savanna, there is a possibility to produce 6 tonnes of biomass/ha during a rainy season. This corresponds to around 1.5–2 tonnes of grain/ha for a crop such as maize. This shows that, generally, there is not a deficit of cumulative rainfall in the savanna. Water deficit for plant growth is primarily due to poor redistribution of rainfall over time, and low plant water availability, due to poor rainfall partitioning (which will be discussed further below).

Even in comparison with other hydroclimatic zones, the semi-arid and dry sub-humid savanna come out as relatively wet. For example, a so-called dry semi-arid savanna with 600 mm of annual rainfall concentrated over a 120-day growing season (limited by rainfall occurrence) has more rainfall than the temperate so-called 'wet' boreal forest ecosystems with a similar length of growing season but limited by temperature during summer. For example, the agro-ecosystems in the boreal zone of southern Sweden receive a meagre 550 mm of annual average rainfall, with only 300 mm falling during the short growing season, which is limited by cold temperatures in spring and autumn. Despite these limitations in water, harsh air temperatures, and low solar radiation, this southern part of Sweden is considered as having a high agricultural potential. Plates 6.1 and 6.2 show two typical ecosystems in the temperate boreal zone and the tropical savanna zone, receiving similar rainfall and having a similar length of growing period. Plate 6.3 shows the same savanna as in Plate 6.2 but now during the dry season.

The conclusion so far is that there is generally enough rainfall in the savanna ecosystem during the growing season, and that savannas during this period are generally wetter than temperate ecosystems. This suggests an important opportunity for increased food production.

Plate 6.1 *Temperate woodland*

How much rainfall is actually used?

Another way to understand the ecohydrological opportunities offered in the savanna is to examine the crop water balance of savanna farming systems to see if there really is a water surplus that can be put to use to benefit the crops. Figure 6.3a gives a synthesized overview of the partitioning of rainfall in rainfed agriculture on the semi-arid savanna, based on research experiences in sub-Saharan Africa. Soil evaporation generally accounts for 30–50 per cent of rainfall (Cooper et al, 1987; Wallace, 1991), a value that can exceed 50 per cent in sparsely cropped farming systems in semi-arid regions (Allen, 1990). Surface runoff often accounts for 10–25 per cent of rainfall as result of heavy rainfall on soils suffering from surface crusting and compaction (Casenave and Valentin, 1992; Penning de Vries and Djitèye, 1991). The characteristics in semi-arid areas of frequent, large and intensive rainfall events on soils with low water-holding capacities result in significant runoff, amounting to 10–30 per cent of rainfall (Klaij and Vachaud, 1992). The result is that productive green water flow as transpiration is reported to account for merely 15–30 per cent of rainfall (Wallace, personal communication).

Of the 75–90 per cent of rainfall that infiltrates into the soil in rainfed production systems on the African savanna, crops use only about 15–30 per cent as productive green water flow. The remaining water returns to the atmosphere as non-productive evaporation, or contributes to local blue runoff water flow, which only partly

Plate 6.2 *Tropical parkland savanna during the wet season*

contributes to blue water flow on the river basin scale. Thus, while groundwater recharge is potentially beneficial for humans and ecosystems downstream, the same conclusion is not automatically true for surface runoff since it may evaporate before reaching a stream.

Studies in semi-arid parts of Syria show that evaporation losses for rainfed wheat under on-farm conditions amount to 35–45 per cent of total green water flow (Zhang and Oweis, 1999). Experience from a semi-arid savanna farming system in China shows similar water flow partitioning, with large non-productive water flow in the water balance (Fig. 6.3 b). This example is from a savanna in Gansu Province in China, which receives an annual rainfall of around 400 mm. While surface runoff is low on the loess soils prevalent in the region, evaporation losses are very high, amounting to 75–80 per cent of rainfall. Productive green water flow accounts for only 15–20 per cent of seasonal rainfall (data from Zhu and Li, 2000, in SIWI, 2001a).

The examples of agricultural rainfall partitioning in the semi-arid savanna discussed above originate primarily from research carried out on research stations, as opposed to research carried out in farmers' fields. As an example of the magnitude of difference, Rockström (1997) showed that merely 4–9 per cent of the rainfall took the productive green water path to contribute to biomass growth of pearl millet. This was done by detailed water flow observations over a period of three years (1994–1996) in a farmer's field in the semi-arid savanna of the Sahel (Niger). The grain yield in this

Note: The temperate woodland has an annual rainfall of 550 mm, a growing season of 120 days and a daily evaporative demand during the growing season of 2–3 mm/day. The tropical savanna has an annual rainfall of 600 mm, a growing season of 120 days, and a daily potential evaporation during the growing season of 5 mm/day.

Photo: Johan Rockström

Plate 6.3 *Tropical parkland savanna during the dry season*

farming system amounted to approximately 500 kg/ha. None of the years had a drought, while all presented more or less severe crop water scarcity due to dry spells, large surface runoff and evaporation flow. In this case the farmer was managing a degraded crop field that suffered from soil crusting, extremely low organic matter, and severe soil nutrient mining, all contributing to the low fraction of productive green water flow. This yield is representative for a large proportion, if not the majority of rainfed agricultural land in the semi-arid and resource-poor savannas of the Sahel.

Surface runoff – a friend and a foe on the savanna

Surface runoff in the savanna is always ephemeral. It flows as rapid storm pulses, often only minutes or hours during and shortly after a rainfall event. The runoff pulse is often dramatic, and gathers high speed and volume in large gullies. Plate 6.4 shows the dramatic effects of water erosion in a catchment in the Lake Victoria basin (Nyakach bay, Kenya). In this example, storm surface runoff flow is generated from a steep

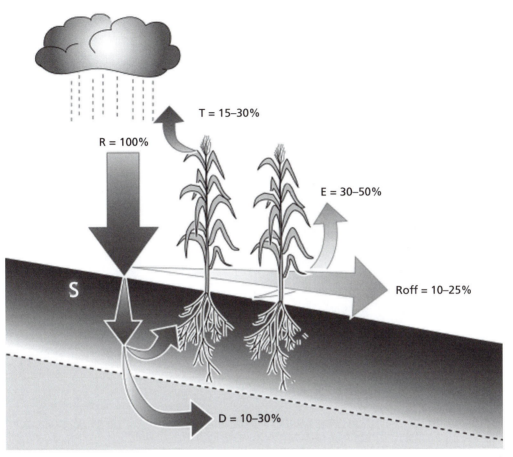

Note: R=Rainfall, T=Transpiration, S=Soil infiltration, D=Deep percolation, E=Evaporation, and Roff=Surface runoff.

Figure 6.3a *General overview of rainfall partitioning in farming systems in the semi-arid tropics of sub-Saharan Africa with data primarily fron on-station research*

escarpment with degraded, shallow soils. Once it reaches lower positions on the gradient from escarpment to lakeshore, the runoff flow causes large soil erosion, where the soil is deep and susceptible to erosion. The result is huge, ravine-like gullies almost 30 meters deep. The highly erosive surface runoff carries high volumes of sediment into the lake, causing serious eutrophication.

As is the case with 'average rainfall', it makes little sense to talk of average surface runoff in savannas. Large, high-intensity storms on wet, crusted and bare soil on steep gradients will generate the largest runoff volumes, while low-intensity storms on flat, dry, non-crusted and densely vegetated soil will generate no runoff at all. Even for a location with the same slope, vegetation and crusting, runoff will differ depending enormously on rainfall intensity, rainfall depth and wetness of the soil. A large rainfall event with high intensity, for example a 50 mm storm over one hour, may generate no

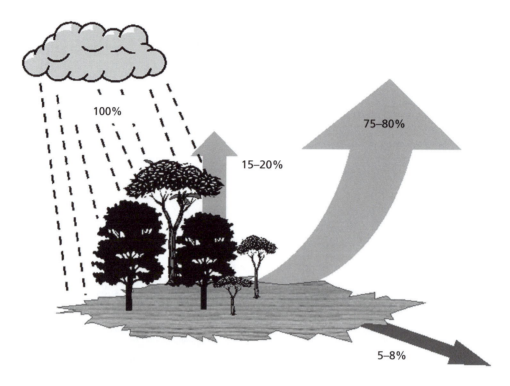

Source: Data from Zhu and Li, 2000, in SIWI, 2001a

Figure 6.3b *Example of on-farm rainfall partitioning for a rainfed farming system in a semi-arid savanna in Gansu Province, China*

surface runoff on a completely dry soil that has recently been tilled, but will generate 50 per cent runoff (50 per cent of rainfall) if the soil is saturated with water. The wide spectrum of surface runoff from one farmer's field in the semi-arid Sahelian savanna is shown in Figure 6.4. As seen from this example, a rainfall event of over 50 mm can generate zero runoff, while a rainfall event of 20 mm can generate 50 per cent runoff.

Water erosion caused by surface runoff from tropical rainstorms constitutes the main agent of land degradation in tropical environments. The colonial powers invested considerable efforts in erosion control in the tropics through terracing, contour bunds and cut-off drains to divert surface runoff out from agricultural lands. This was followed by a strong focus on soil and water conservation during the decades following independence. However, in Africa, the conservation focus was delayed several decades after independence. The colonial focus on physical structures to control erosion, which was carried out with forced labour, resulted in a serious boomerang effect after independence when farmers systematically refused to carry out conservation work since it was so strongly associated with forced labour under the colonial regimes. This has gradually changed, however, and in the 1970s and '80s soil and water conservation experienced a renaissance, as reflected by several authors in many parts of Africa – for

Photo: Johan Rockström

Plate 6.4 *The Ragen gully, Nyakach bay, Kenya*

example, in Kenya (Tiffen et al., 1994; Lundgren, 1993), in sub-Saharan Africa in general (Reij et al, 1996), and in Tanzania (Kangalawa, 2001). A century of land management with a focus on erosion control using soil and water conservation has resulted in an impressive reduction of erosion (Tiffen et al, 1994) but also a narrow and partly erroneous water bias. The focus was, and to a large extent still is, on reducing water erosion by getting rid of surface runoff, regarded as a nuisance and a source of soil erosion.

More recently the opinion on surface runoff has changed, and surface runoff is seen more and more as a valuable 'good' flow, and as potentially useful to manage the high temporal variability of rainfall. The perceptional shift from surface runoff being a 'foe' to being a 'friend' holds tremendous promise for the semi-arid savannas of the world. As was shown by Evenari et al (1971) for the Negev desert, and by Agarwal and Narain (1997) for India, using surface runoff for agriculture in semi-arid and even arid environments dates back several millennia. There are even indications that the farmers of Mesopotamia, where agriculture originated 10,000–12,000 years BP, actually saw surface runoff as a beneficial flow, and harvested it for productive use in farming. In India, indigenous knowledge on water harvesting, where surface runoff is collected, stored, and applied on crops to bridge dry spells, dates back several millennia (Agarwal and Narain, 1997). The knowledge was largely lost with the introduction of modern agriculture in the wake of the Green Revolution, which was based on small petrol and diesel pumps, tapping and lifting groundwater and, where this was possible, river water. Today there is a renewed interest in indigenous water-harvesting practices in which runoff is collected for productive use in, for example, crop cultivation (see Chapter 8).

The Need to Distinguish Droughts and Dry Spells

What we have shown so far is that savannas are not that 'dry' after all, but instead receive relatively large volumes of rainfall (300–1500 mm per year) concentrated over short rainy seasons when the atmospheric thirst is normally lower than during the rest of the year. We have also shown that water scarcity in agro-ecosystems is not necessarily a result of low rainfall but often a result of poor rainfall partitioning in the water balance, resulting in water scarcity in the root zone – in other words, a soil moisture scarcity. Thus, the ecohydrological reality of the savanna is more complex than the simple relationship between annual rainfall, potential evaporation and the occurrence of extreme events such as droughts and floods. The first step towards an ecohydrological analysis more adapted to savannas is to distinguish between droughts and dry spells. The second step is to distinguish between different natural or meteorological conditions and conditions induced by humans.

Meteorological droughts

A meteorological drought occurs when rainfall declines below a minimum threshold required to sustain ecological functions that it normally sustains. This vague definition

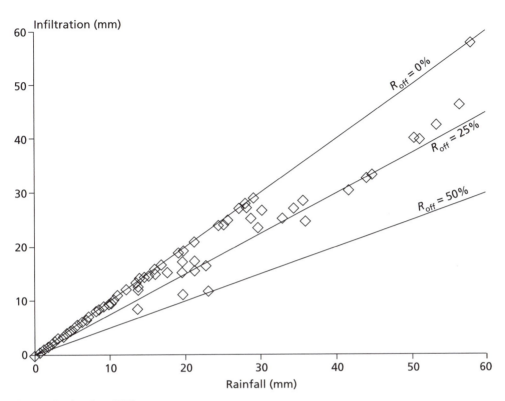

Source: Rockström, 1997

Figure 6.4 *Observed surface runoff in a farmer's field in the semi-arid savanna of Niger (Samadey)*

directly indicates one of the difficulties in the discussion on droughts, namely their occurrence and their impact on human society (Glantz, 1994). Depending on hydroclimatic conditions, a meteorological drought is often defined as occurring when rainfall is 1–2 standard deviations below the long-term average. Here we will define a meteorological drought simply as occurring when the cumulative rainfall over a growing season in a certain ecosystem is lower than the minimum green water requirement to sustain existing vegetation in that system throughout a growing cycle from seed to grain or fruit.

A meteorological drought is a naturally occurring phenomenon. Human societies and natural ecosystems have adapted and developed social and ecological resilience to cope with meteorological droughts over millennia. Ecological adaptations include the distance between acacias in parkland savannas, and the vegetation bands in the tiger bush formations in Australia and West Africa. Social adaptations to meteorological droughts are found in all human savanna societies. We find examples of social resilience to cope with droughts in the Bible, where Joseph advises the Pharaoh of Egypt to store the grain from seven wet years to bridge predicted years of crop failure during the following seven drought years. This strategy of cereal banks to cushion the effects of natural climatic shocks was, until recently, an integral part of farming societies in the Sahel. As shown by Rockström and Ada (1993) this coping mechanism of storing grain from wet years to bridge drought years has collapsed over the last hundred years from the pressure of population growth, resulting in the progressive degradation of the farming.

Similarly, livestock in semi-arid savanna societies have functioned as walking bank accounts or as an insurance mechanism; they are there to be transformed into cash and food during years of water scarcity. As indicated above, even if meteorological droughts can be more or less determined in hydrological terms, their impact on humans must be analysed from a social perspective. As pointed out by Glantz (1994), droughts by themselves seldom lead to famines. Instead, drought is a trigger that can tip a society with low social and ecological resilience into famine-like conditions once it occurs.

Meteorological droughts seem to occur in natural cycles, often over several consecutive years. Furthermore, there is a growing concern at present over the risk of their occurring more frequently due to climate change. The overall message here is that meteorological droughts in themselves are not the primary hydroclimatic problem of the savannas. In the mid-1980s Bradford Morse, former Administrator of the United Nations Development Programme (UNDP) stated that: 'drought itself is not the fundamental problem in sub-Saharan Africa ... the present drought, however, intensified the interaction of the factors impeding development in Africa; it has laid bare the African development crisis' (Glantz, 1994, p12).

The fundamental ecohydrological challenge in dealing with meteorological droughts is to maximize ecological and social resilience to cope with them, and to adopt land management strategies that reduce the occurrence of agricultural droughts and assist in drought-proofing agriculture (Chapter 8).

Human-induced or agricultural droughts

A human-induced drought occurs when land degradation changes rainfall partitioning to the extent that the soil moisture available to plants drops below the minimum green water requirement to carry a plant through a whole growth cycle. Human-induced droughts are generally defined as agricultural droughts because they most often occur (or rather, are most often experienced by humans) on farmland. However, drought conditions can also occur in catchments and river basins where factors other than cultivation or grazing have altered partitioning points in the water balance.

There is very little documentation on the occurrence of agricultural droughts. An example, though, is the ecological disaster during the 1930s Dust Bowl years in the US, which was attributed to meteorological drought conditions. It was later reassessed, relating the drought-like conditions not only to low rainfall but also to disastrous erosion problems attributed to overexploitation of land. Intensive disc ploughing and a lack of soil conservation methods caused wind and water erosion. Aggravated further by drought conditions, the mismanagement of crop land resulted in extensive land degradation and caused a progressive shift in rainfall partitioning towards more storm surface runoff. This resulted in severe water stress and an agricultural drought due to reduced crop water availability in the soil.

The analysis of the on-farm water balance can be used as a measure of agricultural drought occurrence. At least 250–350 mm of the soil moisture available to plants for most food crops in savanna agro-ecosystems is required to enable an absolute minimum grain harvest. For a semi-arid savanna receiving 500 mm of seasonal rainfall, an agricultural drought would thus occur when 30–50 per cent of the rainfall was 'lost' to the roots as surface runoff and percolation. As shown earlier in this chapter, runoff flow of 25–30 per cent of rainfall is not unusual, and significant amounts of water percolate down to the groundwater even in savannas. The result is a high incidence of agricultural droughts.

Dry spells

As shown earlier, savanna rainfall is highly erratic, and most rain falls as intensive convective storms with high rainfall intensity and extreme spatial and temporal rainfall variability. The result is a high risk of intra-seasonal dry spells. Dry spells are short periods of no rainfall, often not more than 2–4 weeks long, causing water stress in plants and affecting growth.

The frequent occurrence of dry spells affecting crop growth, but not necessarily total seasonal or annual rainfall, is illustrated in Figure 6.5 for a semi-arid parkland savanna agro-ecosystem in the Sahel (Niger). Over three rainy seasons (1994–96) pearl millet, the staple food crop in the region, was seriously hit by dry spells. Still, seasonal rainfall was close to the long-term average of 560 mm, in the 490–600 mm range. The dry spells were never longer than four weeks, and hit the crop during germination and early vegetative growth in 1994, during grain filling in 1995, and during flowering in 1996. Crop yields over those three years were extremely low, ranging from 350 to 420 kg grain per hectare. The lowest yield was experienced in 1996 when the dry spell occurred during flowering, which is the crop development stage most sensitive to water stress. The observations coincide with the average yield levels experienced by smallholder farmers in the semi-arid savanna region of the Sahel, where rainfed farming is practised without external fertilization.

The frequent occurrence of dry spells in the savanna zone means that the poor distribution of rainfall over time constitutes a more common cause for crop yield reductions than meteorological droughts. An important point here is that dry spells cause water scarcity without necessarily causing reductions in seasonal or annual rainfall. Meteorological droughts, on the other hand, are always manifested as serious reductions in seasonal or annual rainfall that result in absolute water scarcity due to low cumulative annual rainfall. From the perspective of agricultural water management, an important difference between meteorological droughts and dry spells is therefore that, during a drought, there is not enough water to produce a crop, while in a rainy season subject to dry spells, there is enough water but it is not available at the right time.

From a water management perspective the implication is that while meteorological droughts are impossible to manage, dry spells can be managed. This is why it is important to distinguish between droughts and dry spells.

A dry spell occurs as short periods of water stress, often only a couple of weeks long, during crop growth. Such short periods of water stress can have a serious effect on crop yields if they occur during water-sensitive development stages such as during flowering or yield formation (Rockström and de Rouw, 1997). If actual green water flow is only

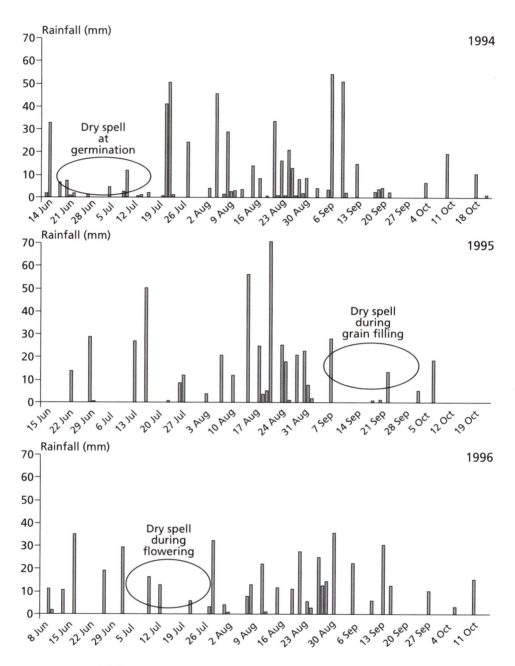

Note: Average rainfall in this parkland savanna is 560 mm. Each rainy season was hit by a dry spell, during germination and early vegetative phase in 1994, during grain filling in 1995, and during flowering in 1996. Crop growth was seriously affected. Still, the seasonal rainfall over this period was close to the average, ranging from 490 to 600 mm.

Figure 6.5 *Dry spell occurrence in a semi-arid savanna agro-ecosystem in Niger (1994–1996)*

half the maximum green water flow, yields will drop by at least an equal relative amount and be reduced to half the maximum yield. When plant water uptake falls to 70 per cent of maximum uptake, plant growth is affected due to soil moisture stress. Research from several semi-arid tropical regions shows that the occurrence of meteorological dry spells far exceeds the occurrence of meteorological droughts. Based on research in East Africa, Stewart (1988) indicated that severe crop reductions caused by a dry spell occur 1–2 out of 5 years, while Sivakumar (1992) showed that the frequent occurrence of seasonal dry spells with a length of 10–15 days were independent of long-term seasonal averages, ranging from 200 to 1200 mm in West Africa.

Besides meteorological dry spells, there may also be agricultural dry spells, which are even more common. They are due to the poor rainfall partitioning that causes short periods of plant water stress. For a maize crop on a clay soil in the Machakos district of Kenya, dry spells that exceeded 10 days occurred in 67–80 per cent of the rainy seasons from 1977 to 1998. For a maize crop on a sandy soil in the same region, dry spells occurred 90–100 per cent of the rainy seasons (Barron et al, 2003).

The impact of water stress caused by dry spells on plant growth and final yield will vary depending on the severity and timing of the dry spell. A prolonged dry spell occurring during flowering can result in complete crop failure, while a short dry spell during early vegetative growth may result in only a very limited effect on the final yield. The crop may be able to compensate for a reduction of the number of plants caused by an early season dry spell with a larger number of panicles and higher panicle weight during later growth stages.

The impact of dry spells on plant physiology is, however, only one factor affecting overall performance of a farming system. The risk of crop reductions and crop failures caused by dry spells also affect farmers' risk perceptions, which in turn form the basis for decisions on investments in labour, fertilization, and pest and crop management.

Coping with droughts and dry spells

The above indicates that a key to improved water productivity in rainfed agriculture in semi-arid and dry sub-humid tropical environments is to mitigate intra-seasonal dry spells. The distinction between meteorological and human-induced droughts and dry spells is necessary not only to understand the ecohydrological challenges and opportunities in the savanna, but also to make wise choices in coping with droughts and dry spells. The matrix in Figure 6.6 summarizes the discussions in this chapter by giving a conceptual framework to distinguish between man-induced and natural droughts and dry spells. The matrix shows the different types of water scarcity, their occurrence and impact on agriculture.

Most of our development attention about water scarcity is on drought management (shaded cell in Figure 6.6). It is not very surprising that many efforts in droughtproofing and drought mitigation have failed – after all, what can really be done? Coping with meteorological droughts must foremost and exclusively deal with social preparedness and coping mechanisms – by assuring that there are institutions, human capacities and capital to bridge meteorological drought with the least human suffering and a minimum of ecological degradation. This last issue is important. The human response to a cycle of meteorological drought years is often increased human pressure on vulnerable

	Dry spell	Drought
Meteorological	*Occurrence:* [2/3 years] Two out of three years *Impact:* Yield reduction *Cause:* Rainfall deficit of 2–5 weeks periods during crop growth	*Occurrence:* [1/10 years] One year out of ten *Impact:* Complete crop failure *Cause:* Seasonal rainfall below minimum seasonal plant water requirement
Agricultural	*Occurrence:* [>2/3 years] > two out of three years *Impact:* Yield reduction/complete crop failure *Cause:* Poor rainfall partitioning leads to low plant water availability Poor plant water uptake capacity	*Occurrence:* [>1/10 years] > one out of ten years *Impact:* Complete crop failure *Cause:* Poor rainfall partitioning leads to seasonal soil moisture deficit to produce harvest

Note: Grey indicates current focus.

Figure 6.6 *Types of water scarcity and underlying causes: distinction between meteorological and human-induced droughts and dry spells*

ecosystems that have become even more vulnerable under the impacts of drought. The first move by a desperate population is to survive on the existing local natural resources. But the marginal vegetation may already be under pressure from grazing, deforestation and serious water stress. The human pressure on a natural resource base, which, due to drought, is at its most vulnerable stage, is thus at a high when it should be at an absolute low to ensure maximum environmental conservation and to give ecological drought resilience a chance to cope with the natural calamity. This was shown clearly for grassland savannas in the Sahel in the mid-1980s. The human response to the consecutive drought years in 1982–84 was a desperate search for food and fodder in marginal grassland savannas. The human pressure increased dramatically when the ecosystem was seriously affected by the prolonged drought and in its most vulnerable condition. The result was severe land degradation, which still persists (Glantz, 1994).

The primary human option is to accept droughts and adapt to them. The options of doing the reverse – mitigating droughts by adapting them to our management priorities – have a very limited likelihood of success. This does not apply to dry spells, and it applies only to some extent to agricultural droughts. However, dry spells are manageable. Surprisingly little attention is given to mitigating dry spells, despite the fact that we can actually deal with them and that we know their serious implications for crop growth.

Dry spells do not occur because there is an absolute lack of water, either from rainfall or in terms of soil moisture. They occur because there is a deficit of water during one part of the plant growth season. Excess water received earlier during the rainy season can compensate for this deficit through the application of different water-harvesting practices (Chapter 8). Agricultural dry spells, and to some extent agricultural droughts, can be managed, as indicated above, through improved crop, soil and water management.

Summary

The focus in this chapter was a close look at a global ecohydrological hotspot in terms of the future challenges to balance water for humans and nature. Although the semi-arid and dry sub-humid tropics are ecosystems characterized by high water-related vulnerability, yet they have the most exigent combination of rapid population growth, poverty, and land use that humans depend on for life support.

We argue that the label 'marginal drylands' often given to semi-arid and dry sub-humid tropical landscape is misleading. Instead, the ecological term 'savanna' should be used in order to better reflect the fact that 'drylands' are not as dry as often perceived. Savannas cover almost 40 per cent of the world's land surface and have, for example in sub-Saharan Africa, an equal portion of the population. Savannas are characterized by a sharp divide between wet and dry periods of the year. This means the perennial life forms have adapted to survive the long dry seasons, while annual life forms generally depend on the wet rainy seasons. The ecohydrological challenge in savannas is not particulary related to lack of water. Rather, the main challenges are adapting to the huge fluctuations of rainfall over time and space, and adapting to the high evaporative demand of the atmosphere.

Water is the primary factor limiting biological life on the savanna, and it has shaped the ecological climax accordingly. While the ecological resilience is inherently low in many savanna environments, human pressure has rendered the ecosystem even more vulnerable through intensive cultivation, grazing and deforestation. The fragile savanna has become more vulnerable even to small environmental shocks. Together with an erosion of social resilience the result over the last century has been disproportionate human suffering compared to the relatively moderate environmental shocks that caused the social disasters. The ecohydrological challenge of the savanna is immense, given the fact that food production has to more than double there over the next generation in order to keep pace with population growth. Enabling such a development while securing ecosystem services is a formidable task.

There is no such thing as average rainfall on the savanna. Unreliable and high intensity rainfall concentrated during short rainy seasons means that the ecohydrological predicament on the savanna is less related to low annual rainfall and more related to a complex set of different ecological causes of water scarcity. A thirsty atmosphere and rainfall concentrated over three to seven months of the year determines the length of the growing period (water scarcity mode A), while the large rainfall variability results in a frequent occurrence of meteorological droughts and dry spells (mode B). Human-induced land degradation, often defined as desertification in its most severe form, causes green water scarcity in the root zone due to poor rainfall partitioning (water scarcity mode C). Finally, population pressure on finite freshwater resources results in increased water crowding, exposing blue water scarcity (mode D).

Special attention is given to sub-Saharan Africa, where the ecohydrological challenges in savanna agro-ecosystems are extensive, both in terms of dealing with inherently vulnerable ecosystems and in facing a future based on a landscape scarred by a recent history of erosion and social and ecological resilience. As an ecohydrological entry point to savanna management, we have distinguished between natural and man-induced droughts and dry spells. The focus is generally on meteorological droughts, which are naturally occurring and form an integral part of the savanna ecology. On the other hand, agricultural droughts occur in savannas as a result of severe deterioration of soil and vegetation. This has the effect of causing severe scarcity of green water to sustain plant growth. Food crops do not fail due to lack of rainfall but because of lack of soil moisture. Dry spells are short periods of water stress during plant growth, which negatively affect final yields. They are extremely common on the savanna, often occurring every rainy season. If they occur during growth phases sensitive to water stress, such as flowering, dry spells may result in complete crop failure. Dry spells are not only very common; they also affect risk perceptions among farmers. Rain, even though not necessarily being the ultimate limiting factor for crop growth, is the only completely random growth factor. This is what makes water the entry point for upgrading food production in savanna agro-ecosystems.

The water balance is a good indicator of savanna resilience, and several examples for savanna agro-ecosystems show that only a small fraction of rainfall is actually used as productive green water flow. Seeking ways of increasing the amount of productive green water flow in savanna agriculture may create an ecohydrological opportunity to improve the productivity of savanna agriculture without jeopardizing the water flows, which sustain ecosystems. The focus of the next chapter is on how to feed a growing population in savanna ecosystems that are prone to water scarcity while securing water flows to sustain ecosystems.

Chapter 7

Water Perspectives on Feeding Humanity

Feeding future populations requires an unprecedented increase in agricultural productivity – unprecedented both in magnitude and in scope. The challenge is to generate more food for vulnerable societies and do it in balance with ecological functions in vulnerable ecosystems.

More Crop per Drop

Water for food accounts for up to 95 per cent of the direct per capita fresh water needs (see Chapter 4). This means that the most urgent freshwater challenge is to identify strategies to feed the additional population of tomorrow and to decrease malnutrition. At the same time it is necessary to safeguard water flow to sustain ecosystem services.

Farmers produce food. The vast majority of farmers, both in terms of area under agriculture and numbers of people living by farming, are found in tropical developing countries. Most are poor, small-scale farmers with limited access to resources and external inputs. These smallholder farmers carry out 60 per cent of global agriculture. The smallholder sector as a whole is responsible for 80 per cent of agricultural production in developing countries, indicating their key role in local food and livelihood security (Cosgrove and Rijsberman, 2000).

Nowhere is this challenge of balancing water for food and water for nature as large as in the savanna ecosystems. This is due to a concentration of interacting factors and processes such as harsh water conditions, high environmental vulnerability, extensive poverty and rapid population growth. We will therefore continue to focus on the semi-arid and dry sub-humid tropics of the world.

Three main questions

The efforts to achieve sustainable freshwater management raise three main questions:

- First, how much water will be needed to produce food in the future?
- Second, which water will be used to produce food – in other words, what is the relative role of irrigation dependent on blue water versus rainfed agriculture dependent on green water?
- Third, how far can improvements in water productivity (more crop per drop) go to reduce the necessity of trade-offs between agriculture and ecosystems?

In this chapter we will focus on the last two questions. The first question is addressed in chapters 3 and 4 and will reappear in chapters 9 and 10, with a focus on implications for ecohydrological landscape management.

Population growth differs enormously between regions. For example, towards 2030, East Asia will reach zero population growth, while sub-Saharan Africa will maintain a growth rate of 2 per cent per year, despite the drastic deceleration of rural growth rates linked to urbanization,[1] and to the HIV/AIDS pandemic (UN, 2003). Still, by 2050, every second baby will be born in sub-Saharan Africa. In 2020, 40 per cent of the world population will live in South Asia and sub-Saharan Africa (Conway, 1997), the two regions subject to the greatest challenges in terms of poverty, malnourishment and water-related constraints.

Added to this immense challenge are the estimated 800 million people in poor developing countries in the tropics now suffering from malnourishment (FAO, 1999). While over the last 30 years the world average calorie intake has increased by almost 20 per cent, 33 countries still have a calorie consumption of under 2200 kcal/person/day. Most of these countries are in sub-Saharan Africa (FAO, 2003).

Even without considering the water requirements, there are deep concerns about the chances or probability of achieving food security for a population of 9 billion people 50 years from now.[2] In 1970, Norman Borlaug, Nobel Prize laureate and the father of the Green Revolution, said that it only solved momentary problems prevailing at the time, and that he had given the leaders of the world 30 years to find solutions to the population problem. In 1992 he added that:

> *Today, they have wasted 22 years during which they did not even discuss the matter. With only a few years left before it will be too late, I warn them: There will not be another Green Revolution.*
>
> Gillard, 2002, citing Cousteau, 1992.

Population growth and improvements in nutrition put a formidable pressure on future food needs.[3] For world cereals, the largest world food commodity, production to meet the demand by 2030 must increase by almost 1 billion tonnes, up from the current level of 1.84 billion tonnes (FAO, 2002). This implies an average growth rate of 2 per cent per annum, which is higher than the preceding three decades. For the regions of the world with most rapid growth of demand, the growth has to be higher even than the impressive growth rates achieved during the Green Revolution of the late 1960s and 1970s.

This huge increase in food production would achieve three out of four requirements: it would feed the additional population, raise nutrition levels from an average of 2600 kcal to 3000 kcal per person and day, and reduce the number of malnourished from 800 to 400 million people. The fourth challenge would remain: to secure an adequate diet for the 400 million people that would still suffer from malnutrition in 2030.

Historical evidence shows that agriculture has been able in the past to produce more than a sufficient amount of food to meet the growing demand of the world population. It is dangerous, however, to extrapolate future achievements due to productivity increases, based on past success. The bulk of food production increase in sub-Saharan Africa over the last 30 years has occurred through expansion of agricultural land. In view of decreasing arable land and freshwater resources per capita, and allowing for the fact that all the best farmland is already under production, the possibility of repeating past production trends is impossibly optimistic.

Three main ways of increasing production

There are three ways to increase crop food production: expand the cultivated land; increase cropping intensity and the number of harvests over time; and improve yields of grain or biomass per unit land. These three means are important not only to understand agricultural development but also to deal with natural resource use.

The first way, expansion of cultivated land, involves a shift in use of freshwater from one ecosystem, perhaps a forest, wetland or grassland, to another ecosystem, for example, agriculture. The expansion may not necessarily involve a shift in the volume of consumptive water use. It may even involve a reduction, as in the case of a shift from a highly transpiring forest to annual crops. It will, nevertheless, involve a shift of ecological water functions to production of an ecosystem good, namely food, on cultivated land.

In terms of the second way to increase food production, cropping intensities have increased progressively over the last century in all farming systems of the world. Population growth has forced a change from shifting cultivation systems based on long fallows to today's predominant system of continuous cultivation. Where environmental conditions permit and where irrigation is possible, several crops per year are often harvested. From a water perspective, increased cropping intensity on cultivated land will generally not have a large effect on ecological functions. It will, however, always require additional fresh water, which may affect the ecosystems that depend on that water.

The third way of producing more food is by increasing yield. This means that more food is produced per unit of soil or water. This is the strategy with the least impact on water-dependent ecosystems. An increased yield would result in more consumptive green water use, but would involve a much lower shift in water flows compared to a shift from one land use to another, or a shift in cropping intensity. From an ecohydrological perspective the minimum impact on freshwater-dependent ecosystems is therefore achieved if food production is attained through yield increases. Increasing cropping intensity is second best, and area expansion is the worst ecohydrological option. Water quality implications of land use changes, however, are also important. Obviously, this ranking assumes that yield increases are achieved through sustainable management changes, which do not result in water quality deterioration.[4]

The analysis above clearly indicates the immense food challenge that faces mankind over the next 50 years. The increase in demand for food will surpass the situation 40 years ago when the Green Revolution, based on water pumps, fertilizers, pesticides and improved crop varieties, lifted large parts of South Asia out of the risk of starvation. The starting point is, however, more precarious today. Less land is available for agriculture, and today we understand that most fresh water is already carrying out a 'job', for humans and for nature, and that each shift in water flow in favour of agriculture is a service lost from nature.

Call for more crop per drop

Behind every kg of food, 1000–3000 litres of freshwater are hidden. Producing 1 billion tonnes more of cereal food, increasing production of livestock and other foods such as vegetables, oil crops, pulses, roots and tubers, will require huge volumes of additional consumptive green water flow. Nowhere is the challenge of achieving the required increase in food production as large as in the regions of the world where four interacting processes coincide: rapid growth of population; the various poverty aspects, such as low purchasing power, poor access to land and low performing land management, which in turn causes a feeling of despair due to hunger; and finally water scarcity. These factors all coincide in the semi-arid and dry sub-humid savanna agro-ecosystems of the world.

Among water professionals the focus on agricultural productivity has been accompanied simultaneously by an increased attention to water productivity. The second World Water Forum in The Hague in 2000 resulted in a new call for water productivity increases. The production of more crops per drop was to be a freshwater strategy to achieve the production of more food for expanding populations while limiting freshwater trade-offs with water-dependent ecosystems (Cosgrove and Rijsberman, 2000). In his speech to the Millennium Conference 2000, Kofi Annan, the Secretary General of the United Nations, underlined the realization of the freshwater challenge lying ahead with regards to food:

> *We need a blue revolution in agriculture that focuses on increasing productivity per unit water – more crop per drop.*
>
> Kofi Annan, Secretary General of the United Nations

Can Irrigation Expansion Solve the Food Challenge?

The Green Revolution involved the large-scale adoption of new high-yielding crop varieties primarily of rice and maize, which needed technical inputs such as fertilizers and pesticides as well as a reliable supply of water to the crop. During the peak of the Green Revolution (1967–1982) average growth rates of cereal yields attained an impressive 2.9 per cent per year. This was achieved through blue water supply for irrigation on all scales, from the adoption of small petrol pumps to lift water from rivers and wells to large-scale irrigation schemes. Without the development of affordable small hand pumps, the Green Revolution in India and parts of South Asia would never have materialized. In a sense, the Green Revolution was thus a blue revolution, because each increase in crop yields required more consumptive crop water use, and a secured water supply functioned as an important incentive for investments in the new crop varieties and methods.

Today, the world is confronted with a new food challenge, at least as large as the one facing Asia in the 1960s. The challenge is to double food yields in one generation, primarily in the savannas of sub-Saharan Africa and Southeast Asia. Is this realistic, and if so, how will it happen, and what are the ecohydrological implications?

Remaining degrees of freedom

Irrespective of opinion on irrigation development, it is clear that the food challenge facing developing countries is so large that all efforts have to be made to exploit every possible means of feeding tomorrow's world population. At present, irrigation plays, and will continue to play, an absolutely crucial role in this respect. In many arid and dry semi-arid regions, irrigation is the only means by which food security can be achieved. We should not forget that half the world's irrigation water is used for paddy rice, predominantly among small-scale farmers in South and East Asia. These represent a very large portion of food consumers in the world. Optimistic outlooks on irrigation (for example, from the UN FAO, 2002) suggest that irrigation will account for almost 40 per cent of farmland expansion from 1995–2030, and between 50 and 60 per cent of the food production increase. In 2030, half of all food and two-thirds of all cereals is expected to originate from irrigated agriculture.

This said, the question still arises: is it realistic to rely so heavily on irrigation as the panacea to feed the future population in developing countries? Put in another way, is a new blue revolution realistic?

We have already seen that the degrees of freedom in increasing human blue water withdrawals are limited by the ceiling of realistic withdrawals of 12,500 km³/year. To this constraint should be added the requirement of securing blue water flow for ecological functions in in-stream aquatic ecosystems. As mentioned in Chapter 4, despite the limited present knowledge of how much water would be required for this, it has been suggested that 40 per cent of the stable runoff flow should be secured. This would correspond to 5,000 km³/year. Present global withdrawals amount to 4000 km³/year, leaving us with a remaining blue water flow of 3500 km³/year. This is the additional blue water flow that can be theoretically appropriated in the future.

In Chapter 3 we also estimated that based on an optimistic projection of irrigation development, the increase in consumptive blue water use could amount to about 600 km³/year from 2000 to 2050, while water productivity improvements may contribute with 200 km³/year to global water needs, ie a total irrigation contribution of 800 km³/year. We will use this figure, which is a contribution to agricultural water needs, as a basis in further analyses in this book. An increase of 600 km³/year in consumptive water use by 2050 coincides with other optimistic outlooks on irrigation, which, for example, suggest a mere 15–20 per cent increase in irrigation water withdrawals by 2025, as a result of efficiency improvements and productivity growth of irrigated crops (Hofwegen and Svendsen, 2000, p36). This would translate to an increase in consumptive use of 260–300 km³/year, or a withdrawal increase of 375–500 km³/year by 2025. Similarly, UNFAO in its optimistic irrigation development scenarios estimates that withdrawals will increase by only 220 km³/year, up from 1840 km³/year to 2060 km³/year. Overly optimistic assumptions for improved irrigation efficiency explain this low figure. An increase of blue water use in irrigation of 600 km³/year on a global scale seems achievable at first glance compared to the 3500 km³/year that is accessible, and would translate into a major contribution to the food security of future populations.

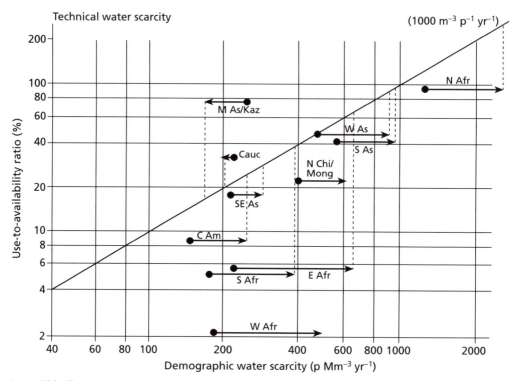

Note: This diagram assumes semi-arid regions secure a per capita blue water withdrawal of 1000 m³/person/year. The vertical axis shows the water withdrawal as a percentage of total water availability. The horizontal axis shows the demographic water scarcity (people per 1 million cubic meters of annually recharged blue water).

Source: Modified from Falkenmark, 1997

Figure 7.1 *Prospects for food self-sufficiency based on a blue water future for the semi-arid regions of the world*

Food self-sufficiency supported by irrigation is far from realistic

A global analysis, however, tells us very little of the potential, in view of the enormous variation between different regions, countries and locations. Falkenmark (1997) studied the validity of food self-sufficiency based on irrigation in regions with semi-arid climates. She assumed that in tropical countries a withdrawal to an availability ratio of 50 per cent constitutes the actual upper limit, due mainly to large evaporation losses from surface water reservoirs. However, it was also assumed that the societies in Africa and Asia within the next 25 years would scarcely be able to achieve more than a 25 per cent mobilization increase of blue water resource.

Figure 7.1 shows the increase needed in blue water mobilization up to 2025, for ten of the world's regions with a semi-arid climate that were discussed in Chapter 5 (see Figure 5.8). The arrows indicate the change in demographic water scarcity over the period 1995 to 2025 – that is, the forced shift of different regions as a result of population growth. The diagonal line indicates an assumed blue water requirement of

1000 m³/person/year (for all activities by humans directly using blue water), which is a fairly typical level of water withdrawal in irrigated countries. The dashed line between the arrow tip (situation 2025) and the diagonal line indicates the shift required, in terms of increased (or for some regions decreased) water withdrawal.

For Southeast Asia it seems possible to satisfy the increased blue water requirement resulting from population growth by increased water development and by a move from an 18 per cent withdrawal ratio to a level close to 25 per cent in 2025. Water saving makes the situation manageable in Middle Asia/Kazakhstan and the Caucasus. In contrast, based on the assumption of continued food self-sufficiency demands, the water requirements in Southern Africa, West Africa, East Africa and North China are rising too fast for society to cope. These regions will have a population of approximately 1.7 billion people in 2025, or 20 per cent of the world's population. The most critical belt is North Africa, West Asia and South Asia, where increased blue water withdrawals to meet food requirements will be most difficult, if not impossible, over the next generation. This suggests that approximately half the population of Africa and Asia will already be facing blue water scarcity in 2025. These regions with blue water scarcity are also included in the regions identified earlier in this chapter as those facing the most serious future challenges in terms of poverty, population growth and food requirements.

The condition of water scarcity in the critical regions is linked either to a substantial present withdrawal (for example, North Africa and West Asia), or to a low coping capability that will severely limit the prospects for a rapid increase of withdrawals (for example, sub-Saharan Africa). For the regions presently with high withdrawals, every additional increase is very expensive and environmentally sensitive. For sub-Saharan Africa, it is difficult to envisage a development at the extremely rapid pace required. Furthermore, the ecological consequences of water resources development will limit the expansion potential. A safe conclusion, from an ecohydrological perspective, is that food self-sufficiency based on irrigation will be difficult to achieve on a regional, country or river basin scale.

Potential to Increase Rainfed Production

The necessary increase in agricultural productivity is unprecedented in relation to the Green Revolution, which increased production of wheat, maize and rice primarily in Asia and Latin America. Now, a doubling of food production in one generation would have to occur in large parts of Asia, Latin America as well as in sub-Saharan Africa. This is an immense challenge, especially in view of the present discouraging statistics from sub-Saharan Africa that reflect a continent that has still to experience its first green revolution.

A future even more challenging than the last Green Revolution

The challenge now is also different in character from the Green Revolution, which was based on the wide promotion of a universal agricultural package and founded on successful crop breeding of rice, wheat and maize in international agricultural research institutes (IRRI the Institute Rice Research Institute in the Phillipines, and CIMMYT, Centro Internacional de Majoramiento de Maiz y Trigo, Mexico). Furthermore, the precondition for success was fertile soils with a stable and secured water supply, because such were the conditions on experimental stations where the new crop varieties had been developed in the first place. According to Conway (1997), writing about the urgent need for a second Green Revolution, the 'new' revolution cannot simply reflect the successes of the first event. Instead a second Green Revolution must:

- be achieved under highly diverse conditions in terms of soil and water variability;
- be adoptable by resource poor farmers;
- be environmentally sustainable.

This requires a stronger on-farm focus in research and development, and a shift from designing high-yielding packages that suit medium- to high-potential agricultural conditions, toward designing site-adapted strategies that suit smallholders who have poor resources, less fertile soils and live in hazardous climates. The Green Revolution was an immense achievement. The challenge ahead clearly shows that another will be even more difficult. The challenge facing mankind now lies, using the terminology of Chambers et al (1989) and Pretty (1995), in the 'pre-modern' agricultural systems of the world[5] – in agricultural systems of the world where former efforts have failed. Moreover, this must happen now, 30 years after the first Green Revolution, when population has roughly doubled. Added to this is the realization, which was not there in the 1960s, that simultaneous care for the environment is critical for our own life support.

Present yield gap

The need to adjust the focus of agricultural development to on-farm conditions is evident from the yield gap between the maximum yields attained in research stations and the actual yields experienced among farmers. The conceptual difference between theoretical yields, maximum yields, achievable yields on-farm, and actual yields, is shown in Figure 7.2.

The potential yield for a given crop and hydroclimate is determined by climatic factors, primarily radiation and temperature (de Wit, 1958). For a maize crop, the present potential yield limit is in the order of 20 tonnes of grain per hectare. This yield level is theoretical only. On-station research yields can be seen as representing what can be produced given local soil conditions and climatic variability. However, farmers generally do not harvest maximum yields. What is possible to produce on-farm is affected by the level of land degradation, which is generally much higher than on research stations where soils are well drained, fertile and subject only to limited erosion problems.

The farmers' reality is also influenced by other constraints such as labour shortage, insecure land ownership, capital constraints, poorly developed infrastructure and markets, and limitation in human capacities. All these factors influence how farming is done, in terms of timing of operations, effectiveness of farm operations such as weeding, and pest management, investments in fertilizers and pesticides, use of improved crop varieties, and water management. What will finally be produced in the

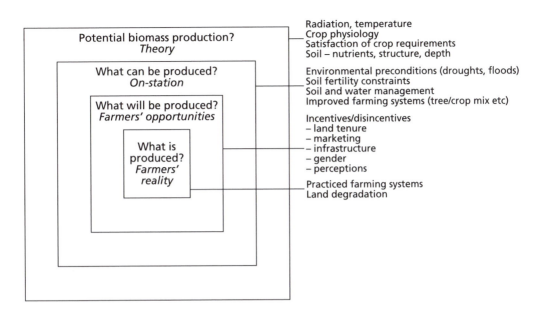

Figure 7.2 *Conceptual distinction and factors determining the difference between potential yields, attainable yields (on-station yields), yield levels possible to achieve on-farm, and the actual yields experienced on farmers' fields*

farmers' fields is thus greatly affected by social, economic and institutional conditions. The yield gap is illustrated in Figure 7.3 for semi-arid savanna agro-ecosystems in countries in Eastern and Southern Africa. The horisontal line shows the average grain yield for on-farm semi-arid rainfed farming in sub-Saharan Africa. Under the same hydroclimatic conditions, on-station yield levels of maize, the staple grain, reach between 5 and 6 tonnes of grain per hectare. This can be seen as the maximum attainable yield given local environmental conditions and using farm operations similar to on-farm conditions, but applying better timing of operations and higher levels of fertilization and pest management, as well as improved crop varieties. Notably, commercial farmers under similar hydroclimatic conditions generally operate at much higher yield levels, around 7–8 t/ha, with yields levels of 10 t/ha of rainfed semi-arid maize being common under conservation tillage in Zimbabwe (Brian Oldrieve, personal communication, 1998). Reported on-farm yields, from government statistics, generally range between 1 and 2 t/ha, reflecting the 'one-tonne agriculture' presently operating in large parts of savanna agro-ecosystems of sub-Saharan Africa.

However, poor smallholder farmers making their living from <5 ha rainfed farms on the savanna often have even lower actual grain yields. Observed on-farm yields are very low, often fluctuating around an average of 0.5 t/ha. These are extremely low grain yields; ten times lower than the maximum attainable from on-station yields. In other words, the yield gap is dramatic.

It remains dramatic even if a degree of caution is required when assessing the differences in Figure 7.3, although the agro-ecological conditions are not directly comparable between smallholder farmers and commercial farms. For example, in

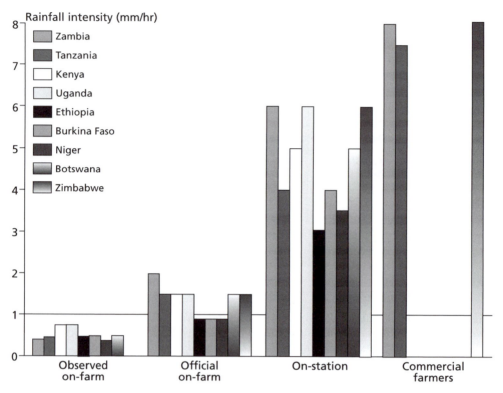

Note: The horizontal line is the average yield level for savanna rainfed agriculture in sub-Saharan Africa. Official on-farm yields originate from government statistics, while observed on-farm yields originate from the authors' own observations among individual farmers in the indicated countries. Yields from commercial farmers originate from large-scale farms practising intensive management and conservation tillage techniques.

Figure 7.3 *Yield gap between actual on-farm yields and maximum yields for staple grains cultivated in rainfed savanna agro-ecosystems: Eastern and Southern Africa*

Zimbabwe, under similar hydroclimatic conditions, the high-potential farmland has, until recently, been cultivated by commercial farmers, while the low productive soils have been in the hands of smallholder farmers. Still, the yield gap is far too large to be explained only by differences in soil conditions.[6]

As shown above, the causes underlying the gap between farmers' yields and maximum achievable yields are complex and related to both social and biophysical factors.[7] It is beyond the scope of this book to discuss all these interlinked factors in any detail. We simply conclude here that an aggregate manifestation of the state of affairs with regard to these complex social driving forces is the actual way by which a farmer manages his or her land. From an agricultural perspective, the impact of social factors has consequences on land management, which are contained on the farm or within the boundaries of a farming system. From an ecohydrological perspective, and especially for tropical farming systems, the impact of social factors on land use is manifested in the on-farm partitioning of rainfall.

Table 7.1 *Biophysical deficiencies affecting yield levels*

Biophysical deficiency	Factors	Manifestation	Hydrological impact	Management
Hydro-climatic deficiency	Seasonal rainfall Rainfall variability in space and time Potential evaporation	Extreme meteorological events: droughts floods dry spell	Low plant available soil moisture	–
Soil deficiency	Soil texture Soil structure Root depth Slope Soil chemical properties	Soil crusting Soil compaction Low water-holding capacity Low fertile soils Contaminated soil	Low plant available soil moisture and low plant water uptake capacity	Tillage Biological soil management
Plant deficiency	Soil nutrient availability Crop Pests and disease	Weak roots Poorly developed canopy	Low plant water uptake capacity	Crop management

Three biophysical deficiencies

The focus is here on the biophysical factors behind the yield gaps. The question raised at this point is what ecohydrological factors can explain the large gap between farmers' yields and attainable yields? The biophysical determinants of crop yields can be divided according to three agro-hydrological deficiencies that contribute to yield reductions (Rockström and Falkenmark, 2000) (Table 7.1).

Hydroclimatic deficiencies set the limits for potential yields, and are manifested as low cumulative rainfall, meteorological droughts and dry spells. Soil deficiencies are manifested by low soil infiltrability and poor water-holding capacity of the soil. Due to weakly developed roots and canopies, plant deficiencies are manifested by poor plant water uptake capacity, which is in turn related to compaction and soil nutrient deficiencies.

As seen in Table 7.1, soil and plant deficiencies are a result of both biophysical parameters, such as soil and plant properties, and of social factors that can have a major impact on land-use management. Two contrasting examples of farming systems from Kenya and Ethiopia may illustrate the links between biophysical deficiencies and social factors that affect yield gaps.

The semi-arid district of Machakos in Kenya has a high population pressure. A good land security situation has made farmers widely adopt management practices that reduce soil and plant deficiencies. Capacity building among farmers and closeness to markets (Machakos is only 100 km from Nairobi, the capital of Kenya) has resulted in intensified agricultural practices.[8] Land degradation has been avoided through the adoption of soil and water conservation methods and diversification of production systems. The result is a farming system that, despite a fivefold increase of the population between 1930 and 1990, has been able to keep soil and plant deficiency at bay (Tiffen et al, 1994).

Northern Ethiopia presents several examples of the impact on soil and plant deficiencies during extended periods of conflict and land insecurity. From the 1950s until the late 1980s (with certain periods of positive developments in between), decades of turbulent conflict and politically organized relocation of people and confiscation of land resulted in large-scale deforestation and degradation of crop and grazing land. Extreme events of storm runoff in the steep highland regions, possibly reinforced by extensive deforestation, still cause complete loss of arable land, as gravel and rocks are washed down the steep slopes and on to crop land. Continuous cultivation with poor tillage practices on low fertile soils sensitive to erosion has increased the deterioration. Yield levels among resource-poor farmers in the Axum area in Northern Tigray are in the order of 500 kg/ha of local tef and maize crops.

Can on-farm yields be doubled over the next 25 years?

The potential role of water management to improve on-farm crop yields depends on to what extent farmers' actual yields are constrained by water availability or by environmental preconditions that affect production. If crop yields are severely constrained by environmental preconditions, such as droughts, or if there is not enough rain to support crop water requirements, then water management has little to contribute. But water management can play a major role in improving yield levels if there is a potential to do so, if constraints are manageable and if there are opportunities to increase rainfall infiltration, soil water-holding capacities and soil fertility.

The yield gap between the farmers' reality and the theoretically attainable yields is both a negative and a positive indicator for present and future land-use management. The negative interpretation is that low yields indicate serious land degradation, in terms of erosion, desiccation[9] and soil fertility depletion. It clearly shows that the natural resource base is in bad shape. On the other hand, the positive interpretation of a large yield gap is that there remains an enormous potential for increasing yields. Yield growth normally follows the general law of progressively diminishing returns (in terms of yield) to increasing input of growth factors such as fertilizer. However, farmers experiencing yields far below the potential, are positioned at the lower end of the production function, where each incremental improvement of growth factors (soil nutrients, water, aeration), will result in a large yield return. This is in contrast to farmers operating close to the maximum level, where improved management will result only in a small incremental increase in productivity.

We know that even with the most optimistic predictions on irrigation development, rainfed agriculture will continue to produce at least half the world's food. In order to meet future demand, rainfed yields will have to double over the next 25 years. Without increases in water productivity, a doubling of yield will require twice as much consumptive green water use. The question is whether there is enough water available on-farm to enable this doubling. Again, if the hydrological conditions permit a doubling in the semi-arid tropical zone, then there is a good chance for a doubling in all hydroclimates with sedentary farming communities.

Rockström and Falkenmark (2000) developed an analytical tool to assess the options available to improve crop yields from a hydrological perspective. In Figure 7.4 the case of maize cultivated in a semi-arid tropical savanna is presented.[10] The X-axis

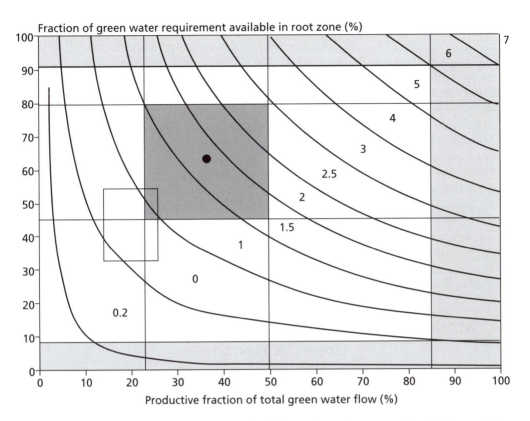

Note: The larger shaded area shows the range of yields experienced on average in sub-Saharan Africa using the rainfall partitioning range in Fig 6.3a. The smaller shaded area shows the yield range on farmers' degraded fields.

Source: Rockström and Falkenmark, 2000

Figure 7.4 *Analysis of the effects of rainfall partitioning and plant water uptake capacity on maize grain yields under semi-arid conditions*

shows the percentage of productive green water flow to total green water flow, or ratio of transpiration (T) to total evaporation (Etot). This is an indicator on grain yield of the impact of crop management such as soil fertility, crop species, timing of operations and pest management. The Y-axis shows the percentage of crop water requirement (CWR) available in the root zone, and is an indicator of the impact of good land management on crop yields because it shows the percentage of rainfall that infiltrates the soil and is accessible to the crop.

The concave lines are iso-lines of equal grain yield in tonnes per hectare (t/ha), with the lowest yield line in the lower left corner, and the maximum yield lines in the upper right hand corner. The grey zone shows upper boundary conditions of the model. The achievable yield level in this case, the semi-arid region, amounts to 5 t/ha of grain. The large grey square shows the range of actual observed yield levels in semi-arid sub-Saharan Africa. The flow partitioning data is taken from Figure 6.3a, which shows a synthesis of research observations on rainfall partitioning for grains under semi-arid rainfed conditions. In Figure 7.4, poor rainfall partitioning gives a vertical drop along the Y-axis and reduces the possible yields by 1–2.5 t/ha. Poor plant water uptake capacity reduces yields by 1.5–3 t/ha. The average experienced yield level on-station amounts to 1.5–2 t/ha. The common on-farm reality is shown by the smaller square with an experienced yield range of 0.5–1 t/ha. In the on-farm case, some 35–55 per cent of crop water requirement is available in the root zone due to high runoff and deep percolation. Productive green water amounts to only 15–25 per cent of total green water flow, which indicates large evaporation losses.

The analysis suggests a broad scope for improving yield levels within the available water balance in semi-arid farming systems. There are seemingly no agro-hydrological limitations to even a large and stable quadruple yield increase from, for example, 0.5 t/ha to 2 t/ha in semi-arid environments. The objective is to maximize infiltration and move upwards along the Y-axis, to mitigate dry spells by increasing the amount of water available over time to plants, and primarily to improve soil fertility management so that the productive green water ratio increases and moves the system to the right along the X-axis.

More Crop per Drop by Reducing Non-productive Green Water Losses

How much more green water would be required to significantly upgrade rainfed agriculture? For that purpose we need to analyse the green water implications of increasing yields, such as the water productivity implications. Water productivity can be defined in several ways. We will define it as the amount of water required to produce one unit of biomass. While we use the term water productivity (WP), other authors prefer the term water use efficiency (WUE), which we will consider an equivalent.

There are two components of green water productivity: total green water productivity related to total evaporation (evaporation and transpiration) and productive green water productivity related to transpiration. It is important to keep in mind that the latter is generally very difficult to influence within a given ecosystem setting, and is largely determined by crop physiology and climatic conditions (Sinclair et al, 1984). This narrows the options for improving water productivity to reducing the other flows in the water balance: soil evaporation, interception, runoff and drainage.[11]

Increasing green water productivity

Generally, a linear relationship is assumed between plant growth and green water flow within a constant hydroclimate, existing soil conditions, and a specific management setting. There are ample empirical data supporting this relationship, which tells us that every incremental increase in crop yield leads to a corresponding increase in green water use (see Figure 7.5). The slope of the line is the green water productivity, or the

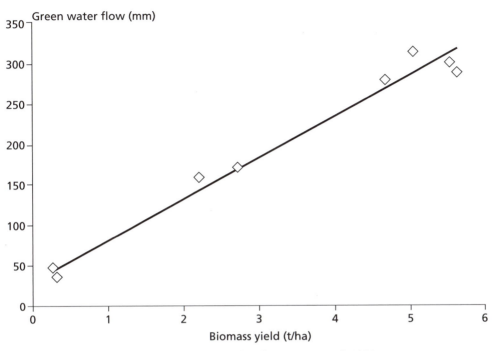

Source: Adapted from Ritchie (1983) based on data from Power et al, 1961

Figure 7.5 *Biomass yield as a function of green water flow*

ratio of green water flow to yield, generally defined in m³/t or mm/kg/ha. This water productivity ratio is generally assumed to apply over the whole yield range (on the X-axis), indicating a constant incremental increase in green water use with every incremental increase in yield. For example, the slope of the line in Figure 7.5 is 50 mm/t/ha, or 500 m³/t, of grain. The intercept, 30 mm/t/ha, or 300 m³/t, shows the amount of non-productive evaporation from the soil occurring early in the growing season when the soil is more or less bare. A doubling of yields from 2 to 4 t/ha would increase green water use from 1300 m³ to 2300 m³ (or from 130 mm to 230 mm).

The linear relationship between yield and consumptive use of water, assumed as universal for all crops but with different intercept and slope, has important ecohydrological implications. It enables us to label each cropping system operating within a certain environmental and management setting with a constant water productivity tag. Based on this constant we can predict water requirements for an increase in yields. Examples of water productivities for a number of crops cultivated in different hydroclimates were discussed in Chapter 3 and presented in Table 3.1. As we showed there, most grain crops in the world have similar water productivities, generally in the range of 1000 to 3000 m³/t, or 100–300 mm/kg/ha (green water flow per tonne grain). The same logic also holds for other land use that generates biomass, such as grazing areas, grasslands, and forests. Here the green water flow is generally considered to increase linearly with increased biomass growth.

Our interest here is to investigate the possibilities of improving water productivity. First, what does Figure 7.5 really mean? Under which conditions does this linearity apply? Green water flow combines two completely different vapour fluxes, which, despite being thermodynamically driven by the same processes (atmospheric demand for water), have completely different ecological functions. Productive green water flow as plant transpiration contributes to the growth of vegetation through root uptake of water and release of vapour from stomata in the leaves. Evaporation, on the other hand, is the transformation of liquid water to vapour either from intercepted water on the canopy surface, open water, or soil moisture with no direct contribution to plant growth.

While transpiration increases linearly with increased plant growth and crop yield, evaporation generally decreases progressively with increased canopy cover, as a result of shading.[12] As was shown in Chapter 4, transpiration is very conservative, and tends to increase linearly with plant growth and crop yield at a rate that is closely related to the physiological characteristics of the plant and the climatic conditions where the plant is grown. Transpiration productivity for a crop in a certain hydroclimate is thus very difficult to influence.

Vapour shift

From a water productivity perspective the goal is to increase the proportion of productive transpiration flow to total evaporation. Reducing evaporation, the non-productive green water flow, in favour of transpiration, can do this. There are two ways of achieving such a vapour shift. The first is by reducing early season evaporation. This can be achieved through easy planting, intercropping (to rapidly develop a canopy cover), mulching and improved foliage. The second is by reducing evaporation flow by increasing the canopy. Alternatively, blue water can be added and converted into productive vapour flow.

Experience shows that improved management can result in a substantial vapour shift, where transpiration and yields increase while evaporation stays constant or is reduced (Viets, 1962; Ritchie, 1983). However, in hot and dry environments with agricultural systems where the crop is sparse and the leaf area never exceeds 2 m^2/m^2, it may be difficult to reduce evaporation flow in favour of improved crop transpiration. This was shown by Daamen et al (1995) and by Rockström (1997) for sparsely planted pearl millet in Niger (Sahel).[13]

Rice presents a special vapour shift problem. Rice is the world's second largest grain crop and is predominantly grown as flooded paddy rice in lowland areas. Evaporation losses are high from the paddy rice systems, as the fields are flooded during land preparation and early growth of the crop. In Asia, green water flow from paddy rice systems range from 4 to 7 mm per day (Tuong, 1999). By reducing the periods of ponding, when evaporation equals potential evaporation from a free water surface, a vapour shift can be produced. This is difficult in this case as rice is sensitive to water stress and the flooding assists in suppressing weeds. However, there are successful examples of upland rice systems, where rice is cultivated without flooding, in the same way as other grains. Yield levels are often lower than paddy rice though, and there is ongoing research to develop high-yielding upland rice, defined as 'aerobic' rice, which can be grown on non-waterlogged, aerobic soil (Tuong and Bouman, 2002).

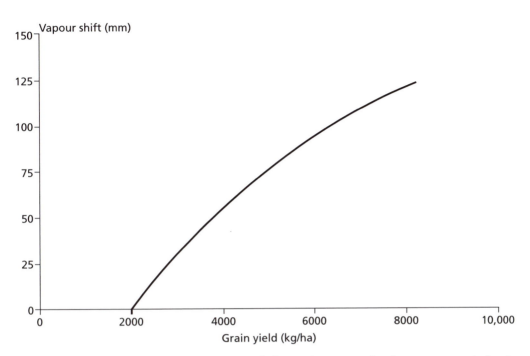

Note: The reduction in evaporation is given in relation to the evaporation from a crop producing 2 t/ha (seasonal E = 167 mm).

Source: adapted from Novak, 1982, and Rockström and Falkenmark, 2000

Figure 7.6 *Vapour shift as a result of increased shading from a denser canopy cover*

A simple rule of thumb may be that a vapour shift is easily achieved when yields start exceeding 2 t/ha (corresponding roughly to a shading or leaf area of 2 m^2/m^2). The options are less obvious in sparsely planted crop systems, especially in dry and hot environments with low yields and low shading. The water savings through a vapour shift can be large, as indicated in Figure 7.6. This figure shows the vapour shift over a yield range from 2 to 8 t/ha in relation to the evaporation experienced at 2 t/ha, in this case a seasonal evaporation of 167 mm. A doubling of yields in this semi-arid savanna environment would give vapour shift savings of 60 mm. With a green water productivity of 80 mm/t/ha (800 m^3/t) grain, this would correspond to roughly 750 kg of grain.

To summarize the options for a vapour shift, the analysis above indicates that reductions in evaporation in favour of transpiration are relatively easy to achieve in farming systems that already operate with relatively high canopy densities. In ecosystems with a dense canopy the energy influx through advection is low. In contrast, a vapour shift is much more difficult to achieve in low-yielding farming systems with sparse canopies. Unfortunately, this indicates that vapour shifts are most difficult to achieve in the agro-ecosystems that are in most need of such a shift – the savannas where present yields are low (< 2 t/ha) and food demand is high.

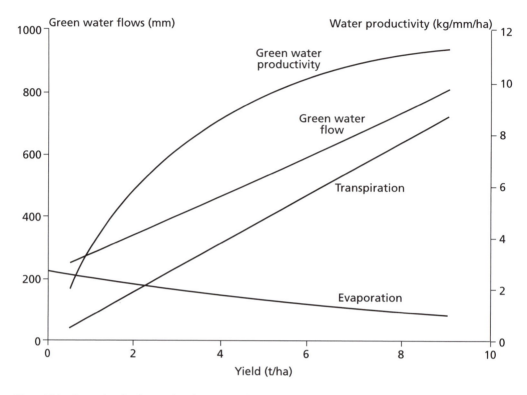

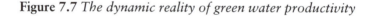

Note: This chart clearly shows the dynamic relationship between green water flow, green water productivity and yield.

Figure 7.7 *The dynamic reality of green water productivity*

Declining evaporation means increasing productive green water flow

The above would suggest that it is difficult to increase green water productivity in savanna agro-ecosystems. However, with increased yield, evaporation declines or remains constant while transpiration always increases. Every yield increase will not result from constant transpiration but from improved green water productivity. The productive green water component of total green water flow will increase as shown in Figure 7.7.

Every management effort in terms of water, soil and crop management will automatically result in improvements of green water productivity at least for a lower yield range (from about 0 to 4 t/ha). This is positive. Instead of the general assumption that some 1500 m³ (150 mm/ha) of consumptive green water is required to produce every incremental tonne of grain, the amount of green water required will actually decrease with every yield increase. Most important, the decrease in water requirement is largest in the lower yield bracket, where evaporation is highest. This shows an interesting path for water productivity improvements in the presently low-yielding rainfed farming systems in the savannas of the world.

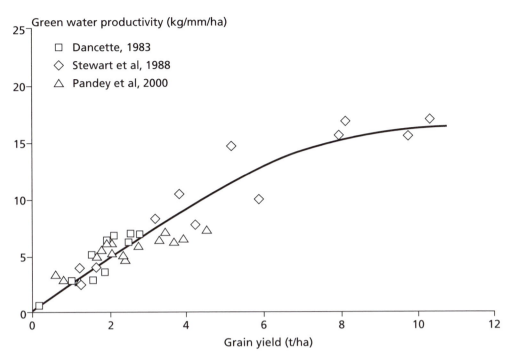

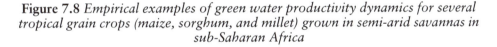

Source: Adapted from Dancette ,1983; Stewart et al, 1975; and Pandey et al, 2000

Figure 7.8 *Empirical examples of green water productivity dynamics for several tropical grain crops (maize, sorghum, and millet) grown in semi-arid savannas in sub-Saharan Africa*

It is important to distinguish between different yield intervals along the dynamic productivity curve in Figure 7.7. When yield levels reach a certain level (approximately around 4–5 t/ha) there is little evaporation occurring. The whole remaining green water flow for every incremental yield increase is productive transpiration. Transpiration is a direct function of climatic variables, root water access, stomata and canopy area, and now linearly related to yield. Thus, the assumption of linearity between yield and green water flow is suddenly valid. At high yield levels green water productivity may therefore be constant. Empirical evidence from various researchers supports the dynamic relationship between green water productivity and yield. As is seen from Figure 7.8, yield data over a wide yield range indicate that green water productivity increases with an increase in yield levels. The data were adapted from several field experiments in savanna environments (Dancette 1983; Stewart et al, 1975; and Pandey et al, 2000).[14]

Management implications

The conclusion from the above is that improving land management is one of the most promising ways of increasing green water productivity, especially in low-yielding

Table 7.2 *Management strategies to improve green water productivity*

Water productivity strategy	Process (refers to Figure 7.9)	Management options	Effect
Vapour shift	[I] Reduce early season evaporation	Dry planting Mulching Zero tillage	Quick crop establishment Reduced evaporation flow Less soil exposure to atmosphere
		Intercropping	Maximize canopy cover
	[II] Reduce evaporation flux with increased canopy	Intercropping Mulching Windbreaks	Reduced energy inflow through advection
		Agro forestry	Reduced energy inflow through advection
Improve T/ET ratio	[III] Increase plant water uptake Maximize productive green water flow	Improved crop varieties	
		Water harvesting Soil and water conservation Soil fertility management Conservation tillage	Dry spell mitigation Maximize infiltration and WHC Maximize plant water uptake Maximize infiltration, WHC and rooting depth
		Intercropping	Maximize transpiration

farming systems with high evaporation flow. Better management will increase crop yields and thereby increase the ratio of productive green water to total green water flow. Improving this ratio will normally imply a simultaneous vapour shift if the hydroclimatic and agricultural opportunity is there. For example, an increased yield (more transpiration), through improved timing of operations and better tillage practices that increase plant available soil water, may simultaneously reduce evaporation as a result of canopy growth. There are several management options available to achieve a vapour shift and to increase the proportion of productive green water flow to total green water flow. These are summarized in Table 7.2.

In the next chapter we will return to the details of land-use practices available to enable water productivity improvements in the farmer's field in line with Table 7.2.

In addition, it is important to note that while both vapour shift and an increase in productive green water in relation to total evaporation will increase water productivity, it is only the vapour shift that truly reduces the amount of drops required to produce a crop. The increase of transpiration through vapour shift comes from a reduction in non-productive evaporation flow. When raising the ratio of productive green flow to total green water flow, the transpiring water can originate from all other flows in the hydrological cycle – from reduced surface runoff and deep percolation, from vapour shift, and from increased extraction of soil moisture. In this latter case, water productivity may increase, but there will always be an incremental increase in consumptive water use (now as transpiration) with increased growth in yields. This increased water use for crops may affect water dependent ecosystems downstream.

Global Assessment of the Water that Can Be Gained

We have now come to a point where we can attempt to assess how far rainfed agriculture can assist in reducing the water trade-offs between water for food and nature. We estimated (in Chapter 3) that even after subtracting the 800 km³/year to be covered by future irrigation development, an additional 4800 km³/year is still required to produce the food to feed the world population in 2050.

There are three questions that now need to be addressed:

- To what extent can vapour shift contribute to more food?
- How much local runoff can be diverted from evaporation and put to productive use?
- How much water may the dynamic character of water productivity save?

To what extent can vapour shift contribute to more food?

The first question is, to what extent can we produce more food with less consumptive green water use? How far could vapour shift contribute to a real increase in crop per drop? The focus here is only on the major cereals in developing countries where the dominant share of tropical agriculture takes place and where there are large evaporation losses – up to 50 per cent of rainfall. The potential for vapour shift is therefore best in these countries. It is also here that the largest share of increased food production will have to occur.

The average yield level of major rainfed cereal crops is currently 2.1 t/ha.[15] Based on the assumption of a reduced growth rate – from 2.5 per cent between 1995 and 2030 (FAO estimate) to 1.5 per cent between 2030 and 2050 – we estimate that the yield level in 2050 will be 3.5 t/ha. The cultivated area is expected to increase from 466 to 535 million ha, at a slow rate of 0.09 per cent/year between 1995 and 2030, and an even lower rate of 0.05 per cent for the period 2030–2050. This will give a total cultivated area under cereals in 2050 of approximately 600 million ha. The production of cereals will then amount to 2100 million tonnes, compared to 1200 million tonnes today, with a projected production in 2030 of 1900 million tonnes.

Early season evaporation (vapour shift option [1] in Table 7.2) for tropical cereals commonly amounts to approximately 150 mm (Singh et al, 1990). This threshold can probably be reduced by 20 mm/ha over a rainy season through mulching, improved timing of sowing, conservation tillage, and intercropping. Applied on 600 million ha in 2050, this gives a possible vapour shift of 120 km³/year.

Present evaporation amounts to approximately 50 per cent of green water flow and could be reduced to 30 per cent through vapour shift resulting from leaf area expansion (Vapour shift option [II] in Figure 7.9). This means that the ratio of evaporation to total evaporation for a yield increase from 2.1 to 3.5 t/ha will decrease from the present 0.49 to 0.31 in 2050. Using the transpiration productivity of 80 mm/t/ha that we used earlier in this chapter for tropical cereals (from Rockström and Falkenmark, 2000), we can calculate the actual reduction in evaporation as a result of a yield increase. Increasing average yield with 1.4 t/ha (from 2.1 to 3.5 t/ha) would reduce evaporation flow by 36 mm/ha (from the present 161 mm to 126 mm on average). Multiplying this by the predicted agricultural area in 2050 (600 million ha) gives an evaporation saving of 214 km³/year, rounded to 210 km³/year. This does not directly appear to be a large volume, but together with the reduction of early season evaporation (120 km³/year), the vapour shift potential is in the same order of magnitude as the whole expected increase in irrigation withdrawals over the next 25 years.[16]

To summarise, vapour shift may diminish future water needs by 330 km³/year (120 km³/year from reduction of early season evaporation and 210 km³/year from reduction of evaporation as a result of denser canopy). This would reduce the green water deficit for food in 2050 from 4,800 km³/year to 4,470 km³/year.

How much local runoff can be diverted from evaporation and put to productive use?

The second way to improve water productivity is to catch local runoff (which would otherwise evaporate further downstream) and use it to increase crop yields. This option implies management of local storm runoff that tends to evaporate in low-lying areas and degraded lands. This is mainly possible in hot tropical environments. It refers to water that does not contribute much to the generation of ecosystem services, although many of the small, seasonal lowland areas, such as the *dambos* in southern Africa, play an important role in maintaining species diversity. Such water can be captured using water harvesting techniques (see Chapter 8) and used for supplementary irrigation for dry spell mitigation.

Crop lands cover 10.5 per cent of the global terrestrial area and we assume an even distribution of them on the different continents. It is not easy to estimate the amount of water available for such redirection of evaporating surface runoff. One way is to assume that the difference in surface runoff coefficients between watershed scale and continental scale is attributed to evaporating surface runoff for crop lands in Africa, Asia, and South America (Table 7.3). The runoff water from crop lands available for surface water harvesting would then be roughly 300 km³/year (Rockström et al, 1999).

How much water may the dynamic character of water productivity save?

The third option to improve water productivity is the easiest: simply increase yield levels. The heaviest demand for increasing yields is in rainfed agriculture, where current average yields in tropical developing countries amount to 2.1 tonnes per hectare. We assume the same yield increase as discussed above, from 2.1 to 3.5 t/ha in 2050. We use the dynamic water productivity relation in Figure 7.7, where less total evaporation is required to generate an additional tonne of grain harvest. The present yield level of 2.1 t/ha then corresponds to a green water productivity of 1,740 m³/t. The future yield

Table 7.3 *Assessment of evaporating surface runoff*

Continent	Precip-itation[a]	Surface runoff[a]	Runoff coefficient, continental scale	Runoff coefficient, field scale	Difference in surface runoff	Evaporating surface runoff (10.5% croplands[b])
	km³/year	km³/year	%	%	km³/year	km³/year
Africa	20780	2480	12	20	1676	176
Asia	32140	9130	28	30	512	54
South America	29355	6450	22	25	889	94
Sum						324

a Data from L'vovich and White (1990).
b The global cropland area is roughly 10.5% of the global terrestrial area.

level of 3.5 t/ha in 2050 would be produced with a water productivity of 1,250 m³/t. We subtract the contribution of vapour shift to this water productivity improvement, in order to avoid double counting of the vapour shift effect. For that purpose we assume a constant evaporation corresponding to the evaporation for the lower yield, which gives us average green water productivity in 2050 of 1300 m³/t. The production of 2100 million tonnes of cereals in developing countries in 2050 would require a consumptive green water use of 2700 km³/year assuming dynamic water productivity. This figure compares to 3600 km³/year if we assume a constant water productivity of 1700 m³/t. Taking the dynamic character of water productivity into account, the increase of consumptive green water use from 2000 km³/year in 1995 would thus be 700 km³/year, compared to 1600 km³/year under the constant productivity assumption. The reduction of consumptive water use compared to the estimate in Chapter 4, which was based on an assumption of constant water productivity, would then be the difference in green water use between the constant (3600 km³/year) and the dynamic estimate (2700 km³/year), equal to a saving of 900 km³/year.

Remaining Water Requirements to Feed Humanity

These discussions began by calculating the additional green water required to adequately feed the world population by 2050. This requirement amounts to a total of 5600 km³/year. The question is from which sources all that water would be provided. Up to this point we have analysed two possible sources: irrigation and possible improvements of water productivity. Irrigation may contribute 800 km³/yr, leaving 4800 km³/yr still unaccounted for. This volume would have to originate from rainfed agriculture. The total contribution from water productivity improvements to future rainfed food production in developing countries, of vapour shift, transfer of local runoff on its way to evaporate to consumptive green water use, and increase of green water productivity through higher ratio of productive to total green water flow, is

Table 7.4 *Total contribution from water productivity improvements*

Water productivity strategy		Flow source	Flow in Figure 7.9	Estimated reduction in green water requirements (km³/year)	Process	Management
Vapour shift (E to T shift)	(A) Reduce early season (B) Reduce E with increased canopy	[E] In-field evaporation	[I]	120 210	Evaporation reduction	Early sowing Intercropping Crop Soil fertility Mulching
Productive use of local runoff		Off-field surface runoff	[II]	300	Runon surface runoff converted to green water flow	Water harvesting for dryspell mitigation
Green water productivity improvement (T/ET ratio increased)		Off-field surface runoff, deep percolation	[II] & [III]	900	Increased plant water uptake	Soil and water conservation Water harvesting Crop, soil fertility management
Total				**1530 km³/year**		

summarized in Table 7.4. As can be seen, the total reduction in green water requirements would amount to 1530 km³/year, which we will round down to 1500 km³/year in the following discussions.

The three different water productivity strategies would all improve green water productivity – that is, increase the amount of crop per drop of green water. Each strategy would, however, affect different water flow components of the on-farm water balance, as indicated in Figure 7.9. Vapour shift affects only the transfer of green water flow from the non-productive to the productive flow, without affecting the water balance as a whole. In Chapter 8 we will briefly investigate the management options available to improve freshwater management in agriculture so that pressure on water-dependent ecosystems is reduced.

We have now discussed all possibilities of meeting the additional water required for food in the future: 5600 km³/year will have to come from irrigation and water productivity improvements in rainfed agriculture. We began with a reasonably conservative estimate of the water for food requirements in 2050 of 12,600 km³/year (with a present use of 7000 km³/year). We have also been relatively optimistic in our estimates of both the irrigation contribution and water productivity opportunities. Our estimate of total green water savings of 1500 km³/year is a very substantial reduction of freshwater requirements for food production, and corresponds to two-thirds of the present consumptive water use in irrigation, or an amount that could fill 15 reservoirs the size of Lake Nasser, behind the Aswan High Dam in Egypt.

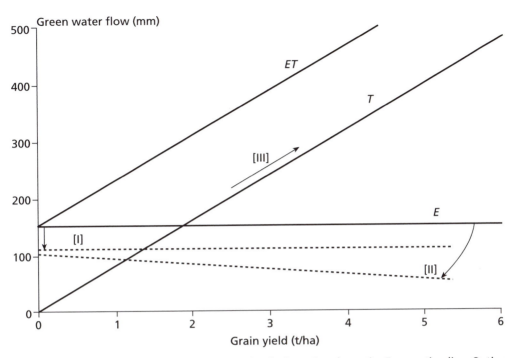

Note: Option [I] to reduce early season evaporation by lowering the entire Evaporation line: Option [II] by progressively lowering evaporation with increased grain yield, resulting in a changed slope of the Evaporation line; Option [III] to increase the ration of productive green water flow (T) to total green water flow (E + T) by moving along the productive transpiration line.

Figure 7.9 *The principal options for improving green water productivity*

The total contribution from irrigation of 800 km³/year (14 per cent) and from water productivity improvements in rainfed agriculture of 1500 km³/year (27 per cent), amounts to 2300 km³/year. The conclusion is that there still remains a large green water deficit of 3300 km³/year or 59 per cent to cover from other sources (5600 – 800 km³/year from irrigation and 1500 km³/year from water productivity improvements). This green water would have to be 'taken' from other ecosystems, through trade-offs such as expanding agricultural land into terrestrial ecosystems, or by diverting runoff water on its way to local streams. This diversion of runoff water would imply a shift in blue water use from its current function of sustaining aquatic ecosystems to supplementing irrigation in rainfed farming systems.

Such a spectacular additional need of green water flow to sustain food production in 2050 underlines the seriousness in the 'new' water scarcity: the green water scarcity. In the following chapters we will discuss the possibilities of achieving the green water productivity improvements we have estimated here, and we will address the goal of balancing the future green water requirement for food with water requirements to sustain ecosystem services.

Summary

Water for food plays a key role in the balance between human development and the needs of the environment. Food production is the world's largest consumer of direct human water use. In this chapter we continued our focus on the world's savanna agro-ecosystems, as these are the regions facing the largest need for water for food production. Agriculture not only depends on large volumes of fresh water, but also on land use. Over the last 30 years intensive use of agricultural land has expanded rapidly at the expense of fallows, forests and natural ecosystems. In order to secure ecological functions and continued generation of important ecosystem goods and services, one of the most important areas of intervention, even from an ecohydrological perspective, is to improve water and soil productivity in agricultural land use. This implies producing more food per unit of soil and water. From a freshwater perspective, this translates into producing more food per unit of consumptive (green) water use. This is an important strategy in order to secure food for coming generations while minimizing the negative trade-offs with ecosystems.

In this chapter we stated that the challenge of water for food production that presently faces mankind is probably the most important in modern history. Unlike the Green Revolution of the 1960s, we are now faced with the task of improving agricultural production in the semi-arid and dry sub-humid agro-savannas of the world. Here, rapid population growth, severe poverty, and the challenge to manage water scarcity coincide with land degradation and ecologically vulnerable ecosystems. The regions of the world that were too poor, too dry, and ecologically too difficult for the methods of the first Green Revolution must now be assisted.

We estimated in Chapter 4, based on the common static assumption of water needs for food, that 12,600 km^3/year of green water will be required to adequately feed a population of 9 billion people in 2050. The additional green water requirement is 5600 km^3/year, compared to today's demand. Irrigation may contribute 800 km^3/year of this additional water for food requirement, leaving 4800 km^3/year to be provided from the development of rainfed agriculture. Can this water be found without seriously affecting water dependent ecosystems?

The 'search for water' in this chapter has focused on the common erroneous assumptions used regarding water productivity. The linear relationship between green water use and crop yields is valid, but it is not possible, as is normally done, to directly translate the slope of the green water–crop yield line to a measure of water productivity for a farming system. The reason is that green water flow involves two vapour flows that tend to move in different directions with increased plant or crop yields. Productive green water flow such as transpiration is directly proportional to both plant growth and yield: more food means more transpiration. Non-productive green water flow, evaporation flow, tends to decrease with increased plant growth and yield, and does not contribute to plant growth. This means that the assumption of a certain water productivity (for constant environment and crop system) over a wide range of yield levels is normally not valid. Instead, each increase in yield level will normally improve the green water productivity, as a result of transpiration becoming a progressively larger proportion of total green water flow. To conclude, water productivity is not static, but highly dynamic, and changes with management practices.

The dynamic character of water productivity offers a number of possibilities to produce more crop per drop of fresh water. It is possible to produce more food with fewer trade-offs with water-dependent ecosystems. We have tried to estimate how effective improved green water use can be in reducing the freshwater requirements for feeding the world population in 2050. In total, we estimate that improved green water management can 'save' 1500 km^3/year in 2050, reducing the remaining green water requirement to feed the world population from 4800 km^3/year to 3300 km^3/year. Despite what we believe to be an optimistic view of the possibilities for improvements of green water productivity, a very large volume of green water flow still needs to be allocated to food production. This is a critical issue, and gives a measurement of the grim ecohydrological situation facing mankind in the 21st century.

Chapter 8

Closing the Yield Gap on the Savanna – The Real World Perspective

Water management that reduces the risk of dry spells may be the most promising way to upgrade rainfed savanna agriculture.

Changing the Farmers' Risk Perception

The world faces the combined challenge of feeding an additional 3 billion people in 2050 and of addressing what has been called 'Conway's hidden food gap'(1997): the malnutrition among the world's poorest people. This will require an additional 5600 km^3/year of consumptive green water use (Chapter 3). This is a tough agricultural goal, particularly as it has to rely to a large degree on increased agricultural productivity, instead of on expanding agricultural land. It is also a major ecohydrological challenge, as every increase in consumptive water use for food may affect ecological functions dependent on water.

In Chapter 7 we estimated how much of this additional green water could be derived from water productivity improvements and be carried out with a minimum impact on ecosystems. We found that irrigation might contribute with 800 km^3/year (or 14 per cent per cent of the future green water requirements for additional food). Even after an exhaustive investigation of the options for water productivity, we estimated a green water saving of 1500 km^3/year or 27 per cent. In spite of this we are still faced with the task of procuring an additional 3300 km^3/year (59 per cent). We will return to the implications of such a large remaining green water deficit for food production in Chapters 9 and 10.

In this chapter the focus is on how water productivity improvements might be achieved on the ground. We continue to concentrate on smallholder farming in savannas, which we consider to be the global hotspot for high population growth, poverty, water scarcity and vulnerability (Chapter 6). Is it possible, given the environmental and social limitations of rural communities in developing countries, to double average yield levels over the next half-century by improving water productivity? How can the consumptive water requirements be reduced by 1500 km^3/year? That saving corresponds to 300 mm/ha/year.

Despite the large expectation on crop per drop improvements in agriculture, the volumes required to feed a growing world population will pose a tremendous ecohydrological challenge. Furthermore, as pointed out by Conway (1997) and discussed in Chapter 7, we are in fact in need of a doubly green revolution, or a green-green revolution, as food production today has to consider two additional factors that were largely absent in the original Green Revolution – namely the necessity to focus on smallholder farmers with poor resources, and the need to balance agricultural development with ecosystem protection.

Mixing indigenous and new ideas

What are the chances of achieving a significant upgrading of rainfed agriculture without compromising the water needs for ecosystems? The answer to this question involves not only technologies and management, but also institutions, markets, policy and human capacities. A common denominator is to promote land-use practices in vulnerable environments that reduce risks in smallholder farming. There is an exhaustive literature on agricultural technologies and methodologies on how to improve agricultural water management, but our aim here is not to repeat such comprehensive work (for example, Barrow, 1987; Reij et al, 1996). Instead, we will focus primarily on the role of smallholder innovations in agricultural water management that aim at minimizing the risk of crop reductions and yield losses caused by droughts and dry spells in savanna agro-ecosystems.

There are two reasons for this focus on the critical role of water: it is a primary limiting factor for crop growth in savanna farming systems, and it is a major factor in determining farmers' risk perceptions. Irrespective of views on sustainable agricultural development, be they founded on a strong belief on modernization with fossil fuel-based inputs or on indigenous know-how and local organic inputs, a starting point is to create incentives for investment in human and other capital. Risk perceptions among farmers are closely linked to the rainfall variability. Farmers hesitate to invest in inputs that require capital, as they are well aware of the extreme variability of rainfall in savanna agro-ecosystems. Water is the only completely random parameter in a rainfed farming system, as it is not possible to influence the supply. Special attention is therefore necessary to promote investments in organic or inorganic fertilization, in hybrid seed, intensified weeding and new tillage systems, and the effective use of labour. Indigenous approaches, despite all their merits in assessing causal complexities and the ability to anchor ownership, will not do the job by themselves. Innovations, genius, and novelty are needed. New and/or locally site adapted technologies are required. Conway (1997) writes:

> *The way forward (in terms of feeding a growing world population) lies in harnessing the power of modern technology, but harnessing it wisely in the interests of the poor and hungry and with respect for the environment in which we live. We need a shared vision based, above all, on partnership, among scientists and between scientists and the rural poor.*

What is needed is thus a mixed development strategy that:

- Acknowledges the potential and important role of science and technology in generating novel and innovative approaches.
- Focuses on local adaptation (social and physical) and adoption (local ownership and capacity building).
- Uses local, indigenous innovations.
- Acknowledges that pragmatism is required in terms of adoption of external inputs, especially of inorganic fertilizers, without which response to water management in soils depleted of nutrients would fail.
- Adopts sustainable agriculture principles in which a maximum effort is made to draw biological resources for soil management, for example, animal and green manure and conservation tillage.
- Bases water management on an integrated catchment management approach that focuses on sharing rainfall between humans and nature.

There are several interesting 'appropriate' innovations originating from science and technology, and also from the commercial agricultural sector, which are already accessible to smallholder farmers. One example is the commercialization of low-pressure drip irrigation technologies, available now to smallholder farmers in the local markets in some parts of Africa. A second example among smallholder farmers in India and Africa is the wide adoption of manual treadle pumps, an indigenous technology that has been technologically refined and transferred to new countries and farming environments. A third example is conservation tillage practices. Conservation tillage, also called conservation farming or conservation agriculture, is a management approach for improved soil and water management that, in the savanna zone, takes the role of a water-harvesting system. It is based on abandoning conventional soil inversion using ploughs in favour of tillage practices such as ripping and sub-soiling that maximizes rainfall infiltration and root development. After decades of science and technology development in close partnerships between farmers and scientists, novel methodologies based on old principles are being adapted and adopted among smallholder farmers in Latin America, Asia and sub-Saharan Africa. There are also several other important areas where external innovations have been introduced to local culture: biotechnology, crop breeding, technologies for groundwater management, precision agriculture techniques, local processing technology, and the introduction of new commercial crops – for example, jojoba and *Opuntia* in arid and semi-arid environments of the Horn of Africa and the Middle East.

Ways to upgrade rainfed agriculture

From a water perspective, there are two main avenues for upgrading rainfed agriculture: to increase the water uptake capacity of plants, and to increase availability of water to plants. Even though these strategies focus on water, the approaches and practices to achieve them are not restricted to water management.

Partitioning of rainfall and uptake of soil water by plants are good performance indicators for all land management practices, especially for plant growth in semi-arid and dry sub-humid ecosystems where water is a major limiting factor for growth. Partitioning of rainfall in the water balance of a crop producing system, a grassland, or

Table 8.1 *Ways to upgrade rainfed agriculture through integrated soil and water management*

Strategy for upgrading	Management	Methodology	Target parameter
Plant water uptake capacity	Soil management	Tillage	Root length and density
		Crop rotation Mulching Organic manures	Crop development
	Crop management	Crop choice Inter-cropping Timing of operations Pest management	
Plant water availability	Soil management	Tillage Soil and water conservation Mulching Crop rotation	Soil infiltrability
		Organic manures	Water holding capacity
	Water management	Water harvesting	Dry spell mitigation

a forested land area will reveal both management performance and water-related ecological resilience. For example, a large amount of surface runoff and a low amount of water uptake by roots indicates that an agro-ecosystem or natural ecosystem has problems of low soil infiltration, low capacity of soil to hold water and weak canopy/root development.

Crop and soil management can improve water uptake capacity (Table 8.1). The target is to maximize depth and density of roots and the development of canopy and grain. Tillage, crop rotations, mulching and the use of organic green manures such as nitrogen-fixing legumes and animal manure influence the structure of the soil, and thereby root development. Likewise, crop choice, inter-cropping, timing of operations and pest management influence plant water uptake capacity. Tillage, which strongly influences both soil conditions and infiltration capacity at the surface, and the structure of the topsoil, also affects plant water availability. Soil and water conservation practices, which focus on maximizing rainfall infiltration, together with crop rotation, mulching and manure management, affect plant water availability. Water management, for example through water-harvesting practices, enable dry spell mitigation, thereby securing water access to plants over time.

Table 8.1 illustrates the need for a systems approach to upgrade rainfed agriculture. Water management is only one way of increasing water productivity. Synergy effects for production improvements can only be achieved in a combination of water, crop and soil management.

Synergy effects of water and nutrients

Water is generally considered the primary factor limiting plant growth in savanna agro-ecosystems. But a prerequisite for improved water productivity is good soil fertility management. There is clear evidence that lack of soil nutrients is often more limiting than lack of water, even with the normal scarcity of water in savannas (Klaij and Vachaud, 1992; Penning de Vries and Djitèye, 1991; Fox and Rockström, 2000; and Buresh et al, 1997). One reason for this, as discussed in Chapter 6, is that water is not as scarce as is often believed. Instead, savannas are ecosystems that receive large volumes of rainfall, but over short periods of time, which results in too much water followed by periods of too little water. An example is a study by Klaij and Vachaud (1992) in a semi-arid parkland savanna environment in Niger, where water fluctuates between scarcity and excess. For a crop of pearl millet on sandy soil in a rainfed system they observed substantial and repeated occurrences of deep percolation beneath the root zone. This occurrence of groundwater recharge in such a dry environment was a sign of water abundance. As deep percolation occurred systematically, they concluded that soil nutrients were more limiting in the crop system than water. There was water, but weak roots and sparse canopy prevented the crop deriving much benefit from it.

These observations show that there was enough water on a seasonal basis, but probably a cycle of excess and deep percolation followed by instances of scarcity during dry spells. This clearly shows that there was no cumulative scarcity of water while in reality there was intermittent scarcity. In a farmer's field on a savanna, the level of water and nutrient stress oscillates like unsynchronized radio waves with a frequency much shorter than a rainy season, more likely on a weekly basis, and often on a daily basis.

The other reason why low levels of soil nutrients can be more limiting for growth, even in semi-arid savannas, is the predominance of inherently low-fertility soils and prolonged soil nutrient mining in smallholder farming. Stoorvogel and Smaling (1990) estimated that nutrient balances in several countries in Eastern and Southern Africa are severely negative and indicate a net loss of soil nutrients in the farming systems. For example, in the Kenyan highlands, the average annual losses were estimated at 73 kg/ha of sodium, 7 kg/ha of phosphorus and 51 kg/ha of potassium. Fertilizer use in sub-Saharan Africa is the lowest in the world, with some 11 kg of fertilizer applied per harvested hectare. Developing countries apply an average of 62 kg/ha (FAO, 1995a).

As a consequence, it is essential that water constraints be addressed in combination with soil nutrient constraints. This is important because investments in water management alone may not generate the payback required to make the effort worthwhile. In a recent study, Fox and Rockström (2003) showed that investment in water harvesting for supplemental irrigation requires a simultaneous investment in soil fertility management in order to generate the economic benefits needed to make efforts in water harvesting worthwhile.

The synergic effects between water and plant nutrients can be illustrated by the work of Breman et al (2001). Figure 8.1 shows yield data from different soil nutrient and water management conditions in Burkina Faso. Farmers' yields in the semi-arid savanna in Ouaigouya in northern Burkina Faso are limited by both water and nutrients, resulting in grain yields in the order of 500 kg/ha. Observations from a wet semi-arid savanna location in Ouagadougou show that even with rainfall up to around 1000 mm/rainy season, yield levels are still low, not much higher than the yields in the

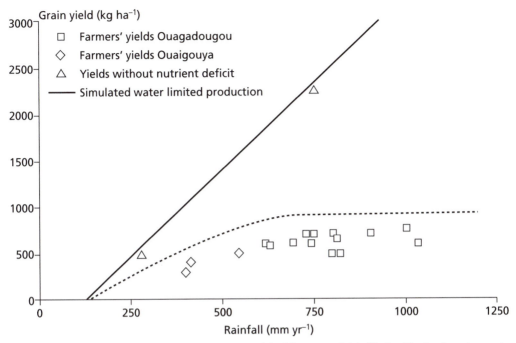

Note: The dotted line indicates the upper threshold of farmers' yields (limited by both water and nutrients).

Source: Adapted from Breman et al, 2001.

Figure 8.1 *Water- and nutrient-limited farmers' yields in Burkina Faso compared to water-limited yield with no soil nutrient limitations*

north, which are limited by water. This suggests that the farming system is strongly limited by soil nutrients, as there is barely any response to increased water availability in the form of increased water uptake by plants. All the excess water probably percolates below the root zone, due to poor water uptake caused by weak roots and canopy development. A crop limited only by water, where nutrients are fully available, yields over 2 t/ha in the case with a rainfall of 750 mm, or almost 1.5 tonnes more than the nutrient-limited crop under the same rainfall. Simulated yield, limited only by water, is shown by the straight line.

A very common experience in resource-poor smallholder farming is that there is no yield response in spite of increased water availability. This is due to nutrient deficiency in the soil. In semi-arid savanna regions of Ethiopia, where land degradation is widespread, it is not uncommon that the staple food crop tef (*Agrostis tef*), grown without fertilization with nitrogen and phosphorus, leads to complete crop failure. The tef crop in these cases is not limited by water constraints, but seriously limited by nutrient stress, as a result of decades of intensive, continuous cultivation on inherently fertile but extremely shallow soils.

The discussion above on soil fertility indicates that synergy effects between water and soil nutrients have the most significant impact on crop productivity. This is applicable also for other factors influencing crop growth, such as choice of crop varieties, pest management, tillage, crop rotations, and intercropping.

Water management that reduces the risk of dry spells may be the most important incentive for investments in rainfed savanna agriculture. This does not only refer to incentives for investing in external inputs such as fertilization, improved seed and pest management, but also for farm management. The latter issue is a primary issue. For example, timing of operations in semi-arid environments is absolutely critical for maximizing the crop response to erratic rainfall (Stewart, 1988; Oldreive, 1993). Early soil preparation and dry planting, which enable a full crop response to the rainfall at the beginning of the rainy season, may make the difference between harvesting a crop or complete crop failure.

Similarly, transplantation of grain crop seedlings at the onset of rains has proven to give double yields in semi-arid savannas as a result of much faster plant growth than normal seed planting. The added water available to plants is large, as up to 20 per cent of the total seasonal rainfall is generally lost due to late planting. Farmers in large parts of India, Sri Lanka and Africa practise dry planting in advance of unreliable rainy seasons (Barrow, 1987). The timing of weeding also affects plant water availability, since weeds consume soil water and influence plant water uptake capacity. They also compete for light and nutrients. But if a farmer's expectations of successfully growing crops are low due to land degradation and the high risk of yield-reducing dry spells, he will not give priority to cultivation but rather will focus on alternative sources of income.

Various water management practices can provide protection against drought and dry spells. The most obvious (and in fact the only) way to drought-proof a crop system is irrigation, which drastically reduces the risk of crop failure due to meteorological droughts and dry spells. This increases incentives for farm investments, and gives higher yield levels than rainfed agriculture. However, our focus here is on the more difficult task of protecting rainfed agriculture practised in savannas from the effects of dry spells.[1]

It is important here to note two points: management influences the impacts of meteorological droughts, and poor management causes agricultural droughts. Many semi-arid farming systems have become increasingly vulnerable to climatic variability through the adoption of drought-sensitive crops and land management practices. For example, the tendency to shift from drought-tolerant millet crops and sorghum to drought-sensitive maize or even rice has aggravated the impact of meteorological droughts, particularly where there is a reduction in seasonal rainfall totals to below the minimum water requirement that enables a crop to complete a full growth cycle from seed to seed. It has also been shown that humans induce drought through poor land management. Decades of intensive disc ploughing at shallow depths, combined with the continuous monoculture of maize on large tracts of land in semi-arid Tanzania, has resulted in compaction, soil crusting, and the exhaustion of soil nutrients. A very small portion of the rainfall infiltrates, but due to the impenetrable plough pans, roots can only access soil water to a depth of <15 cm. The crop suffers from repeated agricultural droughts, even without an occurrence of meteorological droughts. Poor land management causing severe and persistent land degradation has resulted in desertification (Rockström and Jonsson, 1999).

Broadening the Narrow Approaches of the Past

In terms of water management, the link between the farm household and the catchment is particularly important. Much of the focus of agricultural development in rainfed agriculture has been confined to soil, crop and water management within the boundaries of the farm. Such methods are normally considered as soil and water conservation efforts. Off-farm water flow has generally been conceived as a source of erosion to be channelled away from the farm boundary. Instead, a farming systems approach is required, which links the farm household with the catchment.

For several farming systems in the world, land management on a catchment-basin scale is nothing new. There are numerous examples in India of old, traditional river diversion systems, and of runoff concentration in ponds and systems for groundwater harvesting that depend on communal water management on a catchment-basin scale (Agarwal and Narain, 1997). In Eritrea and Ethiopia, sedentary agriculture in arid valleys is made possible through spate irrigation, where storm runoff from high-altitude areas with high rainfall is diverted from large gullies to cropland for flood irrigation in low-lying flat areas with extremely low rainfall. The existence of such systems is often determined by environmental necessity – for example, spate irrigation systems in arid lands, or the water-harvesting systems in the Negev Desert. Without them, the local climate would be too unreliable for sedentary societies to be established in the first place. In savanna agro-ecosystems, rainfed farming can be practised without additional inflow of external water, but at a high risk of droughts and dry spells. Even here there is a local tradition of water resource management, but attention has primarily been on conserving water where it falls on the farmland itself.

The conservation focus of the past

The alarming reports of human-induced land degradation by water erosion can explain the strong emphasis on soil erosion control in the promotion of soil and water conservation. This applies especially to the savanna regions, where the majority of the soils are prone to wind and water erosion (Hoogmoed, 1999, p17). For instance, in rainfed agriculture the strong focus on soil conservation alone is curious, especially in view of the emphasis on irrigation as a key to success in the Green Revolution. It is as if rainfed agriculture by definition relies only on the rain falling on the land, while irrigation relies by definition on blue water supplied to the land.

Soil conservation, including such measures as terracing, contour ridges, strip cultivation and micro-basins aim to control erosion and maximize infiltration of rainfall in situ, within the farmer's field. Soil conservation thus has a moisture conservation effect, which explains why these measures normally fall under the label 'soil and water conservation'. An example of the positive results of soil conservation, but without full benefits of increases in productivity, comes from Kenya.

Farmers in the Machakos district in Kenya widely adopted soil conservation methods and farming diversification, which changed an area of vast land degradation in the 1930s to a reasonably well-conserved landscape in the 1990s. Tiffen et al (1994), showed that increased population pressure in this semi-arid savanna landscape contributed to a remarkable environmental recovery. A backbone to this recovery was the adoption among farmers of the *fanya juu* terracing technique to arrest soil erosion. Its success is undeniable and impressive. In most parts the landscape is now well conserved and supports a larger population than ever before (>100 persons per km²). This is an example of the positive implications of soil conservation, although the success is without the full benefits of improved agricultural productivity. Evidence of significant increases of crop yields is, for example, difficult to find in this region. The reason is that soil conservation alone cannot address the hydroclimatic challenges facing farmers in savannas.

Fundamental role of dry spell mitigation

Mitigation of dry spells is also an important factor to consider in increasing agricultural and water productivity in rainfed savanna farming. Farmers can compensate for dry spells using a wide variety of water-harvesting practices that aim at managing local surface and sub-surface runoff for productive use. Dry spell mitigation may have positive synergy effects on the farming system and is probably necessary for investment in other inputs to be worthwhile. Investing in dry spell mitigation can thus be the entry point for developing a positive spiral of productivity. It may trigger investments in soil and crop management, such as adding more organic matter, application of fertilizer and improvement of soil structure through appropriate tillage practices and crop rotations (Figure 8.2). These, in the long run, can progressively increase the productivity of the soil.

It is probable that the development of a sustainable, highly productive agricultural system can only begin with soil and water conservation. These elements are essential to establish the ecological stability required before embarking on productivity improvements. Dry spell mitigation and reducing the risks of crop failure can then follow, and will function as an incentive to further invest in production factors such as fertilization. As is hypothesized by Hai (Rockström, 2000), the adoption of water management practices such as water harvesting may be more likely among farmers who have already adopted soil and water conservation methods where the ecological preconditions required for full response to water management have already been established.

Linking farm and catchment scales

It makes sense from an ecohydrological perspective to use the geographical unit of a catchment or a river basin as the basis for management. The reason is that this hydrological unit enables the assessment of water availability and water impact from land use upstream on water users downstream. From an ecohydrological perspective, integrated catchment management for improved food production aims both at securing ecosystem goods and services, and promoting sustainable agriculture.[2] However, while a catchment approach based on delineating hydrological units along water divides may make sense to researchers, planners and managers, it may not make a lot of sense to local land users.

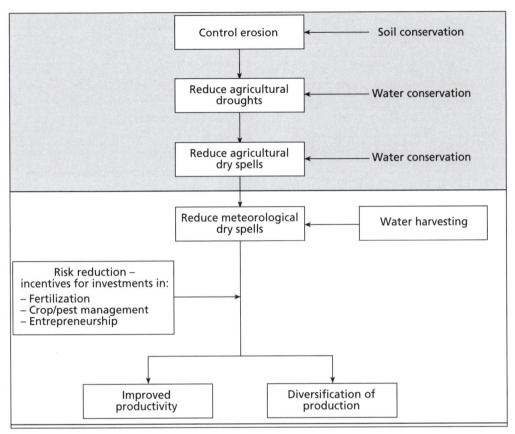

Note: Present focus is shown by the grey area.

Figure 8.2 *The soil and water management continuum in farm systems development*

Our main focus now is to highlight three important elements of integrated catchment management:

- To look at the ecohydrological implications downstream of land-use changes upstream (linking scales).
- To take into account the opportunities evolving from an integrated catchment approach to achieve ecohydrological synergies.
- To link the biophysical dimension with the social dimension.

The full benefits of improved water management for the farm or for the ecosystem can only be experienced if all factors affecting land-use management are addressed. This often requires equal attention to issues like tillage, weeding, pest and soil fertility management, as well as issues related to capital, land tenure and human capacities. Thus, integrated catchment management with a focus on smallholder farming covers production aspects (management approaches), human capacities (skills, incentives),

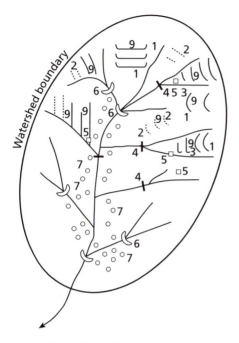

1   Contour trenching
2   Contour stone wall
3   Contour bunds
4   Check dams or gully plugging
5   Farm ponds
6   Percolation ponds
7   Wells
8   Irrigation tanks
9   In-situ moisture conservation measures

Source: Adapted from Sivanappan, 1995

Figure 8.3 *Integrated water management at the catchment scale in India*

financial aspects (capital and marketing), institutional aspects (community organization), and environmental aspects (management of shared natural resources on a spatial scale beyond the individual household).

All these components have to be addressed in order to achieve sustainable land-use practices at the community and catchment level. For example, Figure 8.3 outlines a desirable outcome in an Indian context of integrated soil and water management at the catchment scale (Sivanappan, 1995). Here, water harvesting, soil conservation and soil fertility management are integrated at the catchment-basin level. The aim is to increase agricultural production, generate employment and to reduce land degradation. To achieve this, capacities, institutions, and markets need to be in place. Furthermore, spatial planning of soil and water resources needs to take place at the catchment level. This is challenging, as most land-use planning at present takes place at the farm level. Planning of water use at the catchment level is complex, and there is only a limited institutional and policy foundation to support it. For example, spatial planning on a catchment scale in semi-arid tropical environments will include difficult decisions such as the sharing and management of storm flows in gullies, and ownership of rainfall and rill runoff flow collected in a water-harvesting system.

An example from northern Ethiopia can illustrate the difficulty of addressing water management at the scale beyond the farm level. Here, as in most countries in East Africa, farmers understand that storm runoff in gullies is a serious source of land degradation. However, individual farmers do not own large or rapidly developing gullies, and the gullies are therefore perceived as being the responsibility of the government. In an effort to make productive use of gullies and simultaneously conserve them, privatization of portions of the gullies was introduced (Axum area). The idea was that individual farmers would invest in conservation of the gullies by installing check dams, and then be given ownership to cultivate bananas, a cash crop, in the wet gullies. Initially, however, this innovation was unsuccessful. The reason was that there was no respected institutional arrangement for private ownership of the gullies, which meant that there was no guarantee that capital and labour investments of individual farmers would translate into benefits from the produce. Success was possible only when the benefits were safely attributed to the farmers who were plugging the gullies.

Consumptive water use by crops and downstream ecosystems

Except for productivity increases through vapour shift, increasing food production will always result in an increase of consumptive water use by crops. The relevant starting point for upgrading rainfed agriculture is at the farm level. The first step is to reduce the occurrence of agricultural droughts and dry spells by maximizing rainfall infiltration and minimizing deep percolation. Measures such as contour terracing, tillage, mulching, etc, are used to ensure the highest possible soil moisture availability over time, which is illustrated in Figure 8.4. Over the last 30 years most land management attention has been focused on the farm level. The aim of every farmer is to maximize infiltration and plant water uptake. Of the rain that falls on his or her land, the farmer's interest is to return as much as possible as green water flow, and leave as little as possible to form runoff. The same applies at the sub-catchment scale (for example, at village level), where land management is geared at maximizing consumptive use of water.

The aim of upstream agricultural water management on a farm and catchment scale is thus to hydrologically 'close' each scale – that is, to minimize the generation of blue water flow leaving each scale unit. This is in direct contrast to the expectations of downstream users that upstream catchments must remain hydrologically 'open', to assure that a minimum volume of runoff flow is received downstream.

Surface runoff is generated locally. A pulse of water flow may be generated from degraded foot paths, homesteads and marginal grazing areas, often lasting no longer than a couple of hours after each large rainfall event. Managing this water requires planning capabilities, institutions, a legal framework and human capacity. If this is in place, and the socioeconomic incentives are favourable, then catchment management of ephemeral runoff flow can involve private or community-based water-harvesting systems, such as gully diversions, farm ponds, small dams, contour terracing on a landscape scale, check dams, sand and sub-surface dams (catchment scale in Figure 8.4). The agricultural aim, in terms of water management, is still to minimize blue water flows out of the catchment, and to maximize blue water storage and green water flow within the catchment.

In conclusion, upgrading rainfed savanna agriculture includes two critical components of integrated catchment management:

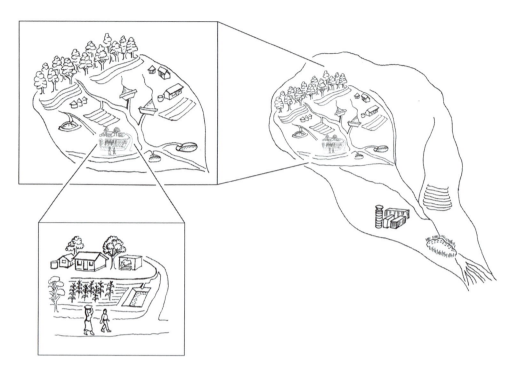

Note: The aim is to hydrologically close each scale, to minimize the generation of blue water flow leaving each scale unit, while the hydrological expectation of downstream users is that the upstream catchment should remain hydrologically open to ensure that a minimum volume of runoff flow is received downstream.

Figure 8.4 *Upstream agricultural water management on a farm and catchment scale*

- The human capacities and the institutional setting required to enable planning and management of water resources for productive purposes beyond the farm scale.
- The capacity to balance rainfall partitioning on a farm and catchment scale in order to secure water for downstream purposes (how to keep the catchment and river basin hydrologically open).

Water Sources for Dry Spell Mitigation

In Chapter 4 we focused attention on both green and blue water flows in water resources management. This is critical not only for securing water flows to sustain ecosystems dependent on indirect blue and green water use, but also for tapping the full potential of improving food production and water productivity in both rainfed and irrigated agriculture. The consequence of an integrated green and blue water approach is that management has its focus closer to the point in the landscape where the raindrop hits the soil. This is different to the conventional approach where focus is on the point where water turns into stable blue water runoff flow in aquifers and rivers. In other words, rain forms the entry point for ecohydrological landscape management.

Water harvesting

For food production a focus on rainfall opens up a wider spectrum of management options compared to a focus only on blue water management. Managing rain where it falls reduces the risk of erosion, as water is a major cause of erosion and the erosive force increases with speed and runoff volume. The water causing the erosion often originates in overland runoff produced on degraded land upstream where the soil surface has low permeability. Runoff will start at the micro-scale as sheet flow, and accumulate into rill flow on small areas within a field (<1 ha). Rills will aggregate into small gullies in a small catchment (generally <5 ha), which then merge into major gullies at the catchment level.

Management practices where runoff is collected and used for productive purposes are defined as water-harvesting systems. These can be grouped into three main types:

- In-situ moisture conservation (soil and water conservation).
- Concentration of runoff to crops in the field, on a field scale (runoff farming) or on a catchment scale (flood water harvesting).
- Collection and storage of runoff water (from roofs and land areas) in different structures (soil, ponds, dams, tanks) for both domestic and agricultural use.

Managing rainfall where it falls also maximizes the benefit of gravitational forces. For example, collecting runoff in a small dam upstream enables gravity-fed supplemental irrigation or water supply for domestic uses downstream. If instead the same runoff is allowed to flow down through the landscape and is captured in a dam reservoir downstream, it is very expensive to lift that water against the force of gravity back to a user upstream. During a farmer-to-farmer extension session on water harvesting, a Kenyan farmer who had adopted roof water harvesting for domestic water supply expressed in a succinct way the value of capturing rainfall upstream (at his house) compared to walking long distances downhill to a river to collect drinking water: 'Before, we let the rain run off and my wife had to carry it back up the hill again; now we take the same water directly from the roof without carrying it' (Kenyan farmer, Rolf Winberg, personal communication).

Managing rain where it falls not only increases the likelihood of reduced erosion and enables more energy-efficient water management: it also increases flexibility in ecohydrological landscape management. Runoff collection can be made in many small reservoirs storing less than 5000 m^3. The spatial distribution of water management is more flexible, with an almost unlimited number of options for small-scale rainwater management, compared to very few options for large-scale blue water management. This gives the opportunity to integrate water resource management more easily with conservation of other ecosystem goods and services.

Despite the opportunities offered by integrating rainwater management to more conventional water resource management of blue water flows, relatively little has been done in this field. In the words of RK Sivanappan (1995): 'Efficient rainwater management is the key for successful rainfed farming, although adequate research information is not available as it is in the case of irrigated agriculture.'

Groundwater for bridging dry spells

Contrary to common belief, the groundwater system is tightly connected to surface water resources. Recharge of groundwater leads to an increase of the groundwater stock, which eventually leads to seepage of groundwater to surface water. During the dry season, rivers are completely fed by groundwater. Consumption of renewable groundwater invariably leads to a reduction of stream flow. The essential difference between surface water and groundwater is the residence time. Surface water has a short residence time, generally leaving the system within a hydrological year (unless large storage works have been constructed). Groundwater has much higher residence times, depending on the size and slope of the aquifers. In flat areas groundwater systems may have residence times exceeding thousands of years. Aquifers with very long residence times (in the order of millions of years) are considered fossil aquifers.

The fact that groundwater has higher residence times makes it special. As a result:

- Groundwater is more reliable – it is there even when it doesn't rain.
- The quantities of water for sustainable use are generally small.
- It is more vulnerable – polluted groundwater remains in the system a long time.
- It has a wide distribution and is often available in situ.

In view of these facts, groundwater is a perfect resource for quantities of high-quality drinking water. It is, however, a limited resource for irrigated agriculture, which generally requires large amounts of water. There are good opportunities, nevertheless, to combine groundwater from shallow wells with rainfed agriculture. Shallow aquifers have a much shorter residence time, and a small stock. During the wet season, groundwater is widely available in shallow aquifers: the same aquifers that communities use for shallow wells. During dry spells, it is possible to withdraw water from these shallow aquifers with low-lift pumps and to use that water for watering gardens or small agricultural plots. In doing so, the farmer may draw down the shallow aquifer completely, but that is not a problem, since the rains following the dry spell will recharge it. On the sandy soils of northern Bangladesh, this approach has led to a substantial increase in production during the dry season. In combination with rainwater harvesting, supplemental irrigation from groundwater may also be a feasible option for savanna environments.

The management of groundwater is much simpler than that of surface water (Savenije, 1998, 1999) – for example, each farmer could have a single well of a limited capacity. Wells can have a relatively low capacity, since the amount of water required to bridge a dry spell is small and generally not more than 20–60 mm (which corresponds to 200–600 m^3/ha). For supplementary irrigation farmers can temporarily exceed the safe yield from a well and pump it dry to bridge a dry spell. A low aquifer capacity often experienced in water scarce areas would prevent full irrigation in the dry season, which is positive as such irrigation is not desirable in water-scarce areas, but it would be more than sufficient for household supply and would allow women in particular to dedicate their time to other economic activities.

Consequently, securing groundwater to bridge dry spells allows farmers to invest in seeds and fertilizers, to use their labour more efficiently, and to conserve their resources. Under such improved conditions, the economic returns from using external fertilizers and of using additional blue water are high.

Upstream blue water – an untapped resource

In Chapter 4 we drew attention to the important role of scale in ecohydrology and water resource management. Blue water flow is conventionally understood as a downstream concept, including the perennial flow of surface runoff in rivers and accessible groundwater. However, water travels a long journey from raindrop to blue water flow, and only a fraction of locally generated runoff upstream will finally end up as blue water flow downstream. (We define the local runoff that evaporates before reaching a perennial river or a groundwater table as 'upstream blue water flow'.)

Local surface runoff is thus the main source of water for upgrading rainfed agriculture in savanna agro-ecosystems. However, not all this surface runoff would evaporate and be considered upstream blue water in the strict sense. Some of the local runoff may eventually reach a river. Quantifying upstream blue water is therefore not easy. What we know is that local runoff flow forms an important water resource base on the local, field and catchment scale, for ecological habitat, direct and indirect human use, and direct ecosystem use. The problem is to understand the partitioning of local runoff into evaporation or upstream blue water, transpiration and groundwater recharge, which can be used further downstream. The opportunity cost of consumptive use of upstream blue water is also not evident. Rockström (1997) showed that a large proportion of storm runoff in a catchment in Niger inundated a lowland and was partitioned between open water evaporation and percolation. Studies in Zimbabwe, on small low-lying seasonal wetlands called *dambos*, which are common throughout Southern Africa, show that groundwater recharge is, in fact, very limited. In Chapter 7 we made a crude estimate of the possible contribution of upstream blue water flow to future food production (300 km^3/year, Table 7.3). As we have shown in this chapter, even small volumes of supplementary water flow in rainfed savanna farming can make a large difference in terms of production, water productivity and risk perceptions among farmers.

The Upstream–Downstream Perspective

There is no space in this book to exhaust the full set of options available to upgrade rainfed agriculture through integrated soil and water management. Instead, here we give a brief glimpse of the opportunity to mitigate dry spells through water harvesting, which is a key entry point to sustainable agriculture in savanna environments.

Effective use of small volumes of blue water

Dry spell mitigation can be achieved through supplemental irrigation of rainfed crops (Oweis et al, 1999; SIWI, 2001a). This water-harvesting strategy adds a blue water flow

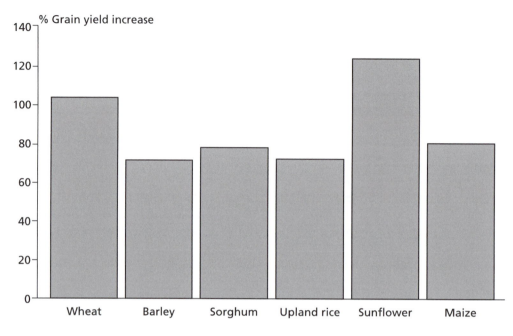

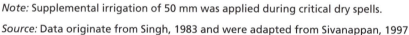

Figure 8.5 *Yield increase for various food crops from supplemental irrigation in savanna agriculture in India*

component, an irrigation component, to a green rainfed system, through storage of blue runoff flow in surface or sub-surface reservoirs, or directly in the soil as groundwater for use during periods of crop water stress. Supplemental irrigation for dry spell mitigation can be one of the most promising strategies for upgrading rainfed agriculture in semi-arid and dry sub-humid savannas. Supplemental irrigation is interesting, since only a limited volume of additional water is required to substantially increase both water productivity and yield levels. Examples of yield increases through supplemental irrigation of rainfed crops in semi-arid savannas are given in Figure 8.5 for several food crops in India. With 50 mm of supplemental irrigation during critical dry spells, yield levels were increased by 70–120 per cent on average.[3] Thus, even small volumes of water (in this case a complementary supply of 500 m³ per hectare equal to 50 mm in rainfed cropping systems) can have a major impact on system productivity if applied at the right time. For sorghum, in the example in Figure 8.5, supplemental irrigation increased the grain yield from 1400 kg/ha to 2100 kg/ha. For a farm household with 1 ha, the additional 700 kg of grain can feed three family members throughout the year.

Successful water-harvesting systems for supplemental irrigation may even have a storage capacity of less than 300 m³. In the dry semi-arid Gansu Province of China (annual rainfall 420 mm), droughts and dry spells are extremely common, occurring

634 times over the last 1400 years (Zhu and Li, 2000). Farmers' staple food yields are on average 1 t/ha. During dry years the yields do not even compensate for the purchase of seed. Farmers are poor, with an annual income of less than US$1 per day for an average five-member family. The region is dominated by flat loess soils with low runoff generation, and only a small portion of the rainfall is used as productive green water flow. Small bottle-shaped sub-surface tanks, with a storage volume of 10–60 m^3 (on average 30 m^3), are used to mitigate dry spells. They are promoted on a large scale among over 1 million smallholder farmers. The impact of these small systems for harvesting water is impressive. Water productivity increases of 20 per cent and yield increases of wheat with 1500 kg/ha are reported (Li et al., 2000).

In Kenya (Machakos District) and in Ethiopia smallholder farmers have adopted similar tanks. These sub-surface spherical tanks with roughly 15 m^3 of storage capacity are used to irrigate kitchen gardens, and enable farmers to diversify sources of income from the land. Such micro-irrigation schemes are promoted together with commercially available low-pressure drip irrigation systems. Cheap drip irrigation kits prevent up to 90 per cent of soil evaporation, and are increasingly adopted among farmers in Kenya, for example. Combining water harvesting with drip irrigation can result in very significant improvements in water productivity (Ngigi et al, 2000).

Small ponds for supplemental irrigation can increase yields and water productivity, especially if they are combined with soil fertility management. In Kenya (Machakos District) and in Burkina Faso (Ouaigouya) farmers have been testing small systems in which surface runoff is collected from 1–2 ha catchments and stored in manually dug farm ponds with a 100–250 m^3 storage capacity (Barron et al, 1999; Fox and Rockström, 2000). In these systems simple gravity-fed furrow irrigation was used. Passion fruit, a cash crop in the region, was grown on the edges of the farm pond and on a wire grid covering the pond in order to provide shading to reduce evaporation losses (Plate 8.1). Small volumes of supplemental irrigation were applied during dry spells (on average 70 mm). Typically for semi-arid agro-ecosystems, dry spells occurred every rainy season, and seasonal rainfall ranged from approximately 200 to 600 mm in the Kenyan location (with two rainy seasons per year) and 400–700 mm in the location in Burkina Faso. In Kenya, one out of five rainy seasons was classified as a meteorological drought (short rains of 1998/99), resulting in complete crop failure. One season at each site (long rains 2000 in Kenya and the rainy season 2000 in Burkina Faso) resulted in complete crop failure for most neighbouring farmers, while the water-harvesting system enabled the harvest of an above-average yield (>1 t/ha). The seasonal long-term average yield levels for traditional farming in both areas are approximately 0.5 t/ha.

The water productivity perspective

From an ecohydrological perspective, increasing yields through water harvesting is not enough for an assessment of water trade-offs between humans and nature. One also needs to focus on the implications of water harvesting on water productivity on a local scale and establish how much water is required per unit of food produced. This is critical, as the amount of water required to produce food will determine the amount of water available downstream to sustain ecosystems. At a catchment scale, we need to look into the upstream and downstream implications of harvesting local runoff water.

Photo: Johan Rockström

Plate 8.1 *Farm pond for supplemental irrigation in Machakos District, Kenya*

An example of the combined effect on water productivity and grain yield of supplemental irrigation from farm ponds is shown for sorghum in Burkina Faso in Figure 8.6a, and for maize in Kenya in Figure 8.6b. Water productivity is given as the amount of grain dry matter produced per mm of water supplied (rain plus supplemental irrigation). Each point represents final grain yield over three years. In Burkina Faso supplemental irrigation alone on shallow soil with low water holding capacity improved water productivity (rainfall + irrigation) over the traditional rainfed practice using zai pits (manual hand-hoeing in small planting pits filled with a soil manure mixture). The increases were on average 37 per cent or from 0.9 to 1.2 kg/mm/ha. For comparison, the corresponding figure for the Kenyan case, on deep soil with high water holding capacity, was 38 per cent or from 2.2 to 3.1 kg/mm/ha (here the traditional practice is animal-drawn ploughing).

The largest improvement in yield and rain water productivity was achieved by combining supplemental irrigation and management of soil fertility through fertilizer application. Interestingly, for both locations, fertilizer application alone resulted in higher average yields than supplemental irrigation without fertilizer during years with gentle dry spells.[4] For seasons with severe dry spells, eg the failing long rains in Kenya in 2000, non-irrigated crops resulted in complete crop failure regardless of fertilizer level. These results indicate that full benefits of water harvesting for supplemental irrigation can only be met by simultaneously addressing soil fertility management.

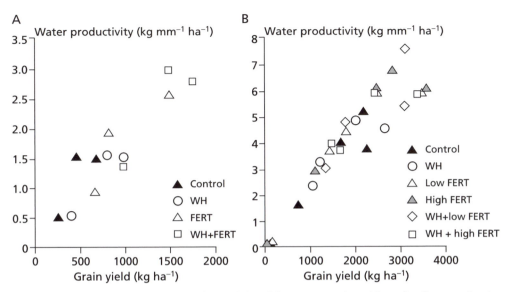

A   Water productivity (kg mm^{-1} ha^{-1})

Control
WH
FERT
WH+FERT

Grain yield (kg ha^{-1})

B   Water productivity (kg mm^{-1} ha^{-1})

Control
WH
Low FERT
High FERT
WH+low FERT
WH + high FERT

Grain yield (kg ha^{-1})

Note: A = Sorghum; B = Maize; Control = traditional farmers' practice with no fertilizer application; WH = supplemental irrigation using water harvesting; FERT = fertilizer application (30 kg/ ha N in Burkina Faso, and two levels in Kenya with Low-30 kg/ ha N and High-80 kg/ ha N).

Figure 8.6 *System water use efficiency (kg grain per unit rainfall + supplemental irrigation) for sorghum in Burkina Faso and maize in Kenya*

An ecohydrological win–win solution

As shown in these examples, integrating water harvesting with soil fertility management resulted in progressively increased water productivity and improvements in yield. From an ecohydrological perspective this is important. It is in line with our discussions in Chapter 7 on the opportunities to use appropriate management to reduce the amount of water needed to produce food while at the same time increase yield levels. This can reduce the need to use in water in agriculture that is presently sustaining ecosystem services.

We can safely assume that the linear relationship between crop yield and transpiration applies in the example in Figure 8.6. Such a linear relationship between yield and consumptive water use implies a constant relationship between water productivity and yield; a constant incremental increase in transpiration is followed by an increase in yield. This means that the yield increase originates from improvements in the amount of 'crop per raindrop'. The yield increase is therefore a result of a reduction in other water flows in the field water balance such as soil evaporation, percolation and runoff. It is important to note though, that while each yield increase generally requires more productive green water flow (more water is needed to produce more food), the point is that for each new kilogram of food a lower relative volume of water is required to generate it.

There are several empirical examples of this important ecohydrological win–win opportunity of using less water for food while food production is increased at the same time. Experiments on maize in a semi-arid Sahelian savanna setting by Pandey et al (2000) showed that as grain yield increased from 1 to 4.5 t/ha, green water productivity doubled from around 3 to 6 kg of grain per mm of green water flow. The yield increase in this case was achieved by adding irrigation water and nitrogen fertilizer. On wheat trials in the Mediterranean region, Zhang and Oweis (1999) showed that both yields and green water productivity are increased when using water harvesting to mitigate dry spells.

Upgrading rainfed agriculture while safeguarding ecological functions that depend on water is important. A focus on the local level where rainfall hits the soil is also important because the field scale and small catchment scale must be the primary focus of attention for management of upstream blue water flow. A remaining question is how much harvesting local runoff affects the availability of water resources and ecological functions downstream.

Summary

In Chapter 7 we quantified the ecohydrological measures urgently needed to feed a growing world population while at the same time securing water for ecological functions. Even though the challenge facing mankind is enormous, with an estimated 5600 km³/year of additional fresh water required, we also showed that there are many opportunities for reducing the ecohydrological trade-offs between water for food and nature. We estimated a potential saving of 1,500 km³/year through various strategies of water productivity improvements, where more crop is produced per drop of water. In this chapter we have addressed the question of how to act on the double challenge of producing more food with less water in the ecohydrologically vulnerable savanna zone.

The bulk of population growth and food deficits occurring in tropical developing countries indicate the magnitude of the food challenge, which requires new approaches in agricultural land and water management. Nothing less than a new, ecohydrologically-anchored Green Revolution is required, and we argue that participatory approaches linked with novel innovations to upgrade rainfed agriculture are urgently needed. Set in the context of integrated catchment management, which is a prerequisite for balancing water resources between food and nature, adaptive and sustainable development can be achieved using various promising small-scale innovations in soil and water management.

Dry spell mitigation is identified as one of the key entry points for upgrading rainfed agriculture. Similarly, while meteorological droughts are virtually impossible to manage through land and water interventions in rainfed farming systems, opportunities are available to reduce the occurrence of agricultural droughts. This is especially the case where water scarcity is related to mismanagement, which creates soil moisture deficits caused by poor rainfall partitioning. Importantly, even if water is not necessarily the primary limiting factor for crop growth even in savanna agro-ecosystems, it is likely the most important entry point to upgrade rainfed agriculture. The reason is that rainfall is the only truly random production factor, and rainfall strongly affects farmers' risk perceptions.

Upgrading rainfed agriculture within the context of ecohydrological landscape management requires a farming systems approach that links the farm household with the catchment. Core elements of this upgrading are productive management of local blue water flows and integration of water and soil management, especially in terms of soil moisture and soil fertility.

With regard to land and water innovations, which have the capacity to upgrade rainfed savanna agriculture, this chapter put special focus on water harvesting practices. These cover a broad spectrum of small-scale techniques and methodologies for productive use of runoff flow on a scale from the field level to the catchment-basin level. Water harvesting offers a broad set of practices to mitigate dry spells and maximise plant water availability. Case examples were presented showing that water harvesting can achieve significant increases in yield and water productivity. More crop is produced per drop of water and per unit land. A key feature behind such win–win effects is a reversal of present trends of human-induced land degradation in favour of a progressive build-up of ecological resilience and soil productivity. Conservation tillage is given as a good example of a soil and water management strategy that aims at returning the soil to conditions similar to its virgin state. In the process it increases both yields and water productivity and it reduces traction and labour requirements. This is important from an ecohydrological perspective. Increasing demand for water for food is a threat towards securing ecological functions that are dependent on water. Every saving of water through 'crop per drop' improvements, and every increase in the productivity of existing cropland, will reduce the pressure of water trade-offs between food and nature.

It is not easy to extrapolate successful examples of upgrading rainfed agriculture in trying to answer the question of whether the large water savings discussed in Chapter 7 (reducing fresh water requirements in rainfed agriculture with 1500 km³/year in 2050) are realistic. Similarly, it is not easy to assess whether a doubling or even tripling of yield levels is realistic over the next two generations. What can safely be said, however, is that there are numerous examples of affordable, socially and environmentally appropriate water management strategies that can double and even triple yield levels in rainfed savanna farming systems. These are most successful if combined with farm management methods in general and soil fertility management in particular. Here, we have given summaries of promising examples, especially on water harvesting, from various parts of the world. Our optimistic outlook is in line with other more comprehensive assessments of opportunities to upgrade rainfed agriculture. For example, in a global study specifically focusing on the potential of so-called sustainable agricultural systems with minimum use of external inputs such as fertilisers and pesticides, Pretty and Hine (2001) clearly showed that there are large opportunities to upgrade such systems. According to their study of 90 development projects around the world a 50–100 per cent increase of rainfed yields were achieved, and in a few cases they were considerably higher. This should be compared to the low 5–10 per cent yield increases achieved in projects on irrigated crops, which had, however, a higher starting yield.

Even though there is an ecohydrological win–win situation for increasing agricultural and water productivity in rainfed agriculture, in absolute terms there will still be a need for more water for food production. The reason is that every incremental increase in food will be followed by a proportional increase in productive green water flow. This is unavoidable. The question that is still valid and largely unanswered concerns increased use of agricultural water upstream and its implications for the availability of blue water to sustain ecological functions. And even after our estimates of how far water productivity can contribute to reduce water for food requirements in 2050, there remains a staggering 3300 km^3/year deficit if we take on the challenge of feeding the whole world population in two generations' time.

It is often argued that virtual water trade can solve this problem by importing food from water-rich to water-scarce countries. Yet food imports already constitute a virtual trade of water, as behind each tonne of, for example, grain, some 1000–3000 tonnes of water are hidden. As shown by Postel (1998) 25 per cent of the world grain trade in the 1990s was already driven by water scarcity, manifested primarily by grain imports to arid countries with high purchasing power. For vulnerable environments in the world, virtual water trading is a less-evident solution. There the majority of the population make their living from agriculture; food demand is high and increasing rapidly; purchasing power is low, and alternative sources of income are few. Our conclusion is that from a socioeconomic perspective all efforts will have to be made to facilitate a process of improved water and agricultural productivity *where the rain falls*. However, the unavoidable deficit between the demand for food and the local production that can be attained will have to be bridged through 'virtual water' trade (ie through imports of food, where the water to produce it originates outside the region of consumption). The challenge will be, however, to follow a productivity path that increases local food production and thereby generates both food and environmental security. The implications for ecohydrological landscape management of this remaining challenge will be addressed in the next chapter.

Part 3
Socio-ecohydrological Balancing

Chapter 9

Finding a Balance Between Water for Humans and for Nature

The challenge is to live with change without destroying the ability of the life-support system to uphold the supply of ecological goods and services in situations of disturbances and variability.

Humans and Ecosystems Depend on the Same Water

The grand, unresolved issue

In Chapter 4 we clarified the fundamental life support functions of water. Green and blue water flows are directly and indirectly involved in ecohydrological functions. These functions form the foundation of direct support for human life, but also the indirect support for the sustainability and resilience of humanity's natural resource base. Food production is our biggest water consumer, and by introducing a generic human water requirement to supply food, we pointed to a close link between food and ecosystems. Approximately 4000 litres of water are required each day to supply an adequate diet for a human being. This is an annual water requirement of 1300 m^3 per person and is almost ten times higher than the per person water needs for domestic and industrial purposes added together.

Feeding an additional 3 billion people and freeing the present 800 million people from malnutrition will require 5600 km^3 of additional consumptive water use in agriculture, assuming present land use. We further estimated that 800 km^3/year of this amount may derive from an increase in irrigation. In chapters 7 and 8 we investigated how much out of these 4800 km^3/year could be provided by improving water productivity in agriculture – by 'more crop per drop' approaches. There we focused on tropical regions, where the bulk of population growth occurs, and more specifically on savanna agro-ecosystems, where options for improved green water use in agriculture may be quite substantial. We showed that more crop per drop might contribute some 1500 km^3/year, leaving 3300 km^3/year of additional fresh water to be found elsewhere. This indicates the scale of future water trade-off, where water flow will have to shift from natural ecosystems to agriculture.

This volume can be considered an indicator of the unresolved ecohydrological challenge facing mankind. It is an amount of water almost as large as the direct global

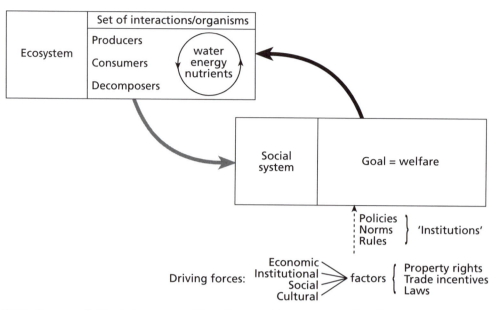

Note: Human activities to improve social welfare are driven by compelling forces and influenced by the institutional system, but involve the production of waste and disturbances influencing the functioning of the ecosystems.

Figure 9.1 *Human dependence on ecosystems offering renewable resources and producing ecological services*

blue water withdrawals at present. From where will this additional volume of fresh water come? Trade-offs between water for nature and humans will be required. In this chapter we will lay the foundation for the 'socio-ecohydrological' management approach needed.

Water and ecosystems

Water plays multiple roles through its many different functions in the dynamics of both ecosystems and social systems (see Chapter 1). It is the determinant and life elixir of terrestrial ecosystems as carrier of nutrients, and it is the habitat of aquatic ecosystems. In social systems, it has vital functions for human life support, such as food production, energy production, as transport medium, as mobile dissolvent, as microclimate moderator, and as an energy carrier on a global scale.

When linking human society and ecosystems, the latter may be seen as essential and dynamic 'actors of production' for social and economic development (Folke, 1997), and the ecological life-support system is essential in interacting both with the biogeochemical cycles and with the water cycles. Ecosystems produce both renewable resources and ecosystem services on which the well-being of human society is based. There cannot be any production of renewable resources and ecosystem services without an ecosystem producing them (see Figure 9.1).

The ecosystem is a biological conception and refers to the interaction between groups of organisms living in a certain biophysical environment. The link to hydrology and water management is the water determinants of a specific ecosystem that is in the water characteristics that determine the habitats, and the growing conditions. Ecosystems are genuinely water-dependent, but the particular type of water is not always specified. Some types of ecosystem, such as forests, bogs or grasslands, are rainwater-dependent. Others, such as certain wetlands, depend on groundwater, or on surface water, for example, floodplains. Ecosystems providing ecological services may be either terrestrial or aquatic. To protect a specific ecological service, such as for instance denitrification, one needs to protect those ecosystems that produce that type of service, in this case wetlands.

When looking at ecosystems from a hydrological perspective, one has also to distinguish between upstream ecosystems and downstream ecosystems. Upstream ecosystems are involved in rainwater partitioning between the evaporating part, the flood flow part and the groundwater part. The downstream ecosystems tend to be victims of river depletion, seasonal changes in stream flow and degradation of water quality.

Three entry points for alterations of aquatic ecosystem caused by water

Since aquatic ecosystems are genuinely blue water dependent, they are very vulnerable to changes in river flow and quality, and therefore to human activities upstream – whether they are river regulations, pollution loads or consumptive water use. Human activities may create many different types of threats to these ecosystems, such as overfishing, pollution, eutrophication and introduction of exotic species. The relevant water-related determinants have to be clarified first in order to protect a particular ecosystem.

Three kinds of human activity threaten aquatic ecosystems. Figure 9.2 shows the causal links between alterations of ecosystem goods and services and the human activities in the landscape, which are related to the supply of food, water and energy, and to the generation of income. Three entry points are involved in these modifications of water in the ecosystem:

- flow control measures to fit flow seasonality to seasonal water demand;
- land-cover changes influencing soil permeability and rainwater partitioning, and consequently the generation of runoff;
- water withdrawals and after-use alterations in terms of consumptive water use and pollution load, respectively.

Since the introduction of agriculture and sedentary societies some 10,000 years ago, humans have exploited and regulated blue water flow in rivers, and therefore have had an impact on the aquatic ecosystem in those rivers. During the last hundred years, the development of rivers has accelerated, in step with the needs of a rapidly increasing world population. At present in-stream blue water flows are seldom completely natural. They are most often subject to some form of artificial regulation, designed to

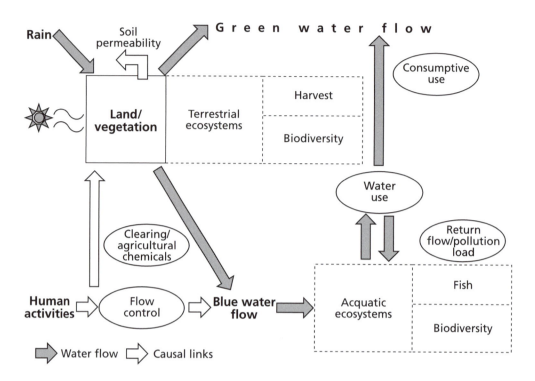

Figure 9.2 *Modification of blue water flow by direct and indirect human activities: flow control structures, consumptive use, and land/vegetation manipulation*

smooth over seasonal and spatial differences in stream flow and to adapting water availability better to water needs. Particular attention has been drawn to the major impact that regulation of blue water flow in rivers has on both average discharge and on the flooding/drying regime of wetlands connected to the river. Storing water behind dams has already reached a massive scale in the developed part of the world, while many developing countries in Africa are still striving to cope with a much larger temporal variability of both rainfall and runoff. The typical per capita storage volumes in sub-Saharan African countries are only 10 per cent or even less, compared to North America (Abrams, 2003). Aquatic ecosystems may also be linked to groundwater. In such cases, over-exploitation of groundwater can affect ecological functions by reducing groundwater discharge and therefore the river flow during periods of the year critical to in-stream ecology (Dunbar and Acreman, 2001).

Terrestrial ecosystems, changes in land use and land cover

Whereas aquatic ecosystems are blue water dependent, the terrestrial ones are green water dependent. They are intimately linked to the rainwater partitioning process, and responsible for most of the green water flow back to the atmosphere. As discussed in Chapter 2, land cover changes tend to alter the rainfall partitioning, the relative proportions of green and blue water flows. They may also alter the relative proportions of fast-flowing storm runoff and slow-flowing low flow originating from groundwater seepage. Terrestrial ecosystems consume large amounts of water – in fact, two-thirds of the precipitation over the continents. Changes in land cover affect the relative proportions of green and blue water flow and the proportions of storm runoff and groundwater recharge that feed rivers with time-stable flow. The impact of deforestation on the local water balance is an issue that has caught considerable interest in hydrological communities (Calder, 1999). The stream flow change is the accumulated result of what happens with the two partitioning points, and the kind of vegetation that replaces the former trees. In the developing world, as stressed in Chapter 1, much attention has gone to the upper partitioning point by highlighting the perceived role of forests as '*water-providing* ecosystems'. Macropores facilitate groundwater recharge in an active process of infiltration. This function may progressively vanish after deforestation, leading to reduced dry-season flow. Where soils are permeable, as is often the case in temperate zones, the lower partitioning point is the more relevant one (Sandström, 1995). The response to deforestation is increased stream flow. Forests are in reality '*water-consuming* ecosystems', a view also reflected in South Africa, where forest plantation as a stream flow reducing activity was incorporated in a new water law.

Thus, while the total runoff increases after deforestation, the principal source of increase is from reduced transpiration. This is a result of the replacement of deeper-rooted trees by crops with more shallow roots. The largest change is a reduction of the delayed flow component, a decrease of the dry season flow (GWP, 1999). The hydraulic properties of surface soil, which determine the rainfall infiltration capacity of the soils, are vulnerable to compaction and loss of organic matter when forests are removed. This results in rapid reduction of groundwater recharge, which impacts the low flow in the river. Of particular importance in forest ecosystems is the proliferation of macropores as a result of root activity, which contributes in great measure to rainfall infiltration. With deforestation these infiltration canals are progressively lost with the deterioration of the biological activity associated with the forest.

Decreasing stream flow or river depletion over time is a well-known and widespread but poorly analysed phenomenon. It is a plausible result of increased consumptive use of water. Unfortunately, current statistics do not provide good overviews of how river discharge has changed over time in different parts of the world. There is only scanty information on the real dimension of the current river depletion in response to human activities. Except for changes caused by climate, river flow may alter over time in two parallel ways. The first is caused by changes in consumptive water use, and the other by changes in land-use. These changes have consequences for altered rainwater partitioning between green and blue water flows, which alter runoff production. Lannerstad (2002) provides numerous examples of streamflow reduction. One set of examples includes river depletion in catchments, including the Nile; the Yellow River and the Huai River, both in Northeast China; the Chao Phraya River in Thailand; the Murray Darling River in Australia; and the Logone River in West Africa. The other group of examples reflects cases where out-of-basin transfer has contributed further to reduced stream flow in the downstream part. Examples of such rivers are the Colorado River (North America), the Aral Sea tributaries, the Indus, the Ganges, and the Jordan.

The results of land-use changes are often strongly felt in ecosystems in semi-arid regions. A concrete example of such vulnerability on a regional scale is the impact that deforestation has had on rainwater partitioning. Gordon (2001) has analysed the consequences of large-scale land-use changes during the past 200 years for river runoff from the Australian continent. These changes altered the partitioning of rainfall and the green water flow. The substantial clearing of the pristine eucalyptus woodlands by European immigrants involved a remarkable decrease in woody vegetation and a corresponding increase in croplands and grasslands. Switching from perennial vegetation to seasonal ones resulted in a reduced green water flow and an increased runoff. The water flow implications were estimated to a 10 per cent decrease in green water flow with a corresponding increase in blue water flow. This increase corresponds almost exactly to the current blue water flow from the continent. These hidden green water flow changes are seen as major causes for the large-scale dryland salinization problems in Australian soils and water systems that are now creating such high costs.

Upstream-downstream linkages – Lake Victoria as an illustration

Hydrological changes made by human action upstream may have strong effects downstream, both on aquatic ecosystems and on riparian communities depending on those ecosystems for their livelihood (see Figure 9.3). Lake Victoria, the world's second largest freshwater lake and the largest tropical lake, offers an illustration. This lake directly and indirectly supports 30 million people who generate a gross annual economic product in the order of US$3–4 billion. The lake produces approximately 170,000 tonnes of fish each year, supporting lakeshore communities in an area with one of the densest (up to 1200 people/km^2) and poorest rural populations in the world.

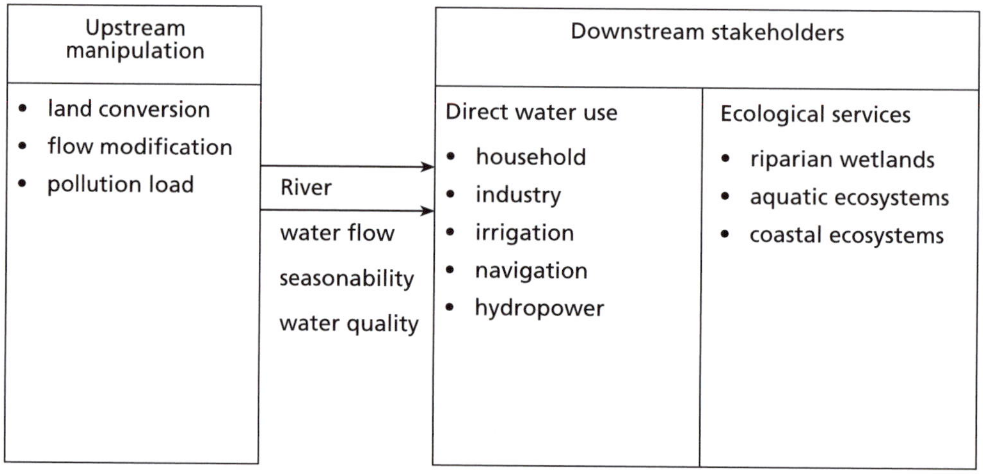

Upstream manipulation	Downstream stakeholders	
• land conversion • flow modification • pollution load River water flow seasonability water quality	Direct water use • household • industry • irrigation • navigation • hydropower	Ecological services • riparian wetlands • aquatic ecosystems • coastal ecosystems

Source: Adapted from Falkenmark, 1999

Figure 9.3 *Conflicting interests in upstream and downstream activities where catchment-based reconciliation methods are needed*

In this region environmental deterioration caused by humans over the last decades has resulted in serious negative impacts. The increased nutrient load going into the lake and the colonization by the water hyacinth (*Eichhornia crassipes*) in the late 1980s have resulted in extensive eutrophication, reduced light penetration, increased evaporation from invading swamp fauna, and reduced biodiversity of aquatic plants and fish species. The invasion of water hyacinths has prevented numerous rural communities from fishing, which was their source of living. The nutrient load originates from several sources; the relative role of these sources is still debated. Possible sources are: sediment flow from water erosion caused by land degradation in rural uplands; waste effluent from urban discharge; loading from atmospheric deposition from forest burning; and wind erosion (ICRAF, 2000). Overgrazing, deforestation and intensive agricultural practices in the upper catchment have increased stormflow and deep gully erosion, which all contribute to sediment loading in the lake. The social and economic consequences are seen both in the disastrous effects of a deteriorated resource base for shoreline fishing communities, and in the reduced social resilience and deteriorated livelihood base of the agricultural communities living upstream.

Learning to Live with Change

Co-evolution

The fact that human activities always involve landscape modifications is now being increasingly acknowledged and is generating a shift in thinking among ecologists. While it is being understood that humanity will have to live with change, the conventional idea of securing 'ecosystem balance' is now being slowly abandoned. The study by van der Leeuw and colleagues (2000) has contributed to this shift. They analysed the co-evolution of society and nature and the relationship between humans and their environment in the Mediterranean region over a 20,000-year period. The studies covered badlands, droughts and flash floods in Spain; salinization and water mismanagement in south Greece; a mix of tectonic activity and human interactions with vegetation in north-west Greece; and 7000 years of human activity in the Rhone valley in France. The result suggested that no single set of natural dynamics could be identified as responsible for the extensive land degradation observed in the different case studies. The outcome was rather the result of a converging set of social processes, interacting with the surrounding environment, a co-evolution of social and environmental processes. The group realized that human reaction to environmental change is less direct than other species, because society has to become aware of the problem before it can consciously respond. The study also questioned the idea of sustainability in the meaning 'to continue living as we do forever', an idea that rests on the assumption that stability is natural and humanly achievable. The long-term perspective of the study, however, suggests this is an illusion. Stability is probably an exception worth particular analysis. The consequence is that rather than assuming stability and explaining change, one needs to assume change and explain stability.

Resilience and biodiversity

Certain key ecological functions are of societal interest to secure. These include the capacity of the life-support system to deliver food, biomass and ecological services of various kinds and to endure disturbances and variability. It is of vital importance to secure these functions. They can be defined as the ecological resilience of an ecosystem that is the capacity to absorb change without loss of stability. There are two kinds of resilience to keep in mind: social resilience, or the coping capacity of society and its institutions, and ecological resilience, which means the coping capability within the ecosystems itself. These two are interdependent.

> *An ecosystem's capacity to absorb change without losing functions is closely linked to its self-organizing ability for renewal and re-organization following a change. When a social or an ecological system loses resilience, it becomes vulnerable to change that could previously be absorbed. Without resilience, ecosystems respond to gradual change by sudden switches to contrasting regimes, triggered by stochastic events like storms, fire, drought or sudden pollution episodes. In a system that has lost resilience, a sudden ecological shock such as a drought, or a social shock like a price change may easily result in a change that can cause societal problems through disruption to previous ways of life. As resilience declines, it takes progressively smaller external events to cause a catastrophe. Reducing resilience in other words increases vulnerability* (Folke et al, 2002).

While resilience is a buffer to disturbance, biological diversity plays an essential role in this buffer capacity – it acts as insurance by providing overlapping functions for restoring ecosystem capacity to generate essential ecological services. Components that can re-establish ecosystems following disturbance are essential to protect (Falkenmark and Folke, 2002): a minimum composition of organisms has to be retained to secure the relations between the primary producers, consumers, and decomposers that mediate the flow of energy, and the cycling of elements and spatial and temporal patterns of vegetation. Loss of biodiversity reduces ecosystem resilience to change. In this situation, the way to proceed is considered to be through adaptive management, which is understood within the context of test-based management responses. Complex (many factors interacting) and dynamic (changes over time and in space) responses from ecosystems to human management interventions bring quick feedback loops, resulting in adaptation of management in tune with ecosystem response. What is meant is an ecosystem management approach based on a close science-based policy development. In a situation where stressed ecosystems tend to change – not gradually but in lurches by surpassing thresholds and in response to surprises and in ways that are seldom predictable – societal reactions have to give room for uncertainties (Holling et al, 1998).

Management has therefore to be adaptive, in other words respond to feedbacks from the environment by a learning-by-doing approach. What is referred to is a science-based trial-and-error management response before the suspected change has advanced beyond reversibility.

The challenge is to act before the crisis phase has accumulated in magnitude and scale. When the ecological crisis has manifested itself, conflicts can be expected due to the societal disruptions caused. Adaptive management deals with unpredictable interactions between people and ecosystems as they evolve together. Resource management policies are tested to see if they work in the sense of reducing the risk perceived.

Three examples of resilience reduction

Three examples might further clarify the phenomenon of resilience. Resilience of *semi-arid rangelands* is dependent on the ability of the landscape to maintain water infiltration, soil water storage, nutrient cycles and vegetation structure. Rangeland vegetation shifts between dominance of grass and of woody plants and shrubs. The shifts are driven by fire and grazing pressure under highly variable rainfall. Human prevention of fire and persistent grazing pressure shifts rangelands towards a less productive woody state (Walker, 1993).

Cloud forests are another example where loss of trees generates shifts in the state of the ecosystem. Condensation of water from clouds in the canopy supplies moisture for a rich ecosystem. If the trees are cut this moisture disappears and the resulting conditions can be too dry for recovery of the forest and the ecosystem services that it provides.

A third example refers to a region's dependence on *moisture evaporated from upwind ecosystems*. The cutting of humid tropical forests decreases the return flow of moisture to the atmosphere, the green water flow. Then the wind-carried water vapour flow also decreases, and so does the rainfall further downwind, which has been fed from that moisture flow (Savenije, 1995, 1996a, 1996b). In the areas in the Sahel that have experienced a severe decrease in rainfall, the ecological services in the terrestrial ecosystem have been reduced, and the opportunities for future social and economic development have been further constrained. The regional scale of the impact has further exacerbated the complexity. The major social and economic effects of clearing forests along the wet West African coastal ecosystems are felt among semi-arid savanna farmers in the Sahel belt, resulting in a higher order of impacts such as poverty and famines.

Ecological resilience typically depends on slowly changing variables such as land use, nutrient stocks, soil properties and the biomass of long-lived organisms (Gunderson and Pritchard, 2002). These variables are tightly coupled to freshwater flows and dynamics, which are in turn altered by human activities. The lesson to be learnt here is that management supported by environmental monitoring should focus on the slowly changing variables, since it is the handling of those variables that may generate undesirable changes. In the past, only the rapid and easily detectable variables have been in focus and supported by environmental monitoring.

Meeting future human needs will have major implications for further intensified land and water use. One implication of the projected population growth will be a large-scale upgrading of safe water supplies and sanitation. Rapidly growing megacities will require huge volumes of bulk water to be transferred from catchments, creating conflicts with local interests in many areas. The problem will involve rather different configurations, dependent on whether the city is situated close to the water divide, where water transfer from a neighbouring basin may be needed; in the foothills; in a river valley; at a river mouth; or on the coastal fringe. One must try to locate where the returns flows are going after use, and what pollution loads have been introduced into the water, because that will have an impact on downstream users. Environmentally vulnerable zones including aquatic ecosystems will also have to be monitored.

Adding the above concerns to the current difficult water situation in the world, it is evident that from the perspective of adaptive management there will be a whole set of important consequences:

- Land use changes with their effects on critical, slow variables (land use, nutrient stocks, soil properties).
- Water reorganization in the landscape with effects on local land use and ecosystems dependent on water.
- Pollution loads, which influence the quality and usability of water for downstream uses and for aquatic ecosystems.

The Challenge of Feeding Humanity

In today's world compelling forces are at work. A 50 per cent population growth is projected for the next 50 years, and the processes of urbanization and industrialization will continue. These changes, discussed in earlier chapters, can be translated into rapidly growing food needs, increasing energy needs, and increasing bulk water quantities to support municipal water supply of a growing number of megacities in the developing world. The results of these pressures for terrestrial as well as aquatic ecosystems will be impossible to avoid. These consequences will have to be assessed so that the trade-off can be clarified and addressed. The effects on river runoff and the aquatic ecosystems dependent on that runoff might be particularly sensitive. We have already discussed in Chapter 7 the challenge of feeding a growing human population, and that the food production implications will involve appropriation of huge additional green water flows. This brings our attention to the risk for even greater river depletion.

Learning from history

The development of agriculture over time offers another illustration of the stepwise reduction of social and ecological resilience. Since the introduction of agriculture in the Middle East some 10,000 years BP, the agrarian evolution has been based on very similar principles in most parts of the world. The original shifting cultivation systems were based on slash-and-burn agriculture with long fallows and a strong element of pioneering or exploitation of virgin land. This type of agriculture has progressively been abandoned in favour of continuous cultivation practices, mainly as a result from the pressure of an ever-increasing population. The interesting aspect of this agrarian development is that the transition from shifting to continuous cultivation is similar for different farming systems in the world. It is, however, completely different in terms of social and ecosystem impact on the present, non-fallow-based farming systems.

The sustainability of shifting cultivation systems is coupled with slash-and-burn practices. It is based on the principle of using perennial shrubs and trees to lift soil nutrients from deep soil layers to the topsoil where the annual food crops take their plant nutrients. As soon as fallow periods drop below a certain critical threshold (generally 10–15 years in the tropics), the fallow-based system collapses since the perennials are not longer able to lift enough nutrients from deep soil layers to compensate for the export of nutrients from the cultivated annual food crops. The abandonment of shifting cultivation resulted in an agrarian crisis, which was solved in the temperate zone through nutrient transfer from animals and later through fertilizers. Today, modern temperate agriculture is more productive than ever before, yielding in the order of 6–10 tonnes/ha, based on an agricultural system that is highly unstable, because it is dependent on fossil fuel from external sources. This explains recent trends of moving back towards an 'agro-ecological' climax with a better balance between animals and crops.

Roughly 100 years after the Euro-Asian development, the increase in population caused the transition from a shifting cultivation system to a largely continuous system in sub-Saharan Africa. The abandonment of a strategy for soil fertility recycling has not been compensated for by the introduction of a new management strategy for soil fertility. Fertilizer use in sub-Saharan Africa is on average below 10 kg/ha (FAO, 2002) and studies in Eastern and Southern Africa show that the farming systems suffer from extensive nutrient mining. The farming systems have dropped down to a new, lower agro-ecological climax, adapted to the 'new' situation of extremely low soil fertility and low organic matter contents, resulting in a 'one-tonne-agriculture' (see Figure 9.4). As suggested in Chapter 7, the maximum attainable climax is 5–10 times higher than the yields experienced at present. The adoption of plough tillage practices that have highly detrimental effects on soil structure and fertility in tropical soils has further speeded up the process towards extremely low on-farm yields. The result is a dramatic loss of ecological resilience, related both to quick cycles, manifested as low levels of soil moisture available to plants, and slow cycles related to soil biology, soil crusting and plant cover.

Over the last 50–70 years many efforts have been made by farmers, extension workers, researchers and donor agencies to address this agrarian crisis. All ingredients of the industrial farming systems (fertilizers, mechanization and pesticides) have been promoted. This has been done together with 'old' indigenous elements in 'new' disguise, such as improved manure management, stalled livestock in zero grazing systems, composting, green manures and short fallows. Today, as opposed to 20 years ago, there is a firm understanding that technology transfer of temperate zone successes alone will not work. Instead, tailor-made, site-specific adaptations, building on indigenous knowledge, are required. The magnitude of the agrarian crisis is so large that development and refinement of indigenous knowledge alone will not be enough. Instead, innovations – often alien innovations that go through a participatory process of local adaptation – are required in all fields of land-use management, such as the handling of crop choice, water, soil, livestock and forests.

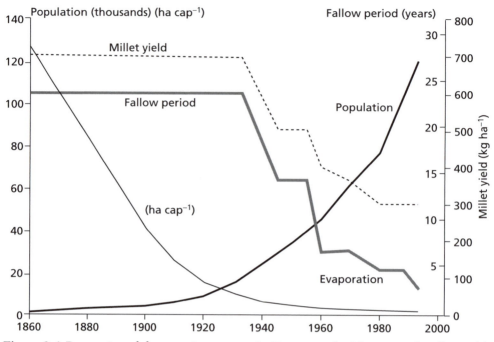

Figure 9.4 *Dynamics of the agrarian system in Zermaganda, Niger: pearl millet yields, population growth, land availability and fallow periods (1860–1993)*

The unavoidable land-use changes

To meet a more than a 50 per cent increase of global food production needed to feed the additional world population and to reduce today's large-scale malnutrition, land-use changes will have to be made, especially in sub-Saharan Africa and South Asia (Dyson, 1994). In Chapter 7 we concluded that an additional 3300 km³/year of green water would be needed but that that amount could not be met by either additional irrigation or increases in water productivity.

From where will all this green water come? The alternative is horizontal expansion of crop production into non-exploited arable land, mainly in Africa and South America. What this expansion would imply is the appropriation of the green water flow now linked to total evaporation from terrestrial ecosystems in savanna grasslands, forests and wetlands, all of which today provide fundamental ecological services. In this situation, guidelines will be needed to find out how such an enormous expansion of land-use change can proceed, and how adaptive management can be of support in avoiding unforeseen surprises.

Two sets of considerations seem to be appropriate here: how to protect particular ecological values tied to specially appreciated local ecosystems, and how to produce the main modifications in terms of identifiable water processes. The protection of ecological values will refer to special geographic coordinates or places, for example to wetlands with endemic species; to grasslands or forests hosting a specific flora or fauna, or maybe endangered species or a biodiversity of particular importance from a long-term perspective.

Land-use change, for example into crop land, will have implications for the two blue/green water partitioning points discussed in Chapter 2. The result will be water consequences in terms not only of altered consumptive use and changing water regime, but also of changes in the feedback of atmospheric moisture that might influence rainfall in downwind areas. All these consequences will produce higher-order effects of various kinds. Some of these may be the slow processes that adaptive management is supposed to address, based on careful monitoring.

In cases where irrigation is expected to increase, one can foresee increased consumptive use of fresh water in terms of blue/green redirection. These green water flows could never be more than 90 per cent of the projection of 600 km^3/year of estimated increase of consumptive water use. A second type of change in consumptive use relate to altered rainwater partitioning on cropped areas. In a global overview, L'vovich and White (1990) made some estimates of changes in water consumption linked to ploughing of earlier virgin land. They came to the conclusion that a combination of clearing, ploughing and cultivation of crops in fact reduced the consumptive use. This conclusion is in agreement with Bonell's experience of deforestation followed by crop planting (GWP, 1999). He linked the change to switching from deep-rooted trees with longer growing seasons to shallow-rooted annual or seasonal crops. The tentative estimate by L'vovich and White (1990) implies that by 1950 the consumptive use from virgin vegetation areas that have been ploughed and cultivated had decreased by as much as 3900 km^3/year (from 6540 km^3/year in its virgin state to 2640 km^3/year in its cultivated state), equal in scale to the gross blue water withdrawals by 1995 (Cosgrove and Rijsberman, 2000).

This raises some interesting conclusions regarding the mobilization of the 3300 additional km^3/year of green water needed to feed the world population two generations from now. If *forested land* were to be appropriated, it would decrease the green water flow in the tilled and cultivated state more than in the virgin, forested state. The transition would contribute to an increased blue water flow.

The effects on consumptive green water use from a conversion from grasslands to crop land are not that easily assessed, and would vary from case to case. While tropical *grasslands* may have annual green water consumption in the range of 700–1000 mm per year, the green water use on cropland in savanna environments may vary within a much wider range, 500–1500 mm. The reason is that green water use in agriculture depends so heavily on the level of agricultural productivity, where high yield levels imply high productive water flows as transpiration. The trade-off would not necessarily be an issue of possible blue water losses but rather one of land-use change and a detrimental loss of ecosystem services. In some areas aquatic ecosystems would gain at the expense of terrestrial ecosystems.

Implications for Management of Catchments

Recent ecological research has clarified the need to change perspective on the approach to ecosystem stability and the possibilities of controlling change. While earlier perceptions assumed that natural systems are stable and that change is possible to control, the current perception is that change is unavoidable. This understanding is essential to successfully address the eradication of poverty and to increase the well-being of populations in poor countries. The co-evolutionary perspective between the development of society and nature is constructive in the sense that it acknowledges the extremely strong forces that are currently at work. Among these is the continuing population growth. The response time has been too long for efforts to curb this growth successfully. Other factors are industrialization to increase welfare and mitigate poverty and urban migration in response to deficient employment opportunities in rural areas. Globalization is also influencing people's expectations and aspirations. The challenge is thus to live with change without undermining the capacity of the life-support system to sustain the development of society.

The catchment as a mosaic of ecosystems and hydronomic areas

As indicated in Chapter 1, the political imperative for society leaders is to cope with environmental preconditions while satisfying the needs of society. Adequate attention has to be paid to the fact that water is very much involved through its many parallel functions. For society, water is necessary for health, food and energy production. It has an important function in producing ecological goods and services in terrestrial and aquatic ecosystems. Water can be the cause of environmental threats from floods, droughts, and diseases. In its lift up/carry away function it contributes to erosion and sedimentation as well as to transport of solutes.

Based on new insights on social-ecological linkages, resource management has to undergo a shift in thinking both in terms of natural science and social science approaches (Folke, 1997). It is essential to learn how to strike a balance between socio-economic development and maintenance of the productive capacity of ecosystems. In doing this, it will be necessary to properly understand landscape functions and interactions under conditions of change and uncertainty. The role of freshwater is particularly important in securing both the system capacity to sustain the production of food as well as to sustain essential ecological services. We have to find out how to bring together water security, environmental security and food security, which are all closely joined through the water cycle. In the past these have been treated as separate issues, but now we need to know how to manage the catchment in order to achieve compatibility between human activities and ecological protection.

In Australia, the approach of the Cooperative Research Centre for Freshwater Ecology group in Canberra is an example of meeting the challenge of living with change. There was evidently a trade-off situation between utilitarian ideas on river water and the perspective of protection of the river ecosystem. They introduced the concept of *working rivers*, defining a healthy working river as a:

> *managed river in which there is a sustainable compromise, agreed to by the community, between the condition of the natural ecosystem and the level of human use. We work our rivers to produce hydroelectric power; we divert their waters for town water, manufacturing and for irrigation; and we farm the rivers' fertile floodplains. Working rivers will not look like, nor will they function in the same way as pristine rivers. In general, the more work the river is made to do, the less natural it becomes. A different compromise may be*

struck between the level of work and the loss of naturalness, depending upon the values that the community places on any river. The river is managed to sustain at the same time an agreed level of work and an ecologically healthy river. It is up to the community to strike the balance (Whittington, 2002).

We need to better understand the mosaic of ecosystems in catchments, how they affect and are affected by human activities, and how they are linked by water flows. Tools and techniques are needed that illuminate, quantify and evaluate the dependence of society on ecosystems and the goods and services that they provide. There is a diversity of management practices that can be based on ecological knowledge, including protection of certain species and habitats, restriction of harvests, management of landscape patchiness and of entire catchments. The implementation of such practices has to be supported both by social mechanisms and institutions, and by increased public understanding and knowledge.

In a river basin with its mosaic of ecosystems and its mix of societal activities, one has to be also aware of hydrological, topographical and hydro-geological differences. IWMI has introduced the concept 'hydronomic zones' (Molden et al, 2001b), which combines the Greek words *hydro*, 'water', and *nomos*, 'law'or 'institution', which are here interpreted as 'management'. These zones are defined primarily on what happens to blue water after withdrawal and use. What happens to the water after the outflows from uses in different basins? Are these return flows recoverable and can they be reused downstream? Or, can they not be recovered or reused because their location means that return flows go to sinks or the water quality has been degraded? There are three zones where the outflow can be used or reused downstream:

- the water source zone in the upstream basin;
- the natural recapture zone where the water drains back to the water system through gravitational flows;
- the regulated recapture zone where the water has to be pumped back.

There are also some other zones in the river basin: the final use zone where there are no further users downstream, and stagnation zones in dead-end or depression areas from where there is no drainage. More important are the zones with particular water requirements for ecological or environmentally sensitive purposes.

What does ecosystem protection mean?

We have to learn to live with changes without destroying the capacity of ecosystems to provide life support. These changes involve two basic categories of human manipulation: change of water components in the landscape and change of land/vegetation components. Both these categories of manipulations will produce side effects, related flow components and blue/green water partitioning. These manipulations also affect water determinants of ecosystems and will therefore generate higher-order ecological change and disturbance of resilience. The side effects tend to develop in several steps:

- Water itself is affected first.
- Then in turn are organisms that depend on water.
- Next are ecosystems of which these organisms are part.
- Then there are effects that occur at a distance due to ecological cascading.
- Finally, the flows of water through the landscape are involved in linking upstream and downstream activities and ecosystems.

One way of addressing the link between integrated water resource management and ecological services is to manage catchments as an asset that delivers a combination of water and ecological goods and services. Some of these services work together, while others are in conflict (GWP, 1999). Hence, intentional trade-offs need to be made, based on the view of humans as an integral part of the ecohydrological landscape. One can even envisage a situation where landowners should be given the task of managing the natural resources for the society as a whole and be paid for that (GWP, 1999). Ecosystem services and water have to be managed in an integrated way and by adaptive management, which is prepared for unexpected dynamics, uncertainty and surprises.

One interesting example of merging management of water, land use and ecosystems is offered by the 'Working for Water Program' in South Africa, which has multiple goals of water conservation, ecosystem conservation and generation of employment (van Wilgen et al, 1998). This is a 20-year programme, involving some 40,000 people clearing the South African landscape of alien invasive plants that are without natural enemies. These plants, originally introduced by forest companies, are a threat to the highly valued *fynbos* ecosystem with its rich floristic biodiversity and ecosystem services found, for example, in the Cape of Good Hope. They also represent an extra consumptive use of water in that they withhold rainfall from runoff production and therefore in essence deplete the river system. The aim of the programme of eradication is to gain another 10 per cent of stream flow. This is in essence a win–win situation, which combines a hydrological and an ecological management goal with an employment goal. It is in that sense an early example of combined socio-hydroecological management. The local community issues related to this programme are addressed together with regional and national interests, and there exists active management of conflicts, trade-offs and capacity building.

It follows from the above discussion that we have to develop ways and means to merge within a socio-ecohydrological catchment frame, the management of water, land use, and terrestrial as well as aquatic ecosystems. This has to be done with full awareness of the different ethical dilemmas involved. Land use and terrestrial ecosystems are green water dependent, while societal water needs and aquatic ecosystems are blue water dependent. Rainfall is the ultimate water resource of the catchment.

Ecological criteria

Criteria will have to be developed to protect the capacity for sustainable production of life support. This means identification of what key functions are essential for the production of goods and services of social, ecological and economic importance. Conflicts of interest and ways of dealing with them must be incorporated. Moreover, resilience has to be secured and water determinants have to be identified: water flows, water pathways, flow seasonality, water table, water quality and chemical characteristics. Water withdrawals by consumptive water use, land use influencing water partitioning, pollution loads and flow control measures will have a direct and indirect impact on these determinants.

For quite some time the risks of decline in ecological functions after river regulations have been known (Dunbar and Acreman, 2001). It is, however, only in recent years that there has been an increased concern for the importance of maintaining in-stream river flow to secure ecological functions in rivers and lakes. In South Africa, this concern has recently been translated into policy. In Australia, thresholds are now being developed to be respected by water managers. Both South Africa and Australia are countries with savanna environments, and both are moving towards a situation where the rivers are more or less fully committed. Therefore, it is seen as urgent to secure a large enough flow as a reserve, which is uncommitted for societal uses, but available in the river for the aquatic ecosystems. However, the quantification of how much water of what quality to secure at what time is still at a rudimentary stage, so it is only a qualitative 'rule of thumb'.

The South African approach stipulates a water reserve, or minimum in-stream flow, defined in the National Water Act 1998 as 'the quantity and quality of water required to satisfy basic human needs and to protect aquatic ecosystems in order to secure ecologically sustainable development and use of the relevant water resource'. Conversely, establishing forest plantations are nowadays seen as a 'stream flow-reducing activity' for which the forest company may even be charged. This reflects the earlier discussed land/water linkages where forest plantations tend to influence the rainfall partitioning processes. A set of critical deterioration thresholds are considered (Geoffrey and Todd, 2001):

- *Limit of naturalness*, defining the upper threshold for un-impacted conditions.
- *Desired state*, interpreted as the deterioration zone within which the water resource remains sustainable. This state reflects the desired ecological values required and the condition within which an ecosystem should be maintained.
- *Limit of acceptability*, which determines the limits under which the deterioration state of the resource remains acceptable and above which interventions are called for. This limit is based on the degree of risk acceptable for interested parties and authorities as result of a trade-off between conservation needs and development needs.
- *Limit of sustainability* at which the deterioration makes the system unsustainable. At this level the ecosystem has consumed its resilience, loses its stability, and changes into a new equilibrium.

This model can be applied to a situation of river depletion in which the river flow has diminished due to upstream consumptive use. The limit of 'naturalness' is the lowest flow during natural drought situations, the limit of 'acceptability' is the maximum acceptable flow depletion, and the limit of 'sustainability' is the lowest acceptable flow below which the resilience of the ecosystem is in danger. The amount of water it is possible to allocate for direct human use in society is the flow within the limit of acceptability. Various approaches exist to quantifying acceptable changes in terms of closeness to the natural state – for example, 75 per cent of the limit of naturalness is still acceptable, 50–75 per cent is marginal, and less than 50 per cent unacceptable. Although this may be simplistic and rigid, it is at least a starting point, easily applicable in catchments with limited hydrological data.

'How much water does a river need to remain healthy?' was the question asked in Australia. Simplistic thresholds were suggested as a rule of thumb (Jones, 2002). For example, the 'two-thirds natural' scenario is being applied as a provisional flow guidance value. If the flow remains greater than two-thirds of the natural flow, the probability of having a healthy river is considered high. If it is greater than half, the probability is moderate, and if the flow is less than half the probability is low. This rule of thumb is to be seen as a starting point for discussion only, since the view is that it should be up to the local community to decide whether the assessed risk is acceptable or not.

The goal of catchment management has to be to protect the basis for the life support system of the region. A crucial consideration will be how to protect the resilience of the catchment's life-support system or, more particularly, the key productive functions of that system. The overriding task here is to find a management adapted to the catchment, with the aim that future options are protected and secured. Collapses must be avoided by action as early as possible. At the same time land and water resources have to be protected for the next generation. The golden rule will be not to allow any discernible degradation to proceed too far or allow it to come too close to a collapse of the ecosystem. Creeping changes that might make these ecosystems switch to a different state have to be averted. At the present level of understanding, this involves focusing on the slow variables that influence the functioning of the ecosystem in question. As already indicated, these variables include land use, nutrient stocks, soil properties, and the biomass of long-lived organisms. All these variables are linked to land use but have in the past been highlighted without any water variables attached (Folke et al, 2002). Since both land use and soil properties are intimately linked to water processes and functions, water variables such as water flow regime, green water flow and water pollution will have to be added at the next level of understanding.

Open versus closed basins

In the trade-off between more consumptive water use for an extended food production and maintaining in-stream river flow for downstream aquatic ecosystems, the remaining degrees of freedom are important in terms of non-committed stream flow. For such considerations, IWMI has introduced the concept of open and closed river basins (Seckler, 1996). The hydrological definition, implications for management and examples of ecohydrological indicators are given in Table 9.1. The concept is that in open river basins there remains a blue water surplus that might be allocated for additional consumptive use ('beneficially depleted') in, for example, food production (Molden et al, 2001b). In a closed river basin, the consumptive use has already reached a threshold of what can be accepted from an ecological perspective, and there is very limited outflow left. All water is already committed to environmental use or beneficially depleted. In this situation, reallocation is the only option when water demands

Table 9.1 *Open/closed/closing basins*

Basin state	Excess water	Increased consumptive use	Examples of ecohydrological indicators
Open	Always	Possible	30% of stable runoff secured for ecosystems Natural fluctuations of river flow
Closing	Only during wet season	Possible only during wet season, requires new storage	Storage and diversions of river flow result in changes in river flow regime < 30% of stable runoff secured for ecosystems
Closed	Never	Only by reallocating water from other consumptive uses	River flow not enough to sustain in-stream ecological functions

Source: Molden et al, 2001b

continue to increase. Basins may also be closing in cases when their water is fully committed during part of the year, typically the dry season, while a water surplus remains during the wet season that can be made accessible through inter-seasonal storage. While there have so far been only limited assessments of the degree of ecohydrological closure of river basins in the world, indications would suggest that in the semi-arid regions there are only few open rivers left with a blue water surplus during the low-flow season. According to Molle (2002), for example, most of the river basins in Thailand, including the Chao Phraya river basin, are now nearing closure.

Summary

In this chapter a fruitful dialogue between water professionals and ecologists has contributed to clarify a set of interrelations between water, humans and ecosystems. Ecologists state that water is much more interesting through its functions and effects than as an abiotic environment supporting aquatic ecosystems. Ecological systems are set in a landscape and linked by flows of water in an upstream/downstream pattern. From a study of land degradation over 20,000 years it was concluded that development has had the form of a co-evolution of society and nature, where the interrelationship has been more one of resonance than of cause and effect.

Humanity's fundamental challenge is therefore to find out how to live with change while securing the capacity of the life-support system to deliver food, biomass and ecological services, and to endure disturbances and variability. Resilience has to be secured to both natural and human-induced disturbances through biological diversity.

A minimum set of organisms has therefore to be retained to secure the relations between primary producers, consumers and decomposers that mediate the flow of energy and the cycling of elements. Here, fresh water provides the foundation for the processes involved. The stepwise development of agriculture over time illustrated this point, passing from shifting cultivation to continuous cultivation, and arriving at different agro-ecological climaxes with 6–10 t/ha in more successful modern systems, and <1 t/ha in less successful African farming systems.

While earlier perceptions assumed that natural systems are stable and that change is possible to control, modern perception stresses that change is unavoidable. The challenge is therefore to live with change without undermining the capacity of the life-support system. One must consider how to protect the resilience of the life-support system of the catchment and the key productive functions of that system. The prime goal is to protect the ecosystems from creeping changes that might allow these systems to switch to a different state with lower ability to absorb variability and unavoidable changes.

Societal changes that will happen in the next 50 years will have major implications for land and water use and unavoidable consequences for terrestrial and aquatic ecosystems. Food production especially will involve appropriation of huge additional green water flows, risking further river depletion. To feed the 2050 world population, the additional green water needs, which are not covered by irrigation expansion and crop per drop improvements, have been assessed at some 3300 km^3/year (see chapters 6 and 7). The gap will have to be met by horizontal expansion into forests and grasslands.

The conflicts of interest will, however, look different in different hydroclimates and will culminate in the savanna regions with their rapidly rising food needs and the restricted blue water availability. Guidelines will be needed to find out how the expansion in terms of changes in land use can be implemented without threatening the production of ecological services. Such guidelines will incorporate the interacting processes of slow and fast variables affecting ecological resilience, and the dynamic role of water in terms of fluctuation, volume and quality, in sustaining ecological functions.

Chapter 10

Towards Hydrosolidarity through Integrated Land/Water/Ecosystem Management

It is time for the world community to address the essential trade-offs between food production for a growing population and the protection of aquatic and terrestrial ecosystems.

Human Life Support and the Millennium Declaration

In a sequence of chapters we have analysed major regional differences in what has been called the water 'predicament'. We focused in particular on the vulnerability of the broad savanna zone in the tropics, which has a rapid population growth and which is suffering from large-scale poverty and malnutrition. This is where the food security will be most problematic in the future. The food production opportunities were analysed from the perspective of the role of water. Although the mainstream recommendation is to import food, that advice is not necessarily realistic even over a long-term time perspective. Instead, we showed that there exists, in fact, a large window of opportunity for a green-green revolution in the savanna zone, based on upgraded rainfed agriculture.

As a conclusion, we have advocated an ecohydrological management approach to better incorporate the many parallel functions of water in both society and ecosystems. Fresh water offers an opportunity for a comprehensive perspective linking water security, food security and ecological security. One way to go forward in securing these three security dimensions is by developing ability for what might be called 'socio-ecohydrological' management of catchments.

The growing awareness of a looming water crisis has created widespread concern for the future in many regions of the world where water sets a fundamental limit to the means to support human life. There have been several warnings that fresh water may actually become this millennium's source of conflict and war. Boutrous Boutrous-Gali, former Foreign Minister of Egypt, expressed this idea in a statement directed to Ethiopia. However, there is little evidence that water has been the direct cause of armed conflict in the past (Wolf, 2000). More recent thinking suggests a different aspect. Kader Asmal, former Minister of Water Affairs and Forestry of South Africa, and Stockholm Water Prize Laureate 2000, suggested that under conditions of water scarcity, water may instead become a catalyst for cooperation (Asmal, 2001).

Increasing expectations on a declining life-support system

The world population continues to grow by some 60 million every year and is projected to continue increasing at the same speed for several decades. At the same time the life-support system is deteriorating due to continued land degradation, water pollution, and unmitigated river depletion. The present situation is the result of trying to manage the closely interlinked system of our life-support base by taking fragmentary approaches and dealing separately with its different components. As a result of natural water-related processes in the landscape, each measure taken introduces problems elsewhere. The right to safe water is declared a human right, but that right seems also to include the right to indiscriminate disposal of wastewater. Water management now concentrates on satisfying water needs without much attention to what happens to the water after use. Many ways of water use involve the addition of contaminants, producing a polluted return flow. Consumptive water use depletes rivers. Atmospheric processes link the consumptive water use and precipitation in downwind regions. Soil desiccation reduces the green water flow, which should feed the wind-driven vapour flow in the atmosphere.

In the UN (2000) Millennium Declaration, government and state leaders of the world tried to address the gloomy situation of the poverty stricken countries. They declared as a goal for 2015 to reduce by half the number of people suffering from lack of access to safe drinking water and suffering from hunger, poverty and water-related diseases. All these factors are closely water-related. The goal to secure safe water for drinking and to improve health will imply searching in the developing world for sources of raw water with an acceptable quality, as well as managing the supply and quality of this water. The second goal of mitigating hunger will have evident implications in terms of trade-offs between increased consumptive use and protection of vital ecosystem services. The eradication of poverty will demand employment and raising incomes in cash crop production and in industry, both extremely water-dependent.

The set of trade-off problems will be most evident in the savanna region, which is the most vulnerable one because of widespread malnutrition and rapid population growth (Dyson, 1994). The ecological vulnerability of the savanna creates problems for food producers. It is the region with the most adverse hydroclimatic conditions for sustaining successful subsistence agriculture. The reasons for this are the unfavourable combination of several factors: a short growing season with unreliable rainfall and frequent dry spells; vulnerable, low-fertile and often unstable soils; considerable risk for recurrent drought years. It is the region particularly vulnerable to human-induced changes in landscape management. In a longer-term perspective, population growth will add water crowding to this list of subsistence challenges.

The particular difficulty in these landscapes is to cope with variability in rainfall. This contrasts sharply with the conventional view among many water professionals who focus on blue water availability. Continents dominated by a few very large river basins, like Africa, may give the impression of being water rich from the conventional perspective of per capita blue water flow. Even if Africa is not water poor in a continental blue water sense, the main objective there is to overcome the green water scarcity problems, particularly in the upstream savannas and tropical forests where rainfall is first partitioned into blue and green water flows.

Trade-offs will be unavoidable

Earlier chapters in this book have clarified how water flows link nature and society. The lesson learnt from the analysis of 20,000 years of human activities suggests that poverty eradication and socioeconomic development will have to involve land-use change in the future as well. A set of key conflicts is apparent in the interaction between nature and society:

- Humans require pure water, but waste production is an unavoidable component of human activities.
- Humanity needs more food, but crop production is water consumptive and expansion will leave less blue water for downstream users and ecosystems.
- The current populations' needs must be satisfied but not at the risk of undermining the life-support system and reduce its potential to solve the needs of coming generations.

The first two conflicting phenomena call for trade-offs between humans and nature and priority setting, as shown below, while the last one calls for the development of criteria for sustainability.

1. Dependence on pure water while increasing pollution during use: Water is often polluted during use, which is a serious dilemma. The result is a long-term build-up of water pollution that has passed from lower to higher concentration levels and from the local to the regional scale, and now approaches even the global scale (Meybeck, 2002).

Fortunately, some ecosystem processes have some purifying capacity, although it is far from the scale now needed. Useful purification components are the biodegradation of organic forms of pollution and the ability of wetlands to absorb pollutants either by sedimentation or denitrification, or by incorporating pollutants such as cadmium into the biomass. Other pollutants are inert and hidden, such as the endocrine disruptors that affect the growth of the offspring of many species, and thus the core of life itself.

In water pollution abatement, the *response time* perspective, that is the time period needed to get rid of a pollution problem, is highlighted by Meybeck (2002) (see Figure 10.1). It is composed of two major components:

- *The social response time*, which contains a whole series of steps: from the first suspicion that there may be a problem, to the making of a political decision to act, to the implementation of that decision by developing the technical capability, to the financing, and finally to taking the necessary technical measures.
- *The hydro-physical response time*, which contains two parts: first the time it takes for a pollution problem to build up by accumulation in a body of water, and second the time it takes to flush away the accumulated pollutants once that the input of them has been stopped. These time delays are related to the renewal time of the water mass in the body of water.

2. More food production may raise consumptive use and reduce runoff: The second dilemma is the trade-off between the need to grow more food for a growing population versus the implications of increased appropriation of green water flow. In Chapter 7

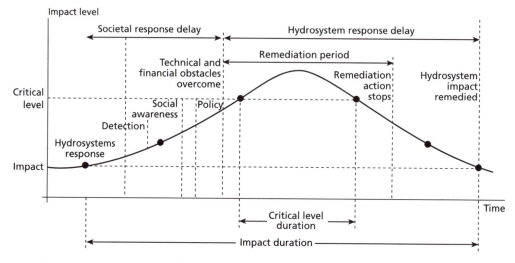

Note: The graph shows schematically how pollution impact changes with time.

Source: Adapted from Meybeck, 2002

Figure 10.1 *Response time delays involved in water pollution abatement: societal response delay and hydrosystem response delay*

we estimated the additional water requirements involved. Figure 10.2 summarizes the options: irrigation with blue water; increased water productivity, which has consequences for runoff formation as it makes it easier for plants to get hold of nearby blue water; expanding appropriation of green water by horizontal expansion of crop fields into areas with natural vegetation such as grasslands, forests or wetlands; and virtual water.

The blue water options and the crop per drop improvements were thoroughly discussed in Chapter 7. The remaining green water needs, by 2050 amounting to altogether 3300 km³/year, were addressed in Chapter 9. The only remaining alternative to securing this volume of water for food production – unless the food needed can be transferred by trade from better-endowed regions – is a horizontal expansion of crop production into tropical grasslands and forests, and to some extent tropical wetlands. Experiences from Australia and Southern Africa suggest that redirecting the blue/green water for large-scale changes to the land surface is by no means uncommon. The situation raises the question of how far we can afford to reduce streamflow. A minimum environmental flow has to be saved from consumptive use for food production purposes and protected in the rivers for the benefit of the aquatic ecosystems.

What are the ecological end points? According to the global assumptions by de Fraiture et al (2001), 40 per cent of the time-stable blue water flow was seen as the minimum to be left uncommitted for in-stream purposes: navigation or environmental purposes. If we take the generally used estimate of global time-stable blue water flow of 12,500 km³/year, humanity is left with the remaining 60 per cent or 7500 km³/year,

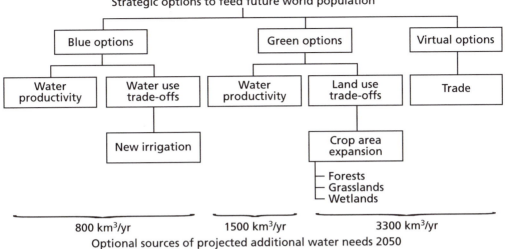

Strategic options to feed future world population

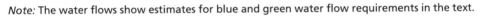

800 km³/yr   1500 km³/yr   3300 km³/yr
Optional sources of projected additional water needs 2050

Note: The water flows show estimates for blue and green water flow requirements in the text.

Figure 10.2 *Overview of alternate sources for additional green water appropriation to feed humanity by 2050*

which represents the maximum acceptable diversion. Furthermore, at least 30 per cent has to form return flow to avoid silting and salinization. Therefore, 5250 km³/year represents the maximum acceptable consumptive use of blue water. After subtracting today's consumptive use, estimated to be some 2600 km³/year in the mid 1990s, we are left with only 2650 km³/year as the remaining potential blue water contribution to feed the world. This is the equivalent of the water consumed in producing food for 2 billion people, in a situation where the projected population growth is 3 billion. This would imply, assuming that all food were produced using blue water, that in the next two generations humanity will reach its ecological carrying capacity.

The conclusion is that it is time for the world community to address this underlying trade off between food production for a growing humanity and criteria for protection of aquatic and terrestrial ecosystems.

The regional dimensions of the trade-offs are important: the most challenging regions are evidently those where a scarcity of blue water already exists (cluster a in Figure 5.8) and savanna regions where green water is scarce. In the former regions, the way forward is to maximize crop per drop in irrigated agriculture and to rely on virtual water through trade. In the latter regions, irrigation remains as an alternative in case more blue water can be made accessible at a reasonable cost. Where this is not the case, due to lack of coping capability, trained manpower or economy, the primary solutions are to maximize crop per drop in rainfed agriculture and to expand horizontally by cultivating new land. We showed in chapters 7 and 8 that there is a large potential in terms of crop per drop improvement in the savanna region. The options for expansion differ considerably between regions. In South Asia all cultivable land is already in use, which means that the remaining options beyond crop per drop are buying foodstuffs

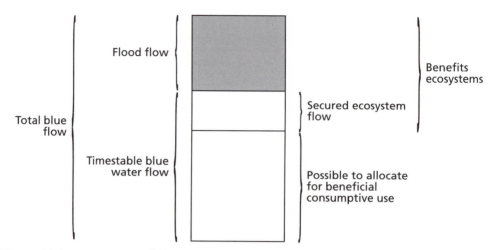

Figure 10.3 *Environmental flow-related approach: different components of blue water flow from the aquatic system protection perspective*

or the expansion of irrigation at the expense of the ecosystems. In Africa much land remains for potential horizontal expansion.

3. Meeting the needs of the present generation without undermining the capacity to meet the needs of future generations: This is the third of the key problems mentioned above. We will return to this issue below.

Catchment scale trade-off between people and ecosystems

The global and regional scales are, however, far from the local reality. People live in catchments and the trade-offs relate to the demands of other interested parties in the same river basin. Figure 10.3 illustrates the approach to blue water availability based on the environmental flow and its different components. It is composed of a flood flow component and a time-stable component. Ecosystem benefits originate from the flood flow plus the uncommitted part of the time-stable flow. The amount that can be allocated for consumptive water uses, including expanding food production, is what remains unallocated of the time-stable flow.

The flood flow is, as stressed in Chapter 1, of vital importance for many aquatic ecosystems, especially in riparian wetlands and floodplains used for pasture. Environmental water flows also include part of the time-stable flow that should be reserved in the river for ecological purposes. We saw in Chapter 9 that different groups have different ideas about how large this part should be. They have developed ideas developing ideas of 'working rivers', criteria for healthy rivers, and rules of thumb regarding the fraction that should be reserved for the benefit of aquatic ecosystems. The trade-off between how much should be reserved and how much can be transformed into more food must be decided, some believe, by the local community. In two Australian examples local decision-making has had different results. In Tasmania, the environmental flow will receive a larger share of the river flow, as contrasted with the Murray-Darling basin on the Australian mainland, which already has the character of a working river. Here the environmental flow is proportionately lower for the simple reason that so much of the flow is already appropriated (Whittington, 2002).

The surplus beyond the environmental reserve is the only blue water resource that can be appropriated for the increasing food production to feed a 50 per cent expansion of humanity. In closed basins where no surplus flow remains to allocate, virtual water is the only way to increased food supply. In this situation the focus will also have to turn to the role of pollution as a destroyer of ecosystems. The only way to give better protection to aquatic ecosystems is to reduce the pollution of river water. Water pollution abatement must therefore become a high-priority activity.

Present Shifts in Thinking and Challenges to the 'Sanctioned Discourse'

Although the blue water approach still dominates, major shifts in thinking are forthcoming. The most constructive one is the important new insight among leading ecologists that our world is characterized by change rather than by a static situation, and that the socio-ecological challenge is to find out how to live with change while learning to protect the productivity of the life-support system. The shift in thinking among hydrologists is what has generated this book: the need to expand the conventional blue water approach so that land use and its water dependence can also be incorporated. In 1999 the International Water Management Institute (IWMI), when developing water accounting categories, introduced the concept of 'water depletion', referring to the consumptive component of water use that renders the water unavailable for further use downstream (Bakker et al, 1999). Its focus, however, remained on the quantity aspects of water use. We are still waiting for a serious discussion in developing countries on the pollution load added by water. Another innovation in water management is the growing attention to the quantity of river flow needed to uphold the basic functioning of aquatic ecosystems, the so-called *environmental flow*.

Tools from the recent past

Methods have been developed for environmental impact assessment (EIA), and it has been stressed in this book that natural water-related processes in the landscape actively translate into environmental side-effects when unavoidable interventions with land cover and water pathways occur. Past approaches to environmental impacts have focused on the biological end effects rather than the processes producing these effects. Environmental legislation has now been introduced in many countries. Upstream/downstream conflicts of interest are being addressed in the UN Convention on the Law of the Non-navigational Uses of the International Waterways (1997). The convention text is not clear, however, about the character of downstream effects. It gives the impression that such downstream harm is exceptional rather than practically unavoidable because of many development-oriented activities upstream (SIWI, 2000). By regarding harm to downstream areas as more of an exception than the rule, adherence to the convention would absurdly constrain intensified food production and water-consumptive human activities upstream. The convention has never entered into force due to lack of adequate ratification. In real life, the set of problems surrounding water sharing in transnational rivers is complicated by inherited perceptions of historic rights to water. Such perceptions are less than helpful in a search for a sharing based on solidarity.

Furthermore, as a follow-up to the recommendations of the Dublin conference on Water and the Environment in January 1992 (ICWE, 1992), there were powerful efforts during the 1990s to develop an integrated approach to water resource management. These efforts represent a major step from the sector fragmentation of past management of water resources (GWP, 2000a). Attention is being paid now not only to technology but also equally to the dimensions of governance such as institutions, legislation and education. The development is paralleled by an action-oriented approach to benefit from lessons learnt through the compilation of the so-called 'GWP Toolbox'. The Integrated Water Resources Management (IWRM) approach remains, after all, rather narrow (GWP, 2000a). It concentrates on seeing water for human support as an economic good and has its main focus on blue water and water quantity.

Considering water as an economic good is about integrated choices

Since the Dublin Conference in 1992, much attention has been paid to the concept of 'water as an economic good'. Because of frequent confusion over water pricing where the prime target remains cost recovery, considerable misunderstanding has remained about what the concept really implies. Instead of economic pricing there is a need for defining a reasonable price, which provides full cost recovery but which safeguards ecological requirements and access to safe water for the poor. Giving a reasonable price to water has the additional benefit that it sends out a clear signal to users that water should be used wisely.

There is an unfortunate contradiction between this principle and the IWRM approach, if the economic principle is interpreted in the neo-classical sense (Savenije and Van der Zaag, 2002). The first aspect of IWRM states that water is not divisible into different types or kinds of water. It may be groundwater at some stage; at a later stage it will become surface water. Earlier in the water cycle it was rainfall and soil moisture. But it all remains the same water. Use of soil moisture diminishes the availability of groundwater; use of groundwater diminishes the availability of surface water, etc. Any use of water, unlike any other natural resources, affects the entire water cycle. Furthermore, water is vital to life for which there is no substitute, and there is no alternative choice to water. The only choice is how to allocate water and to find the most efficient way of using it. Water, then, is immeasurably different from other economic goods. One cannot easily choose another type of water without tapping the same resource. Water is not an ordinary economic good: it is special economic good (Savenije, 2002).

The second aspect of the IWRM approach, which is to consider and balance all sector interests, limits the applicability of neo-classical economic principles as well.

There are important water uses that have a high societal relevance, but a very limited ability to be a source of revenue, particularly for the environmental, social and cultural requirements. Yet most if not all societies respect these interests. Decisions on water allocation seldom appear to be taken on purely economic grounds. On the contrary: governments take decisions on a political basis with strong considerations for social, cultural and sometimes environmental interests. Of course, economic and financial considerations are an integral part of these decisions, but they are seldom the overriding decision variable.

The third aspect, calling for long-term sustainability, makes the application of economic principles in the classical sense even more difficult. Economic analysts can easily demonstrate that the future has no value in monetary terms. The discount rate makes any future benefits or costs further than, say, 20 years ahead valueless and irrelevant. This, like the previous aspect, illustrates clearly that economic thinking in this limited sense differs from attributing societal or personal values to things. Most individuals would agree that personal health, happiness, beauty, safety, the future of your children, education and well-being are more important than money. Societies and, to a smaller extent, the market spend large amounts of money on these qualities of life. Yet it is extremely hard to value these qualities in monetary terms, let alone their future value.

Finally, the aspect of participation requires decision-making processes in which the views of all interested parties are considered. This aspect precludes economic pricing, or at least makes it extremely difficult. Proponents of water markets disagree with this point of view, since they believe that if a market is properly structured and supervised all different interests will be well accounted for. Experience has taught us that this is often not the case. Such an ideal may be possible for certain water sub-systems or sub-sectors such as irrigation. The process becomes very complicated for more complex systems in a multi-sector and multi-interest environment.

In sum, the first (neo-classical) interpretation of 'water as an economic good' led to considerable misunderstanding, one that still continues. Water economics are understood to 'deal with how best to meet all human wants' (Gaffney, 1997), making the right choices about the most advantageous and sustainable uses of water in a broad societal context. This is fully in agreement with the concept of IWRM. Considering water as an economic good is about making integrated choices, not about determining the right price of water. However, we would like to propose that water pricing is the pitfall of the concept 'water as an economic good' (Savenije and van der Zaag, 2002).

The 'sanctioned discourse' is severely delaying a real policy debate

By concentrating on water supply and sanitation in the international water policy debate, 90 per cent of the time is devoted to 10 per cent of the problem (citation from A. Berntell, SIWI). The fact that the perceptions of the expert communities are undergoing a renewal does not mean that one may expect to see new conceptualizations rapidly reflected in a modernized policy framework. There is here – as in the case of water pollution abatement – a response time problem, which is, in this case, linked to the so-called 'sanctioned discourse'. The issues that are discussed are those that are 'politically correct' to debate, or those possible to discuss in light of the level of general understanding in the audience. This phenomenon strictly controls the issues addressed in international communities, intergovernmental as well as non-governmental. In that debate, both the blue water approaches and the water quantity bias still dominate. This situation reflects also the way in which society has been organized, nationally and internationally for several centuries: it cannot easily be modified. The sanctioned discourse has its focus on the same issues as those discussed at the UN Water Conference in Mar del Plata in March 1977, 25 years ago!

The scale and the human dimensions of the issues raised in this book show the urgency of escaping from this dilemma. It is particularly disturbing that very limited attention is directed towards meeting humanity's future food needs. The present approach has left a huge hunger gap unaddressed (Conway, 1997). Especially as 70 times more water is needed to produce the food for one person on an acceptable nutritional level (1300 m^3/person/year) as compared to what is usually indicated as the basic household need of water (50 litres/person/day level).

Combining Social, Ecological and Economic Approaches

There is an urgent need for policy development and management action. Today, there exists massive malnutrition, water-related diseases, deteriorating ecosystems and growing political disputes over international water systems and increasing competition for water in savanna regions. It is probable that our present policies, technologies, and institutions are likely to lead to a future no one will like. At the same time the social forces are strong and these further increase the expectations on the mismanaged life-support system. As we have shown, Herculean efforts will be necessary to secure the future global food supply.

By creating a positive vision of the world in the mid 2000s it is possible to begin crafting the policies and institutions needed to realize the vision. In order to find out how to craft the policies and institutions, a 'backcasting' approach might be helpful by visualizing where we want the world to be then (Falkenmark and Steen, 1995). Once a positive future is described and the end points have been defined, it is possible to analyse what policies, programmes, technologies, and institutions are necessary to move in the desired direction. To reach the desired future, there is a set of perspectives to analyse: the social perspective of what people need and what they will be willing to accept; the ecological perspective of healthy ecosystems dealing with protected areas of particular value; and resilience and the capacity to absorb unavoidable changes and surprises without a change of state. There is also the economic perspective of making economically wise decisions, of necessary financing and cost coverage, and of proper attention to the values that the water system represents and the value added by its wise use.

The social perspective: water-related threats that must be averted

The social perspective involves a set of key issues to be addressed: how can the water resources of a country or region be used to mitigate poverty, generate income for the inhabitants, and secure a reasonable quality of life and economic development from the resources available. There is also the issue of how food supply can be secured by combining local rural production, peri-urban production based on renovated urban wastewater, and the import of food from better endowed regions.

Poverty eradication involves at least three components that are directly or indirectly water related:

- Morbidity reduction through activities that protect health such as safe water supply and sanitation.
- Security of access to food either by achieving national self-reliance through water-consuming crop production, or through the purchasing of food. A combination of these two aspects is also a possibility.
- Secure family incomes, which depend on employment opportunities in a sustainable industrial or cash crop production, which both are both water-dependent.

In order to achieve these grand goals, a whole set of water-related risks that now obstruct poverty eradication and sustainable economic development will have to be avoided through various management efforts:

- *Conflict avoidance*: water-sharing strategies and regulations are needed, as well as reconciliation of stakeholder disputes, encompassing both blue and green water, and based on a universally accepted water ethics.
- *Pollution avoidance*: proper management of waste (liquid and solid) and of water-soluble agricultural chemicals is needed to protect blue water from being polluted beyond limits for safe use.
- *Avoidance of land fertility degradation*: integrated soil/water/nutrient management is necessary.
- *Avoidance of urban water supply collapses*: development and maintenance of the urban water/sanitation infrastructure is necessary, with incorporation into the system of informal areas.
- *Avoidance of crop failure*: Simple drought-proofing technologies based on water harvesting or local runoff collection are also necessary.

It is important to secure social acceptance by the interested parties of the efforts required to meet the different water needs and efforts to avert the various threats. All needs cannot be satisfied at the same time; there are trade-offs to be made and they, too, are not free from conflict. Therefore, interested parties will have to be involved in the planning process, the process of participation will have to be legitimised, and a platform will have to be provided.

The ecological perspective: approaching a realistic view

The concept *catchment-based ecosystem approach* and how it should be understood is unfortunately not very clear. First of all, we have to admit that the concept remains rather lofty and it will have to be further developed to facilitate its constructive use. The catchment contains a mosaic of smaller-scale ecosystems, defined by the abiotic character of the surroundings, which shift as one descends from the water divide to the downstream floodplains and the river mouth area. Ecosystems in different places are internally linked by the water flow through the catchment.

In analysing the measures needed to meet social water needs, a catchment-based approach with proper attention paid to terrestrial and aquatic ecosystems is required. Coordinated development and management of water and land have to be secured to maximize the welfare of vital ecosystems without compromising their sustainability (GWP, 2000b). Unfortunately, the term 'ecosystem' is not very clear when seen from a catchment perspective. The term may be given two complementary interpretations: the life-support system on which human welfare depends, and site-specific landscape components, which have a special social value, for example, a wetland, a forest, a lake or a river stretch.[1]

Such landscape components need to be protected because of interesting endemic species, valuable biodiversity, beautiful landscape or riverscape, or a high social value. It will be essential to secure healthy aquatic ecosystems by avoiding the water pollution that would degrade them. Environmental water flow will have to be secured both as flood episodes and as uncommitted river flow. The terrestrial ecosystems, land cover and land use are also of importance as determinants of runoff production. The more green water they consume, the less will be the rainwater surplus left for runoff production. They are important also for securing groundwater recharge and dry season flow in the river – in short, what we call 'watershed protection'.

From an ecological viewpoint, protection of an ecosystem means to protect it from the risk of collapse or from rapidly changing to a different, unwanted state. Interesting here is what one can learn from the examples of ecological collapses in Chapter 9. A number of examples were given: a cloud forest that collapsed; a semi-arid rangeland that turned from pasture to woody vegetation; a savanna agro-ecosystem that deteriorated to a lower yield level; and a savanna ecosystem that became victim of upwind deforestation through atmospheric moisture feedback. The interventions that caused the disturbance were of two kinds: disturbance of soil/vegetation and of nutrient supply. The indicators of ecosystem collapse appeared as reductions in crop yields and altered vegetation mix . What we can learn from these examples is that water cycling was essential in the ecosystem degradation process. It transmits disturbances, but it also provides a set of different entry points for the disturbance.

The ecosystem approach to a catchment has one major conceptual component, namely the attention to sustainability, which is needed for long-term resilience of the life support system. In Chapter 9 we pointed out that resilience is a key property of an ecosystem. It refers to its capacity to react to change without losing functions and self-organizing ability for renewal after change. The fact that changes are unavoidable makes the resilience aspect essential. Changes may be of natural origin, such as fires and drought years or of man-made origin – for example a change in price for an ecological good, a change of land cover, pollution or climate change. The involvement of water functions in the resilience phenomenon has to be further studied in order to find the links to water management. From an ecological perspective, resilience implies that a minimum composition of organisms has to be retained that can help in re-establishing the ecosystem after a disturbance. This means that biodiversity represents an insurance against unavoidable change in providing a risk-spreading capacity.

The economic perspective: incorporating the full value of water

The economic perspective involved in developing an integrated land/water/ecosystem management is complex. The forces of the economy influence societal wants and expectations. Economic incentives may be used to influence human behaviour in line with what managers find desirable. Infrastructure will have to be financed and the cost for operation and maintenance has to be covered. Economic considerations are also an important component of the decision-making process. The principle of water as an economic good enters here as a way to facilitate the best choice between a set of alternative water allocations and uses. The difference between price and value of water was discussed above. Thus, to avoid the confusion with the *pricing* of water, the focus is now being directed towards the *value* of water. This is a useful tool for management when trying to find efficient, equitable and sustainable ways of handling water resources. It is not the value in a strictly monetary sense that is referred to here but the value for society in its broadest sense, meaning for all water functions and for all water uses. Many of these are in competition. The full value of water can be considered to be composed of:

- The value to the user of the water (food production, industry, household use, fisheries).
- The benefits from return flows (allowing for a second use of the water).
- The benefits from indirect uses (benefits not included in the value to the user).
- The broader societal benefits as spin-off from the water-use function (for instance, employment, regional development, equity, etc, which are not always easy to quantify in monetary terms).
- The intrinsic value of water: water as an economic good, water enhancing the beauty of the landscape, the cultural value of water, the value of it just being there. The intrinsic value is difficult to express in money terms, yet governments and households spend substantial amounts of money on creating an attractive and liveable environment. Water always plays an important role in that regard.

Economists find it difficult to deal with the interconnection between different uses and functions of the water system. The second, third and fourth aspect above could in principle solve that question, but it is complicated to assess them individually because the functions of water in the system are interrelated, as it functions as the bloodstream of the biosphere and also the anthroposphere. Efforts to assess the value of water are often lacking a connection to the properties of the natural water system, which makes it difficult to analyse upstream–downstream dependency. In order to account for the cyclic nature of water in the assessment of the value of water, Chapagain (2000) and

Hoekstra et al (2001) have introduced the *value-flow concept*. This concept aims to provide the missing link between valuation and hydrology. The hypothesis is that the full value of a water particle depends on the path it follows within the hydrological cycle and the values generated along this path. The full value of a water particle in a certain spot at a certain point in time is supposed to be the sum of its in-situ value and all values that will be generated further down along its path. It follows that all values generated by water can ultimately be attributed to rain – that is, no water is worth so much as rainfall, which has all its value creation lying ahead of it.

The Road Towards Hydrosolidarity

Getting away from sector parochialism

In a catchment, water forms the basis of livelihood security for its inhabitants. As a consequence, water has to be managed in such a way that attention can be given to the links between water security, food security and environmental security. The situation is rather different under humid conditions, compared with arid areas. In the humid zone context where water pollution is the dominant problem, upstream/downstream problems are easier to solve: the issue is not one of a zero-sum character. In the semi-arid zone, particularly at high levels of water crowding where many people pollute each flow unit of water, upstream societal priorities influence downstream opportunities. If water for agriculture is given priority, less blue water will be available for downstream users. Similarly, low upstream priority to water pollution abatement will reduce the downstream usefulness of blue water.

We evidently need conflict resolution methods to reconcile the emerging upstream/downstream conflicts of interest. The basis should be general solidarity with focus on beneficial sharing of the joint water resource – that is, the rainfall caught within the water divide. Solidarity means the willingness to restrain one's freedom. Adaptation to the hydroclimatic constraints of a catchment will demand that all the interested parties are prepared to compromise. Principles and rules for sharing will have to be found for the unavoidable compromises between incompatible water interests in a certain catchment. At the very beginning of this process participants will have to consider international conventions, different modes of 'human livelihood rights', long-term productivity of the basin soils, and ecosystem resilience. Adequate management institutions will be crucial: they must be competent to take cross-sector approaches and be able to handle the complexity referred to earlier in this chapter. Societal ability to cope will be another fundamental precondition, involving human ingenuity both in terms of societal approaches and technical solutions.

The complexity involved means that the possibility of reaching the combined goal of water-related human and ecological security will depend on a new generation of responsible and knowledgeable 'hydrocitizens', inspired by the ethical principles of sharing rather than by conventional principles of historic rights or of the selfish capturing of the water resources in a catchment. There are, however, numerous obstacles involved: conceptual obstacles and obstacles in terms of human attitudes and petrified institutions (SIWI, 1999, 2000, 2001b). To overcome these obstacles, an integrated approach to the catchment is essential and would include a necessary base for balancing and reconciling conflicting interests:

- Further developing integrated water resource management to incorporate land use, pollution loads, and vital ecological goods and services.
- Expanding the conventional blue water approach so that the green water flow can also be incorporated. This means considering the rainfall, caught within the catchment, as the basic water resource. That resource represents the water that can be allocated to all water-dependent activities and ecosystems within the catchment.
- Paying attention to the productive water uses in both the green and the blue water branches and to the partitioning both at the ground surface and in the root zone.
- Protecting the soil as much as possible by a vegetation cover, thus minimizing non-productive green water flow.

As we have said above. one crucial task in implementing this new broader approach will be to identify socially acceptable approaches. This will involve: seeking the actions needed to minimize the problems; developing and legitimizing participation rules; creating legislation and institutions to make the proposed solutions possible; and finding incentives and activities needed to secure implementation, including education of all strata in society to make water everyone's business and spread awareness of the need for trade-offs.

Scarcity drives management shifts

As was shown in Chapter 5, the semi-arid climate involves a number of constraints to both crop production (water scarcities A, B and C) and to blue water supply (scarcity D). Three different problems emerge: the vulnerability to pollution loads; the risk for river depletion; and the risk for salinization. Since the high evaporative demand makes most of the rainfall return to the atmosphere as green water flow, there is not much left to form blue water available to dilute introduced waste flows. The first problem, water pollution, will increase as population growth means that the number of people polluting each water flow unit also increases. The second problem, the risk for river depletion, characterizes cases where biomass production and therefore green water flow increases. Even a moderate change in the green water flow may correspond to a big change in an already low stream flow. This difficulty complicates the food security dilemma in poor countries in view of their limited capacity to buy food from abroad. The third problem in these regions is the risk for secondary salinization. This may happen in situations where land-use change involves reduction of green water flow and land first becomes waterlogged, then salinization occurs when the rising groundwater begins to evaporate, leaving the salts behind.

When there is no more water left to be allocated for beneficial consumptive use a crisis might ultimately develop in water-stressed countries. Remaining blue water flow has to be reserved for aquatic ecosystems. In this situation, the water management will have to switch from what we may call 'Mode I', when more water can be mobilized, to 'Mode II', when there is no more to be mobilized. In Chapter 5 we distinguished

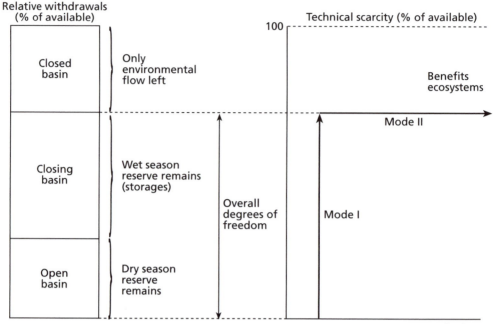

Figure 10.4 *The relationship between water management modes and catchment characteristic*

between two different water stress dimensions: the technical stress dimension expressed in use-to-availability ratio, and the social or demographic stress dimension of water crowding expressed in people per flow unit of water. When these two dimensions were linked we found fundamental differences between the situations in the five separate clusters in that diagram (see Figure 5.8). We were able to distinguish between regions that had more or less reached the 'ceiling' in terms of available water (cluster *a*), those that had a very wasteful water use and were high on the per capita water demand level (cluster *b*), those in the middle of the diagram that are moderate in both senses (cluster *c*), those that are increasingly water crowded but have a large surplus of water left that is difficult to access for economical and capability reasons (cluster *e*), and the water-rich regions (cluster *d*).

If we study such a diagram (see Figure 10.4) we find that the vertical axis will be divided in three portions: the regions with open rivers, the regions with closing rivers where a usable surplus remains but only in the wet season, and the closed rivers, where most of the water is already put to use and what remains has to be left as a reserve for aquatic ecosystems. The border between the closing and the closed rivers is controlled by environmental flow reservations, leaving increased storages as the remaining degree of freedom. In the closed regions there is no surplus for expanding water requirements, since no more storages are acceptable. No more water can be made available except through reallocation. Since the population growth is still quite large in these regions, water resources management will have to move into a new water management mode. In

Mode I, which has dominated water management in the past, focus has been on mobilizing more water to support socioeconomic development, and water management has been characterized by sector approaches. The relevant indicator is use-to-availability ratio, and the technical water stress is the dimension that attracts all interest.

In Mode II, the set of problems is altogether changed. No more catchment water can be mobilized. The only sources are non-conventional ones such as desalination and interbasin water transfers. Water can also be reallocated, for example by water markets, from consumptive to non-consumptive use or environmental flow, from wasteful upstream irrigation to more efficient downstream use. However, with continued population growth, the water crowding increases and so does both the pollution level and the proneness to dispute. Management institutions will therefore have a whole new set of issues to cope with: decisive water pollution abatement, dispute mitigation, water demand control and minimization of water losses.

Increasing food needs will probably have to be supported by import, and by income generation, to make it possible for people to buy their food. Water use for non-consumptive purposes, however, such as municipal and industrial water supply, can continue to intensify as only limited amounts are literally consumed. Wastewater flows can therefore be reused after treatment.The situation is at an impasse in the sense that no more consumptive use and no more water pollution is acceptable. Since consumptive use can also be linked to land-use changes that reduce the generation of runoff, this may be equivalent to a sort of standstill also in terms of land use and land-cover change (except for changes where runoff production would increase). In this situation, attention will move from crop per drop to economic value added per drop.

It is evident that when a country approaches Mode II, the water-related constraints to continued socioeconomic development and the options involved must be properly reflected in national economic planning.

Balancing water for man and nature through a socio-ecohydrological approach

The great complexity of water makes it rational to strive towards a socio-ecohydrologically oriented management distinguishing three lines of action:

- *Securing* water security, food security and ecological security, acknowledging water's life giving characteristics.
- *Avoiding* difficulties in terms of pollution and silting linked to water's lift-up/carry away functions and its mobility, to be achieved by water pollution abatement and soil protection.
- *Foreseeing* unavoidable conflicts and difficulties linked to climatic variability (droughts, floods), and to water's multiple functions and mobility reflected in non-negotiable natural processes in the landscape.

As we have already stressed, the first step in this approach has to be an introductory analysis to clarify the water-related links between the major land uses, water uses and ecosystem services. The crucial resilience capacity of the ecosystem to absorb change without loss of stability must be established. After the introductory analysis, four additional steps will have to follow: setting priorities and identifying basic principles; identifying the action needed; making the needed action possible; and securing its implementation. Broad awareness of land/water linkages and water/ecosystem linkages, particularly in terms of water determinants of important ecosystems in the catchment, will be critical: a land-use decision is also a water decision.

The process also involves ways to achieve social acceptability. In today's policy debate, these steps are generally included in the concept of governance. Adequate ways for participation of main interested parties in a legal arena are important, as is the development of competent institutions able to address issues of complexity to the degree described in this chapter. The necessary modernization of legislation must also be included so that these intricate conflicts of interest can be addressed and enforced. Finally, the financing of the different actions needed, including pricing and economic compensations, must be considered. Guiding principles for conflict reconciliation will be needed. This includes priority setting between different water uses and fundamental ecological services.

Conclusions

In conclusion, we would like to emphasize the following key aspects:

Water is the common denominator in the planet's life-support system. But as water stress increases in catchments because of population growth, urbanization and industrialization, water management will get increasingly complex.

While human livelihood security and pure drinking water, household water, water-dependent food and income generation have to be safeguarded, ecological security must also be achieved with healthy terrestrial and aquatic ecosystems and long-term resilience to unavoidable change.

An integrated approach to land, water and ecosystems gives an opportunity for balancing water for humans and nature. We have showed that the situation calls for conceptual renewals to facilitate the necessary processes involved and to develop the criteria and guidelines needed.

Water as a common denominator

The starting point in our efforts to cope with this complexity is to realize that water is a common denominator of so many functions in the life-support system. Water is essential for life support, for food production, for income generation, for the existence and functions of terrestrial ecosystems and of aquatic ecosystems. Water has two groups of functions in the life-support system, some evident, others hidden. The first group is represented by water flows involved in water supply for society and for plant production. The second group involves three sets of 'consequence-producing' water processes, represented by the rainwater partitioning phenomenon; the 'lift up/carry away' function such as erosion and sedimentation, and water as a mobile solvent; and the transport continuity function based on the water cycle, which produces long cascades of effects.

This central and integrating role of water in the catchment gives an opportunity for integrated management. Here, again, are the basic aspects of water in the catchment:

The ultimate water resource is the rainfall that is caught within the basin. The water moving down the catchment links land use and water; humans and ecosystems; blue water quantity and quality; and upstream and downstream phenomena. The catchment may be seen as a mosaic of partly incompatible water uses, functions and ecosystems. The terrestrial ecosystems are water-consumptive and influence runoff production. The aquatic ecosystems are water-dependent in that the river flow constitutes their habitat. The three security dimensions – water security, food security and ecological security – are linked by water movement and therefore closely interwoven. Components of this complex mosaic are withdrawal sites, sites for consumptive use and return flow partitioning, sites for adding of pollution loads, stretches of in-stream use, runoff modifying terrestrial ecosystems, and aquatic ecosystems dependent on uncommitted flow.

Integrated land/water/ecosystem management

A crucial management tool to be developed is land/water integration taking a catchment-based ecological approach. Although land use and land cover are linked to green water flows, it seems preferable to develop this management around blue water integration as the core since that is where modelling tools are available.

This is what needs to be done:

- The influences of land use have to be incorporated through their role in green/blue water partitioning and in influencing groundwater recharge. Ecological criteria will have to be developed to find the fundamentals for ecosystem health, for local protection needs, for flood episode dependence, and for securing long-term resilience of the life-support system in its totality.
- Combined hydrological/economic models will have to be developed, an area that is currently on the research frontier. Besides cost/benefit analyses, a value flow focus may be helpful, based on the change in value of the rainfall and the green and blue water-related production as it flows down the catchment. This is also an area currently on the research frontier.
- Since trade-offs will have to be an essential component of overall catchment management, it will be essential to secure social acceptance.

Guidelines for hydrosolidarity will also have to be developed on principles of human rights, fairness, equity and equality principles. The process has to incorporate preparedness for change and transient situations, which may need modifications of the management.

Delays in societal response, hydrological responses and ecosystem responses will have to be dealt with. We must be prepared in case of negative events and disturbances such as fires, droughts, floods, pollution episodes and other surprises.

The task involves considerable conceptual challenges, as well. Focus has to be moved from withdrawals of water to what happens to it after use, and to the hydrological functions of the ecosystem that influence groundwater recharge and modify water quality.

Finally, determinants of resilience related to water have to be identified, as well as the involvement of water in the erosion of resilience and the collapse of ecosystems.

Urgent scientific renewal

At present there seem to be two paradigm shifts. One is occurring within ecology and concerns the conceptual framework for understanding, accepting and managing change. The other one is taking place in hydrology and concerns the distinction between consumptive uses of water, as opposed to return flows that may be used again downstream. There is a new focus on rainwater and its partitioning into green and blue water flows and on the recently introduced distinction between open and closed river basins.

The gap between geophysical/engineering and the biological approaches to the life-support system and the human interactions with that system will have to be bridged. The first step has already been taken and the two scientific communities have indeed approached one another:

- The ecologists by stressing that ecosystems regulate both groundwater recharge and dry season flow and that they affect water quality through biochemical processes. There have been numerous innovative initiatives for the management of ecosystems. They have, however, often involved only partial handling of the ecosystem services by taking approaches that involve looking at a single aspect such as management of water to protect ecosystems and management of ecosystems to protect water.
- The hydrologists by focusing on water determinants of ecosystems; on seasonality and certain aquatic ecosystems that depend on seasonal flows; on the fact that terrestrial ecosystems are water consumptive; and on the vulnerability of the savannas to changes in the land cover.

But much still needs to be done. Achieving socio-ecohydrological management of catchments will demand a major renewal of the fragmentation that still exists in science. The two main populations involved, the hydrologists/water managers and the ecologists, will have to meet on an equitable basis (Falkenmark and Folke, 2002). A constructive bridge building through dialogue will be absolutely essential. To take one example among many, a theme for such a dialogue might be to find out what adaptive management and resilience protection would mean in practical terms. The idea is not only to understand the process, but to determine how it can be done. What will be the implications for water management?

Catchment management is evidently developing into an increasingly complex task, and a discussion is necessary on the new concepts and the new research that is needed.

In this field there are many questions and components that will have to be discussed, including ethical considerations. Some are green water related, such as food production modes, site selection of crop fields, deforestation and afforestation, functional diversity and resilience. Blue water questions include selection of sites for water sources and well fields, reservoirs, canals, and pipelines. There is also the important local, national and international problem of upstream/downstream balancing of interests concerning use, water quantities, sustainability and pollution loading.

To be able to do this is finally a question of education. The rapid increase of complexity of water management calls for a rapid change in the educational system to produce the new generation of water managers, hydrologists, ecologists and economists needed. The overall task will be to learn to master the complexity of the multiple functions of water in nature and society.

Many of these questions concern change, and it is therefore important to include not only scientists of various specialisations but also the users, whether in urban or rural areas.

We have discussed the importance of making water everyone's business. This can be achieved through education at all levels of society to make people in general understand and accept the unavoidable change and choices. Various incentives may ease the acceptance, and in some cases sanctions may secure enforcement. But understanding the problems is essential. Therefore, a special target group is journalists in various media who must play a constructive information role on these issues and improve the understanding of unavoidable compromises.

*   *   *

In this book, we have stressed the importance of bridging the gap between hydrology and ecology. We have done this by approaching ecology from a water resources perspective – not the other way around – hence the subtitle, *The New Approach to Ecohydrology*.

We have shown the huge problem of food production if the goal to alleviate hunger now and in the future is to be taken seriously. We have looked at the hunger gap that exists and the probable directions of future development from a perspective of the water requirements for food production.

Much attention has been on the special vulnerability of the savanna zone. We have shown that there remains a large water reserve more or less ready to use, where more food can be produced with relatively less water. This would be a win–win solution, where more food is produced while safeguarding water for vital ecological functions.

Finally we have stressed the importance of creating a new type of water expertise with a capacity to focus on cross-disciplinary issues. This would assist in solving the future complex challenges of dealing with the many functions of water in nature and society.

Notes

Chapter 1

1   The drainage basin catchment is the area inside a water divide. All the rainfall to the catchment is being partitioned between the visible blue water flow, supporting society with direct freshwater services, and the invisible green water flow, supporting plant production in terrestrial ecosystems such as rain-fed croplands. Water is withdrawn to supply cities and industries that return the wastewater loaded with pollutants. Water is also withdrawn for use in irrigated agriculture, from where the part for consumptive use joins the green water flow. The return flow part returns to the river system loaded with salts and leached agrochemicals.

Chapter 2

Introducing Soil Water into the Water Balance Equation

1   Before rainfall reaches the soil, interception may occur, where water is evaporated back to the atmosphere directly from the canopy – from water caught on the leaves and stems of plants and trees. Ponding of water on the soil surface may lead to direct evaporation from the soil (E_p) surface before infiltration. For increased understanding of the two partitioning points, we have chosen to omit these flows in Figure 2.2. However, in dense forests, for example, interception flow can constitute a substantial proportion of the hydrological cycle. In hydrology, interception is often subtracted from rainfall giving the term 'effective rainfall', which is the rainfall that actually reaches the soil surface.

2   Based on an overview of transpiration research from different agro-climatological conditions and for different ecosystems, L'vovich concludes that 'the average expenditure of water for transpiration constitutes at least half of evapotranspiration on land...'

Water Resource Estimates

3   The notion that the water cycle is a balanced closed circuit is adequate for the purpose of our analysis, but in a strict sense there is an unbalanced exchange of water as well, in the form of dissociation of water molecules, dissipation of hydrogen atoms into space, and flow of water from the Earth's interior to the surface.

4   The simple water balance expression being: $P = R + E + G$ giving $E = P - R - G$ (E = total evaporation, P = precipitation, R = surface runoff and G = groundwater recharge).

5   It should be noted that the contrary approach, to derive blue water flow from green water flow calculated from physically and empirically based equations, has also been done, for example, Budyko and Zubenok (1970, in L'vovich, 1979). For areas that do not have streamflow observations the approach has been to use interpolation equations based on empirical estimates of surface and sub-surface runoff coefficients.

Chapter 3

Current Green Water Requirements for Food Production

1   The United Nations world population revision (2002) predicts a deceleration of population growth as a result of lower fertility rates and increased mortality (largely due to the HIV/AIDS pandemic), with an estimated medium projection of 8.9 billion world inhabitants by 2050, compared to previous medium projections of 9.3 billion in 2050. The low and high projections range from 7.4 to 10.6 billion people in 2050. Our estimates of water requirements to cover future needs for food are based on the 9.3 billion projection (UNFPA, 2002), with an increase of 3.3 billion more people between the year 2000 and 2050. We use the rounded number of 3 billion more people by 2050 (2000 to 2050) in our general discussion on population growth, which is slightly higher than the most recent UN revision (UN, 2003) but lower than the previous medium projection (UNFPA, 2002).

2   Defined by the FAO as 'the status of persons whose food intake does not provide enough calories to meet their basic energy requirements' (FAO 2001).

3   Saturation vapour pressure in turn is a function of leaf or canopy temperature. It is commonly assumed that leaf or canopy temperature is close to the air temperature in contact with the canopy.

Additional Water Requirements to Feed Humanity by 2050

4   In our calculation on water requirements to cover future needs for food we have used the figure 3.3 billion additional people in 2050. This originates from FAOSTAT, with UN population data from 2001.

5   Before trying to answer this question, it is important to note a difficulty in interpreting these figures. The year 2000 volume of 7000 km^3/year for use in agriculture includes consumptive green water flow from both irrigated and rainfed agriculture, excluding livestock (ie only plant foods).

6   This estimate is based on FAO's global projection of irrigated land for 2025 of 309 million ha (0.6 per cent per year expansion in 2000–2025 or 42 million ha, of which the totality occurs in developing countries), with a continued expansion rate of 0.6 per cent per year in 2025–2050, arriving at a global irrigated land area of 348 million ha. The increased consumptive blue water use in 2050 is estimated based on an assumed average yield level of 4 t/ha (estimated at 3.6 t/ha for 2025) and a green water productivity of 1700 m^3/tonne, which results in a total consumptive irrigation use in 2050 of 2506 km^3/year, or an increase with 600 km^3/year compared to year 2000.

Chapter 4

Water Flows to Sustain Food Production

1   The data used to develop the map is based on grain production only. Data on blue water withdrawals in irrigation are taken from de Fraiture et al (2001) and Seckler et al (1998) as well as data on areas under rainfed agriculture and estimated grain yields in irrigated and rainfed farming systems. The green water withdrawals were calculated assuming global green water productivity in rainfed grain production of 3,000 m^3/tonne of grain (total evaporation) (FAOSTAT, 1999).

2   For integration we take country level blue water withdrawals in agriculture divided by country level population, giving a per capita volume of blue water use in agriculture. We have based the calculations on the UN medium year 2000 population estimates. Blue water withdrawals are estimates for year 2000.

Green Water Flows Are Sustaining Major Biomes

3   These include grains, legumes and pulses, fruits, vegetables, roots and tubers, fibre crops, sugar crops, oil crops, stimulants, spices, cotton, nuts and fodder crops (Source: FAOSTAT, 1999).

4   This was necessary as the data on permanent grazing land in FAOSTAT, 34 million km^2, was larger than the estimated grassland area (29.5 million km^2) in Rockström et al (1999). Similarly, the forests and woodlands area in FAOSTAT at global level is estimated at 55.5 million km^2, compared to 27.4 million km^2 in Rockström et al (1999). This can be explained by the fact that only a proportion of the grasslands is used for grazing and that there is a large area of permanent grazing within the forest and woodland category (Rockström et al, 1999). Therefore, here (i) the difference in area between FAOSTAT (1999) and Rockström et al (1999) on the forest and woodland category (55.5 – 27.4 = 28.1 million km^2) was assumed to constitute permanent grazing, and (ii) the remainder to attain the FAOSTAT estimated area for permanent grazing (34–28.1 million km^2 = 5.9 million km^2) was assumed to be permanent grazing within the grassland category in Rockström et al (1999). This explains why the annual water withdrawals for the grasslands in this book (12,100 km^3/yr) and forests and woodlands (19,700 km^3/year) are lower than the estimated withdrawals in Rockström et al (1999) (of 15,100 km^3/year for grasslands and 40,000 km^3/year for forests and woodlands).

Chapter 5

The Green Water Perspective

1   The potential evaporation, in simple terms, corresponds to the green water flow from a well-cared-for lawn with an ample supply of water.

Chapter 6

Drylands – the Cradle of Mankind

1   It should be remembered that the classification of hydroclimatic zones, and the threshold rainfall and potential evaporation for different ecosystems, varies with seasonality of rainfall seasons (summer or winter). The reason this is so important is that the potential evaporation during the rainy season is what really affects water availability, because it is only when water is available that the atmospheric thirst for water can translate to real evaporation. Winter rainfall areas, such as the Mediterranean region, have low temperatures and low potential evaporation during the rainy season, which results in lower crop water requirements, which in turn means that sedentary agriculture is performed in 'drier' zones in terms of rainfall. This means, for example, that in strict terms annual rainfall in semi-arid areas with winter rainfall is 500 mm and in semi-arid areas with summer rainfall 800 mm (UNEP, 1992).

Savanna Agro-ecosystems – A Most Difficult Challenge

2   Interestingly, the French forester A. Auberville first used the term 'desertification' in 1949 (Auberville 1949, according to Lal et al, 1998) to describe a general process of degradation that started with deforestation and ended in lands turned into desert. This process did not necessarily have to occur in so-called dryland.

Hydroclimatic Challenges and Opportunities

3   Coefficient of variation (CV) shows the normalized deviation of rainfall from its mean, and is calculated as the standard deviation (SD) divided by the mean rainfall, CV = SD/mean.

Chapter 7

More Crop per Drop

1   In 2025 half of the world's population is expected to live in urban settlements. The transition from a life where livelihoods are secured from land use to an urban life where livelihood is secured through salaries, is also a transition from a situation where children are perceived – from an economic point of view – as an asset (farm labour) to a burden (primarily costs of subsistence and schools, etc).

2   Due to the large uncertainties in population projections, and to the ongoing deceleration of population growth, we have chosen to approximate population by 2050 to 9 billion people (compared to the UNFAO estimate of 9.3 billion given in Chapter 3).

3   According to Evans (1998), the ratio of global cereal yield to world population has been constant since 1950, with the yield level in kg/ha very close to the population (in millions) divided by half. A world population of 9 billion in 2050 would therefore mean a grain yield of 9000/2 = 4,500 kg/ha (Gillard, 2002). This is a significant increase from the present average grain yields in the order of 3000 kg/ha.

4   The huge yield increases over the last 50 years in industrialized countries with the introduction of a fossil fuel-based agriculture after World War II has, to a significant extent, been achieved only with a price of groundwater pollution, soil compaction and reduction in soil biological diversity. There has also been a loss of ecological functions and resilience, caused by excessive application of nitrogen fertilizers and animal manure, improper use of pesticides and intensified use of heavy machinery.

Potential to Increase Rainfed Production

5   Chambers et al (1989) and Pretty (1995) distinguish between three basic categories of agricultural systems in the world. These are the agricultural systems in industrialized countries, the Green Revolution-type agriculture, and the so-called 'pre-modern', 'traditional' or 'unimproved' systems. The industrialized systems are highly mechanized and fossil fuel-based (for both fertilization and traction), while the Green Revolution systems are less capital-intensive but still based on a 'modern' system with fertilizers, pesticides, water supply and crop varieties.

6   Similar yield gap observations can be made for wheat and rice. In 1995, according to FAO-based country comparisons, average paddy rice yields varied between 1.1 and 6.4 t/ha between the lowest and the highest 10 per cent of growers. The 10 per cent of the largest rice-growing countries in the world had an average yield in 1995 of 3.4 t/ha, which is roughly half the highest experienced on-farm yields. The same range for wheat is between 0.8 and 4.8 t/ha, with the 10 per cent of the largest growers in the world having yields of 2.5 t/ha, again roughly half of the achievable on-farm yields. Comparing these inter-country differences with the in-country comparison in Figure 7.3, the indications are that there is a substantial yield gap for the major grains in the world between present and attainable on-farm yields.

7   Social factors are closely related to land tenure, ownership of land, agricultural policy and institutions, human capacity, capital resources such as land, labour and money, risk perception, culture and markets.

8   Intensification is here understood as a reduction of fallow periods resulting in more land under continuous cultivation and an increased use of external inputs such as fertilizers.

9   With the desiccation of soil we mean a process in which soils dry out and lose their capacity to absorb and release water to plants. Soil desiccation is a result of loss of organic matter, compaction and surface crusting, all of which affects soil structure.

10   In this example we have assumed a maize crop with a 120 days growing period, cultivated in a hot semi-arid savanna climate with a seasonal rainfall average of 550 mm and a potential evaporation of 8 mm/day during the rainy season. Water productivity for a productive green water flow as plant transpiration (WP_T) is given as the amount of grain (kg of dry matter) per unit of transpiration (in mm) and unit area (ha). This is used to estimate grain production per unit crop water use, and was set at 12.5 kg/mm/ha, which is a reasonable average for tropical grains (Falkenmark and Rockström, 1993).

More Crop per Drop by Reducing Non-productive Green Water Losses

11   The impact of management on water productivity, particularly in reducing non-productive water flows in favour of productive flows, was outlined by Fischer and Turner (1978, p297): 'Agronomists often report that improved management (for example, fertilization, planting density, etc) and plant breeding have led to substantial gains in water-use efficiency in terms of yield of economic product per unit water supplied. However, it is unlikely that water-use efficiency as we have defined it (total dry matter per unit transpiration) has increased. Most of the gains reported derive from increases in transpiration as a fraction of water supply, due to greater soil extraction and greater plant cover reducing soil evaporation, or from increases in harvest index. Even in the case of forage production, claims that efficiency doubled with nitrogen fertilization of semi-arid pastures could largely reflect savings in soil evaporation.'

12   Shading by leaves results in reduced solar radiation reaching the air space between the canopy and the soil surface, which creates cooler air within the plant system and thus a reduced potential evaporation at the soil surface. This progressively reduces evaporation flow with increased canopy cover. A dense canopy also reduces wind speeds through the canopy and hence the exchange of vapour in the canopy is reduced. This increases the humidity in the air adjacent to the soil surface. The vapour pressure deficit is reduced, which in turn slows down the evaporation process.

13   It should be noted also that early season evaporation is strongly influenced by the number of rainfall events. The largest amount of evaporation occurs from wetted soil immediately after a rainfall event (often hours but up to one day in hot tropical environments). Very soon thereafter the rate of evaporation falls sharply. A large number of small rainfall events may therefore result in higher total evaporation.

14   These experiments were not explicitly focused on water productivity dynamics but rather on yield and green water flow relations. However, as early as 1983, Ritchie investigated the dynamics of green water productivity and yield growth. From a series of irrigation and fertilizer experiments on wheat in the 1960s, he concluded that green water productivity was related to improvements in management, especially increased fertilizer applications.

Global Assessment of the Water that Can Be Gained

15   Including rice (3.7 t/ha) wheat (2.63 t/ha), maize (2.77 t/ha), sorghum (1.04 t/ha), and millet (0.7 t/ha) (FAO, 2002).

16   Furthermore, it is most likely a conservative value, as it does not include vapour shift for canopy growth in other land uses, for example from planting of pulses, legumes, tubers, vegetables and fruits. We also believe that an average reduction of evaporation by 30 mm/ha, resulting in a yield increase from 2.5 to 4 t/ha, is a low estimate. It is a very rough figure, however, as it does not take into account differences in evaporative demand between locations, and the great yield variability. Lower yields can result in higher relative vapour shift if yields are more than doubled.

Chapter 8

Changing the Farmers' Risk Perception

1 It is, in fact, virtually impossible to drought-proof rainfed agriculture. Meteorological droughts occur statistically 1–2 times per decade in a semi-arid savanna. With seasonal rainfall equal to or exceeding 600 mm, there is little that can be done to bridge a drought and secure a crop, since such large volumes of water would be required to bridge a drought, generally in the order of >200 mm of water per hectare, or 2000 m³. This is a very large volume for a smallholder farmer to store. Rather than trying to physically bridge droughts through water management, the strategy is to build social resilience. This includes various types of coping mechanisms on the scale of the individual household, community, society and nation. In many drought-prone rural societies, such social resilience has been largely lost over the last half-century. Growing populations have contributed to an increased magnitude of human suffering as a result of droughts. A more pragmatic water management focus is thus to at least proof agriculture from the effects of dry spells.

Broadening the Narrow Approaches of the Past

2 Sustainable agriculture or farming is generally understood as farming that seeks to make best use of ecosystem goods and services without damaging the environment (Pretty, 2000). In this book, we understand sustainability in the same way: balancing natural resource use between humans and nature. However, we put less emphasis on the necessity to focus on local ecosystem goods and services. For example, in large parts of the developing world, soil nutrient mining is so severe on smallholder farms that fertilizers or a good supply of local, organic sources of soil nutrients are the only viable option to enable a sustainable land management.

The Upstream–Downstream Perspective

3 The yield results from supplemental irrigation originate from a number of experimental trials in India; 16 trials on wheat, 3 trials on barley, 19 trials on sorghum, 4 trials on rice, 4 trials on maize, and 1 trial on sunflower. The data originates from Singh (1983), and were presented and adapted from Sivanappan (1997).

4 A low fertilizer application of 30 kg N/ha was used at both locations, while an additional 80 kg N/ha treatment was tested in the Kenyan location.

Chapter 10

Combining Social, Ecological and Economic Approaches

1 What has to be added here is that we are at present suffering under the rather diffuse use among biologists of the term 'ecosystem' and, in particular, the absence of reference to water in the definition of the abiotic surroundings and the interactions between ecosystem components. A terminological renewal will be essential also for the stakeholder dialogues that will be needed to secure social acceptance of the outcome of unavoidable trade-offs in a certain catchment.

References

Abrams, L (2003) 'Politics and governance at the interface between water and development'. In: 'Balancing Competing Water Uses – Present Status and New Prospects'. The XIIth Stockholm Water Symposium, 2002, issue organized by the Stockholm International Water Institute (SIWI), *Water Science and Technology*, 47 (6) 109–114

Acreman, M (2000) *Wetlands and Hydrology. Conservation of Mediterranean Wetlands*, Nr 10. Tour du Valat, Arles.

Agarwal, A (2000) *Drought? Try capturing the rain*. Briefing paper for member of parliament and state legislatures. An occasional paper from the Centre for Science and Environment. New Delhi.

Agarwal, A (2001) 'Water pollution problems posed by small industries: A case study in India and China'. Proceedings of the Stockholm Water Symposium 2001. *Water Science and Technology*, 45 (8) 47–52.

Agarwal, A and Narain, S (eds) (1997) 'Dying Wisdom. Rise, fall and potential of India's traditional water-harvesting systems'. *State of India's Environment 4 – A Citizens' Report*. Centre for Science and Environment (CSE), New Delhi.

Agnew, C and Andersson, E (1992) *Water Resources in the Arid Realm*. Routledge, London.

Allan, JA (1995) 'The Political Economy of Water: Reasons for Optimism, but Long Term Caution', in JA Allan and JHO Court (eds) *Water in the Jordan Catchment Countries: A Critical Evaluation of the Role of Water and Environment in Evolving Relations in the Region*, School of Oriental and African Studies, University of London.

Allen, SJ, (1990) 'Measurement and estimation of evaporation from soil under sparse barley crops in northern Syria'. *Agric For Meteorol*, 49, 291–309.

Archibold, OW (1995) *Ecology of World Vegetation*. Chapman and Hall, London.

Ashton, P (2002) 'Avoiding conflicts over Africa's water resources'. *Ambio*, 31 (3): 236–242.

Asmal, K. (2001) 'Water is a catalyst for peace'. *Water Science and Technology*, 43 (4): 24–30.

Auberville, A (1949). *Climats, forêts et desertification de l'Afrique tropicale*. Société d'Editions Geographiques et Coloniales, Paris.

Baird, AJ and Wilby, RL (eds) (1999) *Eco-hydrology. Plants and water in terrestrial and aquatic environments*. Routledge, London.

Bakker, M, Barker, R, Meinzen-Dick, R and Konradsen, F (eds) (1999) *Multiple Uses of Water in Irrigated Areas: A Case Study from Sri Lanka*. SWIM Paper 8, International Water Management Institute, Colombo, Sri Lanka.

Barron, J, Rockström, J and Gichuki, F (1999) 'Rainwater management for dry spell mitigation in semi-arid Kenya'. *E Afr Agric For J*, 65 (1): 57–69.

Barron, J, Rockström, J, Gichuki, F, and Hatibu, N (2003) 'Dry spell occurrence and potential impact on maize yields: Rainfall analysis and simple water balance modelling for semi-arid farming systems in Kenya and Tanzania'. *Agric For and Meteorol*, 117 (1–20): 23–37.

Barrow, C (1987) *Water Resources and Agricultural Development in the Tropics*. Longman Scientific and Technical, Harlow.

Boserup, E (1965) *Conditions of Agricultural Growth: The Economics of Agrarian Change Under Population Pressure*, Aldine de Gruyter, The Netherlands.

Bosilovich, MG and Schubert, SD (2001) 'Precipitation recycling over the central United States diagnosed from the GEOS-1 data assimilation system', *Journal of Hydrometeorology*, 2: 26–35.

Breman, H, Groot, JJR and van Keulen, H (2001) 'Resource limitations in Sahelian agriculture'. *Global Environmental Change* 11: 59–68.

Brismar, A (1996) 'Water-related productivity constraints and desertification in the tropical/subtropical drylands. A literature analysis'. Master Thesis. Dept for Systems Ecology, Stockholm University.

Budyko, MI (1986) *The Evolution of the Biosphere*. D. Reidel Publishing Company, Dordrecht, The Netherlands.

Buffagni, A (2001) 'The use of benthic invertebrate production for the definition of ecologically acceptable flows in mountain rivers'. In: MC Acreman (ed) *Hydro-ecology: Linking Hydrology and Aquatic Ecology*. International Association of Hydrological Science (IAHS) Publication no.266. IAHS Press, Wallingford.

Buresh, RJ, Sanchez, PA and Calhoun, FG (eds) (1997) *Replenishing soil fertility in Africa*. SSSA and ASA. SSSA Special Publication No 51.

Calder, IR (1999) *The Blue Revolution. Land use and integrated water resources management*. Earthascan, London.

Casenave, A and Valentin, C (1992) 'A runoff classification system based on surface features criteria in semi-arid areas of West Africa'. *J of Hydrol*, 130: 231–249.

CFWA (1997). *Comprehensive Assessment of the Freshwater Resources of the World*. UN and Stockholm Environment Institute. World Meteorological Organisation, Switzerland.

Chambers, R, Pacey, A and Thrupp, LA (eds) (1989). *Farmer First: farmer innovation and agricultural research*. Intermediate Technology Development Group, London.

Chapagain, AK (2000). *Exploring methods to assess the value of water: A case study on the Zambezi basin*. Value of Water Research Report Series No.1, IHE Delft, The Netherlands

Chaplin, MF (2001) 'Water: its importance to life'. *Biochemistry and Molecular Biology Education*, 29: 54–59.

Cole, MM (1986) *The Savannas: Biogeography and Geobotany*, Academic Press, London.

Conway, G (1997) The Doubly Green Revolution. Food for all in the twenty-first century. Penguin Books New York.

Cooper, PJM, Gregory, PJ, Tully, D, and Harris, HC (1987). Improving water use efficiency of annual crops in the rainfed farming systems of West Asia and North Africa. *Expl Agric*, 23: 113–158.

Cosgrove, WJ and Rijsberman, FR (2000) *World Water Vision – Making water Everybody's Business*. Earthscan, London.

Cousteau, J-Y (1992) 'Convince to conquer'. *Calypso Log*, 3–6 August.

Daamen, CC, Simmonds, LP and Sivakumar, MVK (1995) 'The impact of sparse millet crops on evaporation from soil in semi-arid Niger'. *Agric Water Manage*, 27: 225–242.

Daily, G (ed) (1997) *Nature's Services: Human Dependence on Natural Ecosystems*. Island Press, Washington, DC.

Dancette, C (1983) 'Estimation des besoins en eau des principales cultures pluviales en zone soudano-sahélienne'. *L'Agronomie Tropicale*, 38 (4): 281–294.

de Fraiture, C, Molden, D, Amarasinghe, U and Makin, I (2001) 'PODIUM: Projecting water supply and demand for food production in 2025'. *Phys Chem Earth (B)*, 26 (11–12): 869–876.

De Groen, MM and Savenije, HHG (1996). 'Do land use induced changes of evaporation affect rainfall in Southeastern Africa?' *Phys Chem Earth (B)*, 20 (5–6): 515–519.

de Wit, CT (1958) 'Transpiration and crop yields'. *Agric Res Rep*, 64 (4): 88.

Doorenbos, J and Kassam, AH (1986) 'Yield Response to Water'. FAO Irrigation and Drainage Paper No. 33. FAO, Rome.

Doorenbos, J and Pruitt, WO (1992) 'Guidelines for predicting crop water requirements'. FAO Irrigation and Drainage Paper No. 24. FAO, Rome.

Dunbar, MJ and Acreman, MC (2001). 'Applied hydroecological science for the twenty-first century'. In: MC Acreman (ed), *Hydro-ecology: Linking hydrology and aquatic ecology*. IAHS Publication No. 266, IAHS Press, Centre for Ecology and Hydrology, Wallingford.

Dyson, T (1994). 'World population growth and food supplies'. *International Social Science Journal*, 141: 361–385.

Eagleson, PS and Segarra, RI (1985). 'Water-limited equilibrium of savanna vegetation systems'. *Water Resources Research*, 10: 1483–1493.

Engelman, R and LeRoy, P (1995) *Sustaining water. An update*. Population Action International, Washington DC.

Evans, LT (1998). *Feeding the Ten Billion*. Cambridge University Press, Cambridge.

Evenari, M, Shanan, L and Tadmor, NH (1971) *The Negev, the Challenge of a Desert*. Harvard University Press. Cambridge, Mass.

Falkenmark, M (1975). 'Yttre vattenomsättning i större svenska sjöar'. *Vatten*, 1: 72–90.

Falkenmark, M (1986). 'Fresh water – Time for a modified approach'. *Ambio*, 15 (4): 192–200.

Falkenmark, M (1999). 'Forward to the future: A conceptual framework for water dependence. Volvo Environment Prize Lecture 1998'. *Ambio*, 28 (4): 356–361.

Falkenmark, M (1989) 'Water scarcity and food production in Africa'. In: D Pimentel and CW Hall (eds) *Food and Natural Resources*. Academic Press, San Diego.

Falkenmark, M (1997) Meeting water requirements of an expanding world population. *Phil Trans R Soc Lond B*, 352: 929–936.

Falkenmark, M (2000) 'A European perspective on sustainable consumption of fresh water: Is getting rid of pollutants realistic and affordable?' In: Li et al (eds) *Towards Sustainable Consumption. A European Perspective*. The Royal Society, London. pp477–83.

Falkenmark, M (2001) 'The greatest water problem: The inability to link environmental security, water security and food security'. *Water Resources Development*, 17 (4) 539–554.

Falkenmark, M Anderson, L, Casterson, R, Sundblad, K, in collaboration with Baldidor, C, Gardiner, J, Lyle, C, Peters, N, Pettersen, B, Quinn, P, Rockström, J and Yapijakis, C (1999) *Water – A reflection of land use. Options for counteracting land and water mismanagement*. Swedish Natural Science Research Council, Stockholm.

Falkenmark, M and Ayebotele, NB (1992) 'Freshwater resources'. In: J Dooge (ed) *An Agenda for Science for Environment and Development into the 21st Century*, International Council of Scientific Unions, Cambridge University Press, Cambridge.

Falkenmark, M and Chapman, T (eds) (1989) *Comparative Hydrology – An Ecological Approach to Land and Water Resources*. UNESCO, Paris.

Falkenmark, M and Folke, C (2002) 'The ethics of socio-ecohydrological catchment management: towards hydrosolidarity'. *Hydrology and Earth System Sciences*, 6 (1): 1—9.

Falkenmark, M and Lindh, G (1976) *Water for a Starving World*. WestView Press, Boulder.

Falkenmark, M and Lundqvist, J (1997) 'World Freshwater Problems – Call for a New Realism'. Background Report 1, Comprehensive Assessment of the Freshwater Resources of the World, Stockholm Environment Institute, Stockholm.

Falkenmark, M and Lundqvist, J (2000). 'Editorial: Towards hydrosolidarity. Focus on the upstram-downstream conflicts of interest', *Water International*, 25 (2): 168–71.

Falkenmark, M and Mikulski, Z (1994) 'The key role of water in the landscape system. Conceptualisation to address growing human landscape pressures'. *GeoJournal*, 33 (4): 355–63.

Falkenmark, M, Lundqvist, J and Widstrand, C (1989) 'Coping with water scarcity requires micro-scale approaches: aspects of vulnerability in semi-arid development'. *Natural Resources Forum* 13 (2): 258–67.

Falkenmark, M and Widstrand C (1992) 'Population and Water resources: A Delicate Balance'. Population Bulletin, 47 (3), Population Reference Bureau, Washington, DC.

Falkenmark, M, and Rockström, J (1993). 'Curbing rural exodus from tropical drylands'. *Ambio*, 22 (7): pp 427–37.

Falkenmark, M, and Steen, P (1995). 'To change direction. How to find the new water resources agenda towards a desirable future'. Proceedings, Stockholm Water Symposium 1995, Stockholm Water Company. Stockholm.

Falkenmark, M, Rockström, J and Savenije, H (2001) 'Feeding eight billion people: time to get out of past misconceptions'. *Water Front*, 1: 7–9.

FAO (1986) *African Agriculture: the next 25 years*. Food and Agricultural Organization, Rome.

FAO (1995a).*World agriculture: Towards 2010. An FAO study*. Food and Agricultural Organization, Rome.

FAO (1995b) 'Land and water integration and river basin management'. Proceedings of an informal workshop 31 Jan-2 Feb, 1993. *Land and Water Bulletin*. Food and Agricultural Organization, Rome.

FAO (1997) 'Food production: the critical role of water'. World Food Summit. Technical Background Document 7. Food and Agricultural Organization, Rome.

FAO (1997) 'Irrigation in Africa – A Basin Approach'. FAO Land and Water Bulletin 4. Food and Agricultural Organization, Rome.

FAO (1999) 'Review of the state of the World Fisheries Resources; Inland Fisheries'. FAO Fisheries Circular No. 942. Fisheries Department, Food and Agricultural Organization, Rome.

FAO (2000) 'New Dimensions in Water Security'. AGL/MISC/25/2000. Food and Agricultural Organization, Rome.

FAO (2001) 'The State of Food and Agriculture 2001'. Food and Agricultural Organization, Rome.

FAO (2002a) 'Agriculture: Towards 2015/30. Technical Interim Report'. Food and Agricultural Organization website http://www.fao.org/es/esd/at2015/toc-e.htm .

FAO (2002b) *World Agriculture: Towards 2015/2030 – An FAO Perspective*, Earthscan, London.

FAOSTAT (1999) UN Food and Agriculture Organization Statistical Database, http://apps.fao.org, FAO Statistics Division, Rome

FAOSTAT (2002) UN Food and Agriculture Organization Statistical Database, http://apps.fao.org, FAO Statistics Division, Rome

Fischer, RA and Turner, NC (1978) 'Plant productivity in the arid and semiarid zones. *Ann. Rev. Plant Physiol*, 29: 277–317.

Fischer, G, van Velthuizen, H, Shah, M and Nachtergaele, F(2002) 'Global agro-ecological assessment for agriculture in the 21st century: Methodology and Results'. Research Report, International Institute for Applied Systems Analysis (IIASA), Austria.

Folke, C, Carpenter, S, Elmqvist, T, Gunderson, L, Holling, CS, Walker, B, Bengtsson, J, Berkes, F, Colding, J, Danell, K, Falkenmark, M, Gordon, L, Kasperson, R, Kautsky, N, Kinzig, A, Levin, S, Maeler, K-G, Moberg, F, Ohlsson, L, Olsson, P, Ostrom, E, Reid, W, Rockström, J, Savenije, H and Svedin, U (2002) *Resilience and Sustainable Development: Building Adaptive Capacity in a World of Transformations*. International Council for Science (ICSU), Series on Science for Sustainable Devlopment No 3., Paris, p37.

Folke, C (1997) 'Ecosystem approaches to the management and allocation of critical resources'. In: PM Groffman and ML Pace (eds) *Successes, limitations and frontiers in ecosystem science*, Cary Conference 1997, Institute of Ecosystem Studies, Millbrook and Springer Verlag, New York.

Folke, C, Jansson, Å, Larsson, J and Costanza, R (1997). 'Ecosystem appropriation by cities'. *Ambio*, 26: 167–72.

Fox, P and Rockström, J (2000) 'Water harvesting for supplemental irrigation of cereal crops to overcome intra-seasonal dry-spells in the Sahel'. *Physics and Chemistry of the Earth, Part B Hydrology, Oceans and Atmosphere*, 25 (3): 289–96.

Fox, P and Rockström, J (2003) Supplemental irrigation for dry-spell mitigation of rainfed agriculture in the Sahel. *Agric Water Manage*, 1817: 1–22.

Freistühler, E, Giers, A, Schultz, GA and Bauer, HJ (2001) 'A technique to predict the hydro-ecological effects in an ecological assessment of water projects'. In: MC Acreman (ed) *Hydro-ecology: Linking Hydrology and Aquatic Ecology*. IAHS Publication no.266. IAHS Press, Wallingford.

Gaffney, M. (1997), 'What price water marketing?: California's new frontier'. *American Journal of Economics & Sociology*, 56 (4): 475–521.

Geoffrey, L and Todd, C (2001) 'Defining thresholds for freshwater sustainability indicators within the context of South African water resource management'. In: *Second WARFA/Waternet Symposium*, Cape Town, October 30–31, 2001.

Gillard, B (2002). 'World population and food supply. Can food production keep pace with population growth in the next half-century?' *Food Policy*, pp47–63.

Glantz, MH (ed) (1994). *Drought follows the plough: cultivating marginal areas*, Cambridge University Press, Cambridge.

Gleick, P (ed) (1993) *Water in Crisis – A guide to the World's Fresh Water Resources*. Oxford University Press, Oxford.

Gleick, P (1996). 'Basic water requirements for human activities. Meeting basic needs'. *Water International*, 21: 83–92.

Gleick, P (2000) *The World's Water 2000–2001. The Biennial Report on Freshwater Resources*. Island Press, Washington, DC.

Gordon, L (2001) 'The interplay of freshwater flows, terrestrial ecosystems and society'. Licentiate in Philosophy Thesis 2001: 6, Dept of Systems Ecology, Stockholm University, Stockholm.

Gunderson, LH and Pritchard, L (ed) (2002) *Resilience and the Behavior of Large Scale Ecosystems*. Island Press, Washington, DC.

Gustafsson, Y (1977) Variations in rainfall as a natural constraint in agriculture. *Ambio*, 6 (1): 34–35.

GWP (1999) 'How to bring ecological services into integrated water resource management'. Seminar Stockholm 15–17 November 1999, Beijer International Institute of Ecological Economics, Royal Swedish Academy of Sciences, Stockholm.

GWP (2000a) 'Integrated water resources management'. TAC Background Paper No. 4. Global Water Partnership, Stockholm.

GWP (2000b) *Towards Water Security: A Framework for Action*. Global Water Partnership, Stockholm.

Haddadin, MJ (2001). 'Water scarcity impacts and potential conflicts in the MENA region'. *Water International*, 26 (4): 460–70.

Hadley, R (1975) *Classification of representative and experimental basins*. UNESCO, Paris.

Heyns, P (1993) 'Water management in Namibia'. In: *Proceedings of the Workshop on Water Resources Management in Southern Africa*. Victorial Falls, 5–9 July. World Bank, Washington, DC.

Hoekstra, AY, Savenije, HHG, and Chapagain AK(2001) 'An integrated approach towards the value of water: a case study of the Zambezi basin', *Integrated Assessment*, 2.

Holling, CS, Berkes, F and Folke, C (1998) 'Science, sustainability and resource management'. In: *Linking Social and Ecological Systems*. Ch 13 (eds) F Berkes, C Folke and J Colding, Cambridge University Press.

Hoogmoed, WB (1999) 'Tillage for soil and water conservation in the semi-arid tropics'. Doctoral Thesis. Wageningen University, The Netherlands.

Huntley, BJ and Walker, BH (1982) 'Introduction'. In: BJ Huntley and BH Walker (eds) *Ecology of Tropical Savannas*, Springer, Berlin.

ICRAF (2000) *Improved land management in the Lake Victoria Basin: Linking land and lake, research and extension, catchment and lake basin. First report of progress and results, July 1999–March 2000.* ICRAF and Ministry of Agriculture and Rural Development, Nairobi, Kenya.

ICWE (1992) 'The Dublin statement and report of the conference'. International conference on water and the environment: development issues for the 21st century, 26–31 January 1992,. Dublin.

Jaeger, L (1983) 'Monthly and areal patterns of mean global precipitation'. In: A Street-Perrott A Beran and R Ratcliffe (eds) *Variations in the Global Water Budget*. D. Reidel Publishing Company, Dordrecht, The Netherlands.

Jones, G (2002) 'Setting environmental flows to sustain healthy working rivers'. *Watershed*, Cooperative Research Centre for Freshwater Ecology, Canberra.

Kangalawa, RYM (2001) 'Changing land-use patterns in the Irangi Hills, Central Tanzania – A study of soil degradation and adaptive farming strategies'. Thesis, Dept. of Physical Geography and Quarternary Geology, Stockholm University.

Klaij, MC and Vachaud, G (1992) 'Seasonal water balance of a sandy soil in Niger cropped with pearl millet, based on profile moisture measurements'. *Agric Water Manage.* 21: 313–30.

Korzuon, VI, Sokolov, AA, Budyko, MI, Voskresensky, KP, Kalinin, GP, Konoplyantsev, KP, Korotkevich, ES, Kuzin, PS and Lvovich, MI (eds) (1974) *World Water Balance and Water Resources of the Earth*. Chief Administration of Hydometeorological Service under the Council of Ministers of the USSR. USSR National Committee for the International Hydrological Decade, Leningrad.

Lal, R, Hassan, HM and Dumanski, J (1998) 'Desertification control to sequester C and mitigate the greenhouse effect'. In: NJ Rosenberg, RC Izaurralde and EL Malone (eds) *Carbon Sequestration in Soils, Science, Monitoring and Beyond*. Proceedings of the St. Michaels Workshop, December 1998, Battelle Press, Columbus, Ohio.

Lannerstad, M (2002) 'Consumptive water use feeds the world and makes rivers run dry'. TRITA-LWR Master thesis, Royal Institute of Technology, Stockholm.

Large, ARG and Prach, K (1999) 'Plants and Water in Streams and Rivers'. In: AJ Baird and RL Wilby (eds) *Ecohydrology*, Routledge, London.

Leach, G (1995) *Global Land and Food Supply in the 21st Century*. Stockholm Environmental Insitute, Stockholm.

Leakey, R and Lewin, R (1992) *Origins reconsidered – In search of what makes us humans*. Abacus, London.

Leopold, LB and Davis, KS (1968) *Water*. Life Science Library. Time-Life International, The Netherlands.

Leprun, JC and da Silveira, CO (1992) 'Analogies et particularités des sols et des eaux regions semi-arides: le Sahel de l'Afrique de l'Ouest et le Nordest brésilien', in E Le Floch, M Grouzis, A Cornet and J-C Bille (eds) *L'aridité Une Contrainte du Développement*, ORSTOM, Paris, pp131–54.

Li, F, Cook, S, Geballe, GT and Burch, WR (2000) 'Rainwater harvesting agriculture: an integrated system for water management on rainfed land in China's semiarid areas'. *Ambio* 29: (8).

Loomis, RS, and Connor, DJ (1992) *Crop Ecology: Productivity and Management in Agricultural Systems*. Cambridge University Press.

Lubchenko, J (1998) 'Entering the century of the environment: a new social contract for science'. *Science*, 279: 491–96.

Lundgren, L (1993) 'Twenty years of soil conservation in Eastern Africa'. RSCU/Sida, Report No. 9, Nairobi, Kenya.

L'vovich, MI (1974) 'World water resources and their future'. Mysl, PH, Moscow, p 263.

L'vovich, MI (1979) *World water resources and their future.* (Translation by the American Geophysical Union). LithoCrafters Inc. Chelsea, Michigan.

L'vovich, MI and White, GF (1990) 'Use and transformation of terrestrial water systems'. In: *The Earth as transformed by Human Action.* Turner II, BL, WC Clark, RW Kates, JF Richards, J Matthews and WB Meyer (eds) Cambridge University Press/Clark University. New York.

Meybeck, M (2002) 'Riverine quality of the Anthropocene: propositions for global space and time analysis, illustrated by the Seine river', *Aquatic Sciences*, 64: 376–93.

Mitsch, WJ and Gosselink, JG (2000) *Wetlands.* John Wiley & Sons, Inc, New York.

Molden, D, Rijsberman, F, Matsuno, Y and Amarasinghe, UA (2001a) 'Increasing the productivity of water: a requirement for food and environmental security'. Dialogue Working Paper 1. IWMI, Colombo, Sri Lanka.

Molden, DJ, Sakthivadivel, R,and Keller, J (2001b) 'Hydronomic zones for developing water conservation strategies'. IWMI Research Report. IWMI, Colombo, Sri Lanka.

Molle, F (2002) 'Reform of the Thai irrigation sector: is there scope for increasing water productivity?' In: JW Kijne (ed) *Water Productivity in Agriculture: Limits and Opportunities for improvement.* CABI, Wallingford.

Morales, C (1977) 'Rainfall variability – a natural phenomenon. *Ambio*, 6 (1): 30–33.

Nash, L (1993) 'Water quality and health'. In: PH Gleick (ed) *Water in Crisis.* Oxford University Press.

National Research Council (1991) *Opportunities in the Hydrologic Sciences.* National Academy Press, Washington, DC, pp35–37.

Nemec, J (1983) 'The concept of runoff in the global water budget'. In: A Street-Perrott, M Beran and R Ratcliffe (eds) *Variations in the global water budget,.* D. Reidel Publishing Company, Dordrecht, The Netherlands.

Ngigi, SN, Thome, JN, Waweru, DW and Blank, HG (2000) 'Technical evaluation of low-head drip irrigation technologies in Kenya'. Research report, Nairobi University and the International Water Management Institute, Nairobi, Kenya.

Novak, MD (1982) 'Quasi-analytical solutions of the soil-water flow equation from problems of evaporation'. *Soil Sc Soc Am J*, 52 (4): 916–24.

Oldreive, B (1993) *Conservation Farming for communal, small-scale, resettlement and co-operative farmers of Zimbabwe. A farm management handbook.* Mazongororo Paper Converters (Pvt) Ltd, Zimbabwe.

Olsson, L (1993) 'On the causes of famine, drought, desertification and market failure in the Sudan'. *Ambio*, 6: 395–403.

Ong, CK, Odongo, JCW, Marshall, FM and Corlett, JE (1996) Principles of resource capture and utilisation of light and water. In: CK Ong and PA Huxley (eds) *Tree-crop interactions – a physiological approach*, CAB International, Wallingford, 73–158..

Oweis, T, Hachum, A and Kijne, J (1999) 'Water harvesting and supplemental irrigation for improved water use efficiency in the dry areas'. SWIM Paper 7, International Water Management Institute, Colombo, Sri Lanka

Pandey, RK, Maraville, JW and Admou, A (2000) 'Deficit irrigation and nitrogen effects on maize in Sahelian environment. I. Grain yield and yield components'. *Agric Water Manage.* 46: 1–13.

Penning de Vries, FWT and Djitèye, MA (eds) (1991) *La productivité des paturages sahéliens. Une étude des sols, des végétations et de l'exploitation de cette resource naturelle.* Pudoc, Wageningen, The Netherlands.

Pielou, EC (1998) *Fresh water*. The University of Chicago Press, Chicago.

Pimentel, D, and Houser, J (1997) 'Water resources: agriculture, the environment, and society'. *BioScience*, 47 (2): 97–107.

Postel, SL (1998) 'Water for food production: will there be enough in 2025?', *BioScience* 48 (8): 629–38.

Power, JF, Grunes, DL and Reichmann, GA (1961) 'The influence of phosphorus fertilization and moisture on growth and nutrient absorption by spring wheat: I. Plant growth, N uptake, and moisture use'. *Soil Sc Soc Am Proc*, 25: 207–10.

Pretty, J (1995) *Regenerating Agriculture: Policies and Practices for Sustainability and Self-reliance*. EarthScan, London.

Pretty, J (2000) 'The promising spread of sustainable agriculture in Asia'. *Natural Resources Forum*, 24: 107–21.

Pretty, J and Hine, R (2001) *Reducing Food Poverty with Sustainable Agriculture: A Summary of New Evidence*, Final Report from the 'Safe World' Research Project, University of Essex, UK, p133.

Rapp, A (1974) *A Review of Desertization in Africa: Water, Vegetation and Man*. Secretariat for International Ecology, Stockholm.

Raskin, P (1997) *Comprehensive Assessment of the Freshwater Resources of the World. Water Futures: Assessment of long-range patterns and problems*. Stockholm Environmental Institute, SEI, Stockholm.

Redman, CL (1999) *Human Impact on Ancient Environments*. The University of Arizona Press, Tucson.

Reij, C, Scoones, I and Toulmin, C (eds) (1996) *Sustaining the Soil. Indigenous Soil and Water Conservation in Africa*. Earthscan, London.

Ripl, W (1995) 'Management of water cycle and energy flow for ecosystem control. The energy-transport reaction (ETR) model'. *Ecological Modelling*, 78: 61–76.

Ritchie, JT (1983) 'Efficient water use in crop production: discussion on the generality of relations between biomass production and evapotranspiration'. In: *Limitations to Efficient Water Use in Crop Production*, ASA-CSSA-SSSA, Madison, Wisconsin.

Roberts, J (1999) 'Plants and water in forests and woodlands'. In: AJ Baird and RL Wilby (eds) *Ecohydrology*, Routledge, London.

Rockström, J and Ada L (1993) *Diagnostic sur le système agraire du Zarmaganda Central (Niger)*. Mémoire finale, Institut National Agronomique, Paris/Grignon (I.N.A.-P.G.), Chaire d'Agriculture Comparée et de Développement Agricole, Paris..

Rockström, J (1997) 'On-farm agrohydrological analysis of the Sahelian yield crisis: rainfall partitioning, soil nutrients and water use efficiency of pearl millet'. PhD thesis, Dept of Systems Ecology, Stockholm University.

Rockström, J (2000) 'Water resources management in smallholder farms in Eastern and Southern Africa: an overview'. *Physics and Chemistry of the Earth, Part B: Hydrology, Oceans and Atmosphere*, 25 (3): 279–88.

Rockström, J and Falkenmark, M (2000) 'Semi-arid crop production from a hydrological perspective – Gap between potential and actual yields'. *Critical Rev Plant Sc*, 19 (4): 319–46.

Rocksröm, J, Gordon, L, Folke, C, Falkenmark, M and Engwall, M (1999) 'Linkages among water vapor flows, food production and terrestrial ecosystem services', *Conservation Ecology* 3, (2): 5. www.consecol.org/vol3/iss2/art5

Rockström, J and Jonsson, L-O (1999) 'Conservation tillage systems for dryland farming: on-farm research and extension experiences'. *E Afr Agric For J*, 65 (1): 101–14.

Rockström, J and de Rouw, A (1997) 'Water, nutrients, and slope position in on-farm pearl millet cultivation in the Sahel'. *Plant and Soil*, 195: 311–27.

Rodriguez-Iturbe (2002) *Water Front*, No 2, Stockholm International Water Institute, Sweden

Sandström, K (1995) *Forests and Water – Friends or Foes? Hydrological Implications of Deforestation and Land Degradation in Semi-arid Tanzania*. Linköping Studies in Arts and Science. No 120. Linköping University, Sweden.

Savenije, HHG (1995) 'New definitions for moisture recycling and the relationships with land-use changes in the Sahel', *Journal of Hydrology*, 167: 57—78.

Savenije, HHG (1996a) 'The runoff coefficient as the key to moisture recycling'. *Journal of Hydrology*, 176: 219–25.

Savenije, HHG (1996b) Does moisture feedback affect rainfall significantly? *Physics and Chemistry of the Earth*, 20: 507–13.

Savenije, HHG (1998) 'How do we feed a growing world population in a situation of water scarcity?' In: *Water – The Key to Socio-economic Development and Quality of Life*, SIWI, Stockholm.

Savenije, HHG (1999) 'The role of Green Water in food production in sub-Saharan Africa'. FAO conference on 'Water for Food in sub-Saharan Africa' 1999, www.fao.org/waicent/FaoInfo/Agricult/AGL/AGLW/Africvis.htm

Savenije, HHG (2002) 'Why water is not an ordinary economic good, or why the girl is special'. *Physics and Chemistry of the Earth*, 28 (11–22): 741–44

Savenije, HHG, and van der Zaag, P (2002) 'Water as an economic good and demand management, paradigms with pitfalls'. *Water International*, 27 (1): 98–104.

Seckler, D (1996) 'The new era of water resource management. From 'dry' to 'wet' water savings'. Research Report 1. International Water Management Institute, Colombo, Sri Lanka.

Seckler, D, Amarasinghe, U, Molden, D, de Silva, R and Barker, R (1998) 'World water demand and supply, 1990 to 2025: scenarios and issues'. IWMI Research Report 19, IWMI, Colombo, Sri Lanka.

Seckler, D, Molden, D and Sakthivadivel, R (2002) 'The concept of efficiency in water resources management and policy'. Paper presented at the IWMI Water Week, 12–16 November, 2001, Colombo, Sri Lanka.

Shiklomanov, IA (1993) 'World fresh water resouces'. In: P Gleick (ed) *Water in Crisis – A Guide to the World's Fresh Water Resources*. Oxford University Press, Oxford.

Shiklomanov, IA (1996) 'Assessment of water resources and water availability in the world'. Scientific and Technical Report to the UN Comprehensive Freshwater Assessment. State Hydrological Institute, St Petersburg, Russia.

Shiklomanov, IA (ed) (1997) *Assessment of water resources and water availability in the World*. Stockholm Environmental Institute and World Meteorological Organisation, Geneva.

Shiklomanov, IA (1997) *Assessment of water resources and water availability of the world*. Background Report to the Comprehensive Assessment of the Freshwater Resources of the World. Stockholm Environment Institute and World Meteorological Organisation, Geneva.

Shiklomanov, IA (2000) 'Appraisal and assessment of world water resources'. *Water International*, 25 (1): 11–32.

Sinclair, TR, Tanner, CB and Bennett, JM (1984) 'Water-Use efficiency in crop production'. *BioScience*, 34 (1): 36–40.

Singh, RP (1983) 'Farm pond project'. Bulletin No 6, AICRP, Hyderabad, India.

Singh, RP, Parr, JF and Stewart, BA (eds) (1990) 'Dryland agriculture: strategies for sustainability'. *Advances in Soil Science*, 13: 373.

Sivakumar, MVK (1992) 'Climate change and implications for agriculture in Niger'. *Climate Change*, 20: 297–312.

Sivannapan, RK (1995) 'Soil and water management in the dry lands of India'. *Land Use Policy* 12 (2): 165–75.

Sivannapan, RK (1997) 'State of the art in the area of water harvesting in semi-arid parts of the world'. Paper presented at the international workshop on water harvesting for supplemental irrigation for staple food crops in rainfed agriculture, 23–24 June, Stockholm University.

SIWI (1999) 'Towards upstream/downstream hydrosolidarity'. Proceedings, SIWI/IWRA Seminar, Stockholm August 14. Stockholm International Water Institute, Stockholm.

SIWI (2000) 'Water security for multinational water systems. Opportunities for development'. Proceedings SIWI Seminar, August 19. SIWI Report 8, Stockholm International Water Institute. Stockholm.

SIWI (2001a) 'Water harvesting for upgrading of rainfed agriculture. Problem analysis and research needs'. SIWI Report No 11. SIWI, Stockholm.

SIWI (2001b) 'Water security for cities, food and environment – Towards catchment hydrosolidarity'. SIWI Seminar, 18 August. SIWI Report 13. Stockholm International Water Institute. Stockholm.

Sivakumar, MVK (1992) 'Climate change and implications for agriculture in Niger', *Climate Change*, 20: 297–312.

Stager, JC and Mayewski, PA (1997) 'Abrupt early to mid-holocene climatic transition registered at the equator and the poles'. *Science*, 276: 1834–36.

Stewart, JI, Misra, RD, Pruitt, WO and Hagan, RM (1975) 'Irrigated corn and grain sorghum with a deficient water supply'. *Trans ASAE*, 18: 270–80.

Stewart, JI (1988) *Response farming in rainfed agriculture*. The WHARF Foundation Press, Davis, California.

Stoorvogel, JJ and Smaling, EMA (1990) *Assessment of Soil Nutrient Depletion in Sub-Saharan Africa: 1983–2000, Vol 1: Main Report*. Report No. 28. Winand Staring Centre Wageningen, The Netherlands.

Tiffen, M, Mortimore, M and Gichuki, F (1994) *More People, Less Erosion – Environmental Recovery in Kenya*. ACTSPRESS, African Centre for Technology Studies, Nairobi, Kenya.

Tuong, TP (1999) 'Productive water use in rice production: opportunities and limitations'. *J of Crop Production*, 2 (2): 241–64.

Tuong, TP and Bouman, BAM (2002) 'Rice production in water scarce environments'. In: JW Kijne (ed) *Water productivity in Agriculture: Limits and Opportunities for Improvement*. CABI, Wallingford.

Tyree, MT (1999) 'Water relations of plants'. In: AJ Baird and RL Wilby (eds) *Ecohydrology*, Routledge, London.

UN (2000) Millennium Declaration of the United Nations. A/RES/55/2, 18. New York, September.

UN (2003) *World Population Prospects: The 2002 Revision Highlights*, United Nations Population Division (UNPD), New York, p22.

UNCED (1992) United Nations Conference on Environment and Development. Rio de Janeiro, June.

UNEP (1992) World Atlas of Desertification, Edward Arnold, London.

UNESCO-WWAP (2003) *Water for People, Water for Life: The United Nations World Water Development Report*, Berghhan Books, UN World Water Assessment Programme (WWAP), UNESCO, Paris, p543.

UNFPA (2002) *The State of the World Population 2001*, United Nations Population Fund, New York

United Nations (1997) Convention on the Law of the non-navigational uses of international Waterways, 21 May, 1997. A/RES/51/229, 8 July 1997, United Nations, New York.

van Hofwegen, P and Svendsen, M (2000) *A Vision of Water for Food and Rural Development: A Report to the 2nd World Water Forum*, Delft, The Netherlands, p82.

van der Leeuw, SE (2000) 'Land degradation as a socionatural process'. In: RJ McIntosh, Tainter, JA and McIntosh, SK (eds) *The Way the Wind Blows: Climate, History and Human Action*, Columbia University Press, New York.

van Wilgen, BW, Le Maitre, DC and Cowling, RM (1998) 'Ecosystem services, efficiency, sustainability and equity: South Africa's working for water programme'. *Trends in Ecology and Evolution*, 13: 378.

Viets, FG (1962) 'Fertilisers and the efficient use of water'. *Adv Agron*, 14: 223–264.

Wainwright, J, Mulligan, M and Thornes, J (1999) 'Plants and water in drylands'. In: AJ Baird, and RL Wilby (eds) *Ecohydrology*, Routledge, London.

Walker, BH (1993) 'Rangeland ecology: understanding and managing change', *Ambio*, 22: 80–87.

Wallace, JS (1991) 'The measurement and modelling of evaporation from semi-arid lands'. In: MVK Sivakumar, JS Wallace, C Rénard and C Giroux (eds) *Soil Water Balance in the Sudano-Sahelian Zone*. Proceedings of the International Workshop, Niamey, Niger, February. IAHS Publication No. 199. IAHS Press, Institute of Hydrology, Wallingford.

Wheeler, BD (1999) 'Water and plants in freshwater wetlands'. In: AJ BAird and RL Wilby (eds) *Ecohydrology, Plants and Water in Terrestrial and Aquatic Environments*, pp127–180, Routledge, London.

Wolf, AT (2000) *Trends in Transboundary Water Resources. Lessons for Cooperative Projects in the Middle East*. Proceedings SIWI Seminar 'Water Security for Multinational Water Systems – Opportunities for Development'. Stockholm International Water Institite (SIWI), Stockholm, pp95–109.

Waterlow, J, Armstrong, D, Fowden, L and Riley, R (eds) (1998) *Feeding a World Population of More than Eight Billion People. A Challenge to Science*. Oxford University Press, Oxford.

Wetzel, RG (1999) 'Plants and water in and adjacent to lakes'. In: AJ Baird and RL Wilby (eds) *Ecohydrology*, Routledge, London.

Wheeler, BD (1999) 'Water and plants in freshwater wetlands'. In: AJ Baird and RL Wilby (eds) *Ecohydrology*, Routledge, London.

Whittington, J (2002) 'Working Rivers', *Watershed*, 24: 3–5, Cooperative Research Centre for Freshwater Ecology, Canberra, Australia.

Widstrand, CG (ed) (1980) *Water Conflicts and Research Prioroties. Part 2, Water and Society*. Conflicts in Development. Pergamon Press. London.

Viets, FG (1962) 'Fertilizers and the efficient use of water'. *Adv Agron*, 14: 223–64.

Wood, PJ, Agnew, MD and Petts, GE (2001) 'Hydro-ecological variability within a groundwater dominated stream'. In: MC Acreman (ed) *Hydro-ecology: Linking Hydrology and Aquatic Ecology*. IAHS Publication No.266. IAHS Press, Wallingford.

Wood, S, Sebastian, K and Scherr, SJ (2000) *Pilot Analysis of Global Ecosystems – Agroecosystems*. International Food Policy Research Institute and World Resources Institute, Washington, DC.

World Commission on Dams (2000) *Dams and Development. A New Framework for Decision Making*. Earthscan. London.

World Water Commission (2000) *A Water Secure World*. Commission Report. World Water Council, Marseille.

World Water Council (2000) *World Water Vision: Commission Report – A Water Secure World. Vision for Water, Life and the Environment*, Commission Report from the Water Commission on Water for the 21st Century to the World Water Council, World Water Council, France, p70.

Zhang, H and Oweis, T (1999) 'Water-yield relations and optimal irrigation scheduling of wheat in the mediterranean region'. *Agric Water Manage*, 38: 195–211.

Zhu, Q and Li, Y (2000) 'A breakthrough of the dry farming – rainwater harvesting irrigation project in Gansu, China'. Paper presented at the Stockholm Water Symposium, 14–17 August.

Index